Putting Linguistics into Speech Recognition

CSLI Studies in Computational Linguistics

This series covers all areas of computational linguistics and language technology, with a special emphasis on work which has direct relevance to practical applications, makes formal advances, and incorporates insights into natural language processing from other fields, especially linguistics and psychology. Books in this series describe groundbreaking research or provide an accessible and up-to-date overview of an area for nonspecialists. Also included are works documenting freely available resources for language processing, such as software, grammars, dictionaries, and corpora.

Series edited by Ann Copestake

CSLI Studies in
Computational Linguistics

Putting Linguistics into Speech Recognition

THE REGULUS GRAMMAR COMPILER

Manny Rayner, Beth Ann Hockey & Pierrette Bouillon

with contributions by

Nikos Chatzichrisafis, Marianne Santaholma & Marianne Starlander

FOREWORD BY

Aravind K. Joshi

CSLI PUBLICATIONS
Center for the Study of Language and Information
Stanford, California

Center for the Study of Language and Information
Leland Stanford Junior University
Printed in the United States
10 09 08 07 06 1 2 3 4 5

Library of Congress Cataloging-in-Publication Data

Rayner, Manny.
Putting linguistics into speech recognition :
The Regulus grammar compiler /
by Manny Rayner, Beth Ann Hockey and Pierrette Bouillon,
foreword by Aravind Joshi.

p. cm. – (CSLI studies in computational linguistics)

Includes bibliographical references and index.
ISBN 1-57586-526-2 (pbk. : alk. paper)
ISBN 1-57586-525-4 (cloth : alk. paper)

Catalog entries and call number can be found at
http://cslipublications.stanford.edu/

∞ The acid-free paper used in this book meets the minimum requirements of the American National Standard for Information Sciences—Permanence of Paper for Printed Library Materials, ANSI Z39.48-1984.

CSLI was founded in 1983 by researchers from Stanford University, SRI International, and Xerox PARC to further the research and development of integrated theories of language, information, and computation. CSLI headquarters and CSLI Publications are located on the campus of Stanford University.

CSLI Publications reports new developments in the study of language, information, and computation. Please visit our web site at
http://cslipublications.stanford.edu/
for comments on this and other titles, as well as for changes and corrections by the authors and publisher.

To our parents
who introduced us to language and science

— M.R., B.A.H.

A mes parents
qui m'ont donné le goût des langues et de la science

— P.B.

Contents

Foreword

Language models are necessary in speech recognition systems to reduce the search space. A widely used approach involves the extraction of a statistical language model from a corpus. It is well known that grammar-based recognizers tend to be brittle. So at first sight one might wonder what Manny Rayner, Beth Ann Hockey, and Pierrette Bouillon (RHB) are up to in *Putting Linguistics into Speech Recognition: The Regulus Compiler* (PLSR)?

A key point of RHB is that for certain type of applications, such as controlled language user-initiative (CLUI) spoken language dialogue systems, spoken language recognition by itself is not adequate. Spoken language understanding is needed. Grammar therefore becomes necessary. It also becomes useful for language modeling by overcoming the sparseness of data problem, which is quite characteristic for CLUI spoken language dialogue systems. So in this domain, language resources such as grammars also become useful for recognition. It is interesting to note that although broad-coverage grammars have a long and honorable history in computational linguistics, when they are used in spoken language processing, they have been used only to interpret the text produced by the speech recognizer. They are not used for the language modeling task. The language models used in the recognizers themselves are much simpler and there is no attempt to exploit the complex structured information in the grammars. Some relatively recent examples are LinGO English Resource Grammar (Stanford) used in the Verbmobil project and SRI's Core Language Engine grammars in the Spoken Language Translator system. There is something unsatisfactory about this situation. If grammar-based linguistic constraints were relevant to speech understanding, why would they not also be relevant to speech recognition?

PLSR presents the first coherent program, as far as I know, for using a large resource grammar to support development of speech recognition. During the construction of this resource RHB have taken certain aspects of large scale grammars in systems such as, for example, CLE (SRI), LinGO (Stanford) in Verbmobil, and the XTAG system (UPENN), without committing to any one particular system, a good engineering decision. The work described here is not just a proposal but it has already led to the technology used to create successful speech applications, including the first spoken dialogue system to be deployed in space. RHB systematically go through all the key points needed for fully understanding their approach. They give a detailed description of the grammar and the algorithms used to compile it into a speech recognizer, present empirical evaluations showing how various factors affect recognizer performance, and also demonstrate that, at least for certain classes of applications, these grammar-based systems are superior to the data-driven competitors. A substantial part of PLSR is devoted to a detailed step-by-step tutorial on the Regulus system, showing the readers how they themselves can use the system.

PLSR will appeal to a wide variety of audiences. The detailed tutorial material and the numerous examples will give linguists and computational linguists, who are not familiar with speech technology, the information they need to start building speech enabled systems. The tutorial sections could also be useful to software engineers, who are neither linguists nor speech scientists. Developers, who are already using grammars in their spoken dialogue systems, will find here a method that could offer faster development times and easier grammar maintenance. The theoretical sections in Part II of the book provide information about which aspects of grammar design are important for speech recognition performance, and where grammar-based systems perform most successfully. Part II is also valuable to speech scientists interested in the merits of using grammar-based speech recognition, and anyone needing to fine tune a grammar for speech recognition. An excellent hands-on course in spoken dialogue systems could also be designed around the main chapters of PLSR.

RHB deserve our thanks for making the software open source, and thus available to the largest possible community. If you are at all interested in grammars or speech applications, I encourage you to read this wonderful book. I know you will enjoy it.

Aravind K. Joshi
University of Pennsylvania, Philadelphia PA

March 20 2006

Acknowledgments

The first version of Regulus was implemented at the Netdecisions Technology Center in Cambridge, England, under funding initially from Netdecisions and later from Fluency Voice. We would very much like to thank Netdecisions and Fluency, and especially Charles Mindenhall and Ciaran Coyle, for their decision to make the system Open Source and thus freely available to the research community. Funding for later versions of the system has been provided by NASA Ames Research Center, the NASA Intelligent Systems Project[1], and the Swiss National Science Foundation (Fonds National Suisse de la Recherche Scientifique; FNRS) under the MedSLT and IM2.MDM projects[2]. We are grateful for the support they have provided. None of this work could have been carried out if we had not had access to the Nuance platform. We would like to thank Nuance Communications for making it available to us, both for Regulus and for several other Regulus-related projects.

The software we describe has been implemented by several people, not all credited here as co-authors. The Regulus SpeechServer (Regserver) and the example Java application in Chapter 3 were written by Nikos Chatzichrisafis. The parser compiler used in the Regulus development environment was written by John Dowding. The Regulus `batchrec` tool in Section 4.7.3 was written by Genevieve Gorrell while visiting NASA Ames Research Center; she also used it to perform an initial version of the experiments in Section 11.4. The Regulus translation engine in Chapter 6 was developed under the MedSLT project by Manny Rayner and Pierrette Bouillon. The grammar compaction and empty productions elimination code described in Chapter 8 was written by Dave Carter, while visiting NASA Ames. The original version of the general English speech grammar in Chapter 9 was based on the Gemini grammar described in (Rayner et al., 2000c), which was developed at NASA Ames by Manny Rayner and Beth Ann Hockey. The remaining Regulus software was mostly written by Manny Rayner.

An early version of Part I was presented as a tutorial at the ACL 2004 conference by Manny Rayner and Beth Ann Hockey. An initial version of the Regulus unification grammar to CFG compiler was described in (Rayner et al., 2001a), and Chapter 12 is largely based on material taken from Section 4 of (Rayner et al., 2005e) and (Rayner et al., 2005a).

[1] NRA2-38169

[2] Project numbers 105212–101592, 105212–109417 and 51NF40–104677.

The book itself owes its existence to the patient encouragement we have received from Ann Copestake and Dikran Karageuzian, our editors at CSLI Press. Thank you Ann and Dikran, and we apologise for all the unrealistic time estimates and missed deadlines. Genevieve Gorrell and Yukie Nakao read through complete drafts of the manuscript, and gave us many useful comments. Other people who provided good criticism when we needed it include Ann Bies and Dave Carter. Among his numerous contributions, Dave can also include suggesting the book's title.

Last but absolutely not least, we would like to thank the members of the Regulus user community for constructive and intelligent feedback on the system itself. If Regulus isn't better, it's because we haven't yet had time to implement all the things they've asked for. In this connection, we would particularly like to mention Marita Ailomaa, Yalina Alphonse, Ascander Dost, Dominique Estival, Genevieve Gorrell, Sridhar Gudihala, Hitoshi Isahara, Kyoko Kanzaki, Maria Kaplanidou, Ian Lewin, Yukie Nakao, Bruna Novellas, Justin Nuger, Thang Tran Manh and Andrew Zschorn.

1

Introduction

Manny Rayner, Pierrette Bouillon and Beth Ann Hockey

1.1 What this book is about

One of the key problems in building a spoken dialogue system is achieving high-quality automatic speech recognition. Accurate recognition in the general case of any speaker saying anything is not currently possible. However, useful applications such as dictation, call routing, automated telephone banking or airline flight information query are feasible with current technology, if the advantageous aspects of these tasks are properly exploited. Dictation systems must recognise a large vocabulary, but can use adaptation to a particular user's speech, and are trained from huge collections of sample data. Call routing systems must also deal with large vocabularies and cannot use speaker adaptation. The task is possible, however, because it only involves sorting the input into one of a small number of categories ("classification"), rather than full understanding. Commercial telephone systems for telephone banking or flight information constrain the range of the user's language by controlling the interaction with a series of carefully designed requests for bank account numbers, transaction types, destinations or flight numbers. For instance, if an airline booking system says "What is your departure date, for example 'June fifteen'?", then most users will respond appropriately, making the recognition task relatively straightforward. Table 1 shows several types of speech understanding applications, categorised along various dimensions.

Regulus, the subject of this book, is an Open Source software platform, which can be used together with the commercially available Nuance Toolkit[3] to build speech recognisers for yet another type of application, which we will refer to as *controlled language user-initiative*

[3] `http://www.nuance.com`

	Vocabulary size	Understanding	Speaker independent	Training data (words)	Typical user	Dialogue initiative
Large Vocabulary Dictation	10^5	Words only	no	10^8–10^9	Expert	User
Call Routing	10^4–10^5	Classify	yes	10^5–10^6	Naive	User
Commercial Telephone Systems	10^2–10^4	Slot Filling	no	10^3–10^5	Naive	System
Travel Booking (ATIS)	10^3	Complex/ Slot Filling	yes	10^5	Naive	Mixed
Controlled Language User-Initiative	10^2–10^3	Complex/ Slot Filling	yes	10^3–10^4	Expert	Mixed/ User

TABLE 1 Various kinds of spoken dialogue systems

spoken dialogue systems. In order to explain what we mean by this, an example is in order. Suppose that we wanted to build a speech interface that controlled a mobile robot. If we used the menu-driven (*system-initiative*) dialogue architecture typical of commercial phone systems, a sample interaction might be something like the following:

Robot: What should I do? You can say "move", "pick up object", "check status"...

Human: Move.

Robot: Should I move right, left, straight on, or at an angle?

Human: Left.

Robot: How far should I go? Say a number of metres.

Human: Four metres.

Robot: Moving. What should I do? You can say "move"...

Human: Check status.

Robot: What status would you like to check? You can say "tires", "battery"...

Human: Battery.

Robot: My battery is at 58% charge. What should I do...

This slow and unnatural dialogue is not very satisfactory. Ideally, we would like the user to be in control (a *user-initiative dialogue strategy*) and tell the robot what to do using natural free-form commands:

Human: Well, so now you need to move right — I mean left — about, ah, about three or four metres.

Robot: I'll move a bit more than three metres left, correct?

Human: Good. Now, how much charge do you have left on your battery?

Robot: It's at 58%.

The problem with the second approach is that it is very difficult to implement. If we try to build a system that attempts to handle this broad a range of possible commands, we will find that many words will typically be misrecognised, and that even when they are correctly recognised, the robot will often misunderstand. In Regulus, we focus on an intermediate solution halfway between the two extremes we have sketched above. We put the user in control of the dialogue ("user-initiative"), but only permit them to use a constrained ("controlled") range of language:

Human: Robot, move three point five metres to the left.

Robot: Moving three point five meters left.

Human: Check battery level.

Robot: Battery level is 58%.

Since the language is restricted, it is feasible to write a grammar which precisely specifies what the user is allowed to say to the speech recogniser. This general approach to speech recognition is called *grammar-based language modelling*; as with most methods, it has both advantages and disadvantages.

On the positive side, grammar-based recognisers can be built using only modest quantities of example data, and are typically very accurate when the user stays within the coverage of the grammar; as we explain in the next section, the grammar cuts down the space of possibilities that the recogniser needs to search. An architecture of this kind is well-suited to "expert" users who will interact with the system frequently, and will have time to learn what they can and cannot say to it. This is in particular the case for the two most substantial applications which have been built using Regulus. NASA's Clarissa procedure browser (Rayner et al., 2005d, Clarissa, 2006), which in June 2005 became the first spoken dialogue system to be deployed in space, is designed for use on the International Space Station. Astronauts are almost perfect users for grammar-based speech recognisers; they are highly intelligent, willing to invest time in learning to use the system, and in most cases come from an aeronautics background where use of controlled language is the norm. Similarly, Geneva University's MedSLT (Bouillon et al., 2005, MedSLT, 2006) is an Open Source medical speech translator designed for use by doctors. Doctors are not quite as good users as astronauts for the type of system we are considering here, but they share many of the same properties. They are usually well educated, and accustomed to being presented with new kinds of technology. In areas where there are many foreign patients, the doctor is also strongly motivated to learn to use the system[4].

On the negative side, grammar-based recognisers are brittle; recognition is rarely good if the user wanders outside the grammar's coverage. Also, the process of building them can easily become expensive in terms of human effort. In early projects using this kind of methodology (Moore et al., 1997, Lemon et al., 2001), construction of an explicit recognition grammar was a major task, which required specialised expertise in both computational linguistics and software engineering. The resulting grammars were hard to maintain, and did not port easily to new domains. This contrasts poorly against the currently more popular alternative of directly extracting a statistical language model from a corpus of examples. Although it is laborious and time-intensive to collect the large quantities of training data needed, the training process itself is well-understood.

The fundamental idea behind Regulus is to reduce the effort required to build grammar-based recognisers, by providing a high-level implementation framework and basing the process to as great an extent as possible on reusable resources. This book presents a comprehensive description of the Regulus platform, and is divided into two parts. Part I is an extended tutorial introduction, which explains how to use Regulus to build grammars, recognisers, and simple spoken dialogue and speech translation systems; the presentation is organised around several example applications which can be downloaded from the companion website. Part II describes the theoretical ideas on which Regulus is built, and

[4]The original idea for the MedSLT project was suggested by a doctor based in the Bay Area, where a substantial proportion of the population does not speak English.

also presents empirical evaluations. First, however, we will give a brief overview of speech recognition, and define some of the terms which we have so far been using informally; we will then describe how Regulus fits into the larger picture.

1.2 Speech recognition and language models

A speech recogniser takes a speech signal as input, and transforms it into an output which consists of a list of words. In order to do this, it requires three main kinds of knowledge. First, there is *signal processing*, which converts waveforms into digital representations. Next, it needs an *acoustic model*, which specifies how utterances in the language are realised as digital representations of waveforms. Signal processing and acoustic modelling are big subjects, which are not discussed in this book; we will assume that you already have a speech recognition platform available, containing components that handle these first two tasks. Some parts of the acoustic model will be visible to you. In particular, you will have a *pronunciation lexicon*, which associates each individual word with one or more lists of phonemes. For example, a pronunciation lexicon for British English would say that the word "water" can be pronounced as either [watə] or [watɹ], while a pronunciation lexicon for American English would also have [watə][5] plus the more common pronunciation [warɚ]. (The machine-readable encoding used by Nuance represents this second pronunciation as `w O ! *r`). Other parts of the acoustic model will not be accessible: for example, the relationship between the phonemes and the waveforms is complicated, and cannot be described without advanced statistical techniques. In most of this book, we will specifically assume that you are using the Nuance speech recognition platform, and obtaining your acoustic model as part of a Nuance "Language Pack".

Knowing how words relate to sounds isn't enough, however. If recognition is to be at all efficient, we also need a *language model*, which specifies which words the application is supposed to be able to recognise, and in what orders they are allowed to occur. The intention is to restrict the search space to a manageable size: instead of the whole space of possible lists of words in the language, the recogniser only needs to consider the ones specified by the language model. A language model might for instance represent the fact that "water" is a noun, and that nouns are only allowed to occur in certain contexts. Figure 1 shows schematically how the different knowledge sources involved in the recognition process are combined.

[5] American English also has r-less dialects, for example Boston.

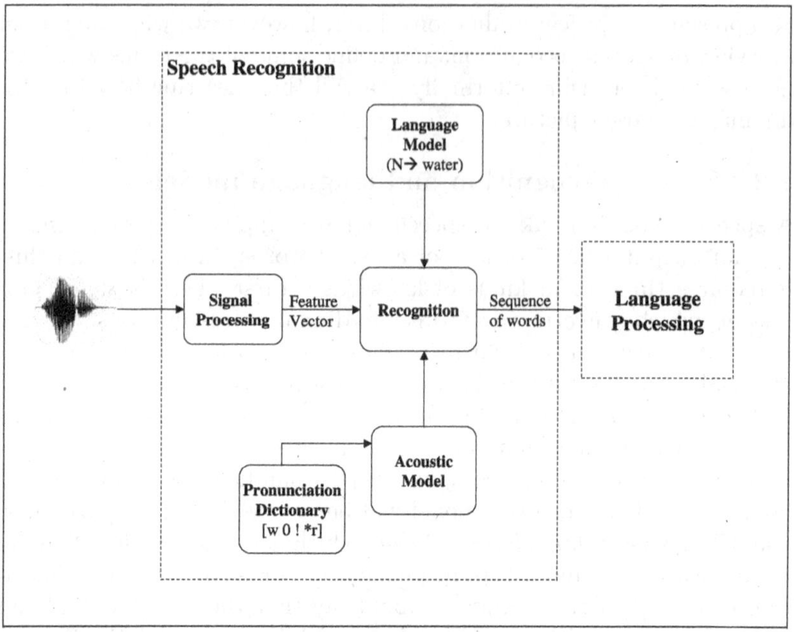

FIGURE 1 The generic speech recognition process

All of the above is very abstract: let's look at a specific example. Suppose that we want to build a recogniser that can handle ordinary British English spoken numbers, like "four", "eighty one", "one hundred and sixteen", and so on. The acoustic model, which we're assuming that someone else has already constructed, will encode information such as the fact that "eighty" is pronounced [ɛiti], and that the phone /i/ is typically realised as a sound wave with the characteristic pattern of a low first formant (F1) and a high second formant (F2), as can be seen in the spectrogram in Figure 2.

A simple way to define the language model would be to say that we will only look in the input signal for the small set of words, like "one", "twelve", "fifty" "thousand" or "and", that can occur in numbers. Another way of putting this is to say that the utterance is constrained to consist of an arbitrary list of number words. This is already going to help us a good deal. Instead of having to consider the hundreds of thousands of words that exist in English, we will only have to take account of a few dozen.

We can however do better than just restricting ourselves to sequences of number words. If we permit any arbitrary sequence, we might for

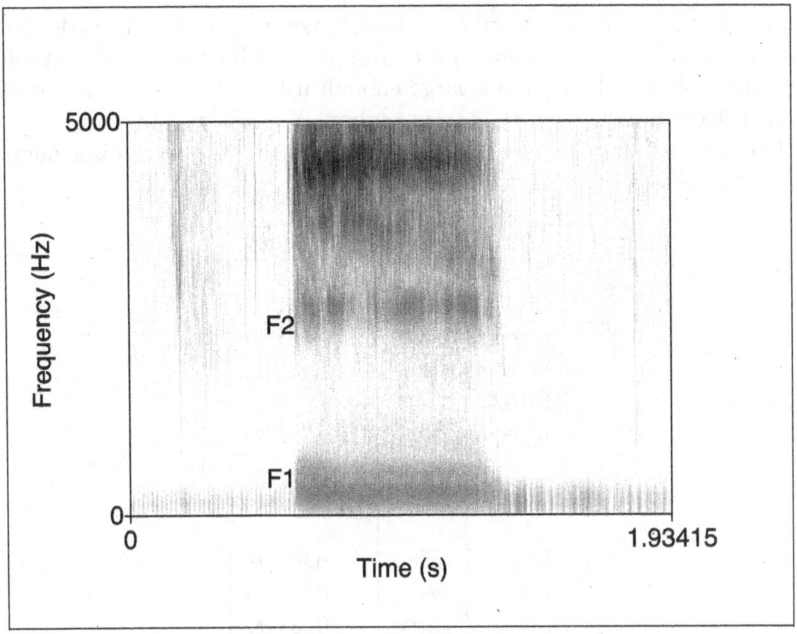

FIGURE 2 Spectrogram of [i]. Dark bands represent formants. As is characteristic of [i], F1 is very low, nearly at the bottom of the spectrogram, and F2 is very high

example misrecognise "fifty nine" as "fifteen nine". (Try saying these two phrases aloud: you'll find they sound almost identical). However, "fifteen nine" isn't a well-formed English number. If we restrict our language model further, so as to allow some sequences of number words but not others, the recogniser will have fewer possibilities to consider, and will be able to deliver better performance.

How could we specify the difference between acceptable and unacceptable sequences? There are two basic approaches we can follow: *data-driven*, or *rule-based.* This book will be mostly concerned with the rule-based approach, but since the data-driven one is quite wide-spread, particularly in research systems, we describe it first. Later on, we will spend a considerable amount of time comparing the two approaches.

1.2.1 Data-driven language modelling

If we are following the data-driven (also commonly referred to as "corpus-based" or "statistical") approach, we obtain a large list of valid numbers, and then we extract statistics from this list. A simple way to do this would be to compile a *bigram grammar*; this is essentially a table, which for each word lists the relative frequencies of words that can follow it. Figure 3 shows an example of what part of this table might look like. If we had a large enough list to start with, we would most likely find that "fifty" is reasonably often followed by "nine", but that "fifteen" hardly ever is. It is plausible that the recogniser ought to be able to find this information useful.

Word	Next	Frequency
...	...	...
fifteen	one	7 700
fifteen	two	6 000
fifteen	three	3 800
fifteen	four	900
fifteen	five	800
...	...	...
fifteen	nine	2 200
...	...	...
fifty	one	630 000
fifty	two	626 000
fifty	three	623 000
fifty	four	577 000
fifty	five	696 000
...	...	...
fifty	nine	428 000
...	...	...

FIGURE 3 Part of simple bigram grammar for English numbers. For each word, we give the number of times it was followed by each other word in the original data-set.

Extracting the kind of statistics in Figure 3 is of course only going to be possible if we have a large amount of data to analyse. (The numbers here were obtained by querying Google.) If we had less data available, we could also consider building a *class bigram model*. We group together all the number-words which are intuitively similar into a *class*: for example, the digit-words "one", "two", ... "nine" intuitively have similar properties, so we could group them into a class called `<Digit>`. Similarly, the words "eleven", "twelve", ... "nineteen" form a class which we could call `<Teen>`, and "twenty", "thirty", ... "ninety" form another class we could call `<MultipleOfTen>`. We can now build a bigram table where the entries are not words but classes, and the frequencies show how often a word of one class is followed by a word of another class.

Figure 4 shows part of a class bigram table.

Word	Next	Frequency
...	...	...
`<Teen>`	`<Digit>`	8
...	...	...
`<MultipleOfTen>`	`<Digit>`	921
...	...	...

FIGURE 4 Part of a simple class bigram grammar for English numbers. We abstract number words into classes; for each class, we give the number of times it was followed by each other class in the original data-set.

There are many ways in which this very basic sketch can be extended. We could consider longer sequences than just two words, or two classes: if we use three-word (class) sequences, we talk about *trigrams*, and in the general case *N-grams*. There is also an extensive literature on methods for addressing the problem of data sparseness; class N-gram models are just one of the simplest ideas.

A good introduction to the theoretical issues can be found in Chapter 6 of Jurafsky and Martin (2000). When we describe practical experiments on data-driven language modelling in this book, we will use the Nuance SayAnything© tool, which provides a user-friendly interface supporting construction of class N-gram models. We will have more to say about this in Chapter 12, but until then we mostly shift the focus to rule-based methods.

1.2.2 Rule-based language modelling

Data-driven language modelling is attractive in some ways, but also has its disadvantages. We have already mentioned the most obvious one: we need a substantial amount of data, in order to extract the frequency counts and other statistics. If we are trying to build a recogniser for a new domain, we will in most cases not have any data at all until the project is well under way. Another more subtle problem is that N-grams only capture local constraints on the input. This is easiest to see with bigrams. For example, suppose we want our little number grammar to deal with three-digit numbers like "two hundred and five". Our bigram or class bigram frequencies will tell us that digits like "five" can quite often be followed by the word "hundred". However, if we are in the middle of recognising "two hundred and five", and we've just reached the "five", we don't want any possibility at all of getting a second "hundred" — this comes from the overall structure of English numbers, which says that a three-figure number can only contain at most one occurrence of "hundred". It's certainly not impossible to try and model this kind of constraint using N-gram or other data-driven methods, but our intuition tells us that it should be possible to define explicitly which structures are permitted. The simplest way to do this is by writing a *context free grammar* (CFG) .

```
MAIN --> NUMBER

NUMBER --> ONE_TO_NINETY_NINE

NUMBER --> DIGIT hundred

NUMBER --> DIGIT hundred and ONE_TO_NINETY_NINE

ONE_TO_NINETY_NINE --> MULTIPLE_OF_TEN DIGIT

ONE_TO_NINETY_NINE -->
   DIGIT | TEEN | ten | MULTIPLE_OF_TEN

DIGIT --> one | two | ... | nine

TEEN --> eleven | twelve | ... | nineteen

MULTIPLE_OF_TEN --> twenty | thirty | ... | ninety
```

FIGURE 5 Context Free Grammar for English numbers up to three digits

Figure 5 shows a CFG for English numbers of up to three digits. There are two kinds of symbols: *terminals* like `hundred` or `three`, written in lower case, which denote concrete words of the language, and *non-terminals* like `NUMBER` or `DIGIT`, written in upper case, which denote symbols for different types of phrases. Each rule has a left hand side consisting of a single non-terminal, and a right hand side containing zero or more symbols, which can be any mixture of terminals and non-terminals. The arrow should be read as "can be" or "can be composed of". So for example

```
TEEN --> twelve
```

means "A phrase of type `TEEN` can be the word `twelve`" and

```
NUMBER --> DIGIT hundred
```

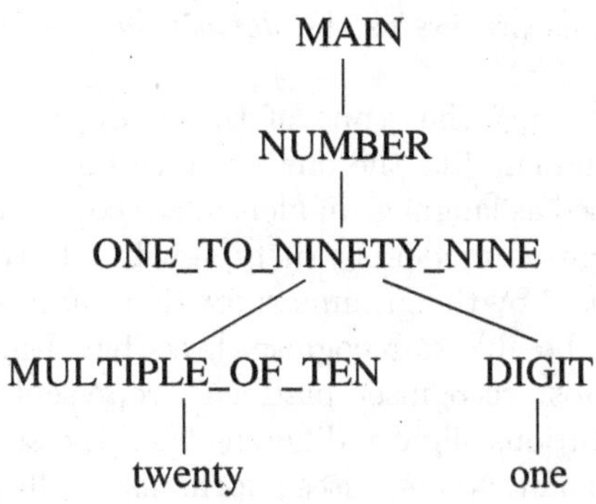

FIGURE 6 Derivation tree for "twenty one" in toy number grammar

means "A phrase of type NUMBER can be composed of a phrase of type DIGIT followed by the word hundred". The vertical bar | denotes disjunction, so

```
ONE_TO_NINETY_NINE -->
    DIGIT | TEEN | ten | MULTIPLE_OF_TEN
```

means that a phrase of type ONE_TO_NINETY_NINE can be a phrase of any of the types DIGIT, TEEN or MULTIPLE_OF_TEN, or the specific word ten.

The distinguished symbol MAIN is defined[6] to be the *root* of the grammar, from which we derive all the possible permitted strings by successive application of rules. For example, we can check that "twenty one" is a legal number as follows. We first use the rule

```
MAIN --> NUMBER
```

to rewrite MAIN into NUMBER. We then use the rule

```
NUMBER --> ONE_TO_NINETY_NINE
```

to rewrite this into ONE_TO_NINETY_NINE. Next, we use

```
ONE_TO_NINETY_NINE --> MULTIPLE_OF_TEN DIGIT
```

[6] Any symbol could be used as the label for the root of a grammar. In this book, we will mostly use the convention (common with the Nuance platform) that the root symbol is MAIN. Another common choice is SIGMA.

to get `MULTIPLE_OF_TEN DIGIT`. We rewrite `MULTIPLE_OF_TEN` to `twenty` to get `twenty DIGIT`; finally, we rewrite `DIGIT` to `one` to get `twenty one`. We can show this process as the *derivation tree* or *parse tree* in Figure 6.

The details are beyond the scope of this book, but it is possible to convert CFG grammars like the one we have just seen into a form where they can be used as language models in a recogniser. A recogniser equipped with a language model of this type will only try to recognise strings that are covered by the grammar; for the grammar in Figure 5, the recogniser would be able to recognise three-digit English numbers, and nothing else. Most recogniser platforms represent Context Free Grammars using notations slightly different from the standard one we have shown. In particular, Nuance uses a formalism called GSL (Grammar Specification Language). We will see examples of GSL in the next chapter. It is also possible to combine CFG grammars with the data-driven language modelling ideas described earlier, by adding probabilities to the grammar rules; logically enough, we call these Probabilistic Context Free Grammars (PCFGs). The Nuance platform provides tools that allow a CFG to be transformed into a PCFG.

We have mentioned some of the advantages of rule-based, as opposed to data-driven language modelling: we are not so dependent on availability of training data, and it is easier to capture long-distance constraints. Unfortunately, a little experimentation with CFGs quickly reveals some serious disadvantages too. The most important one is that it is very difficult to write a good CFG language model for any kind of reasonably complex domain.

Different arguments can be advanced as to why this is. In particular, one sometimes sees the claim that data-driven approaches are more suitable for handling the ungrammatical or disfluent constructions (hestitation, false starts and so on) that are typical of spontaneous speech. This is true, but for controlled language applications it is in our opinion not the most relevant objection. Truly spontaneous and unprompted speech is very hard to recognise and understand using any currently available methodology, and the error rates are usually too high to build applications that offer interesting performance for this kind of input. To us, it seems closer to the truth to say that the problem is primarily lack of appropriate software tools. Writing a rule-based language model is in many ways similar to writing a program, and from this point of view CFG is an embarrassingly primitive programming language. Since we are limited to unstructured atomic categories, it is reasonable to think of it as a programming language which doesn't even have variables — it is hardly surprising that it will be difficult to write clean, well-structured code.

In the world of programming languages, this is a common situation; the standard solution is to define a more expressive high-level language, which compiles down into the original low-level formalism. In the next section, we will explain how Regulus fits into this picture.

1.3 What Regulus does

Regulus raises the level of abstraction when writing CFG language models. Specifically, we use feature grammars as a more abstract way to represent CFGs. We will go into much more detail in the next chapter, but for now we will give an immediate example in order to provide motivation. Suppose we want to build a command and control application, which lets us manipulate objects on a PC desktop using voice commands. There will be some operations, like "open", "close" and "resize", which apply to windows, and others, like "delete", "copy" and "print", that apply to files. If we are using a CFG language model, it might contain rules like the following:

```
COMMAND --> WINDOW_VERB WINDOW_NOUN
COMMAND --> FILE_VERB FILE_NOUN

WINDOW_VERB --> open | close | resize
FILE_VERB --> delete | copy | print

WINDOW_NOUN --> window | browser
FILE_NOUN --> file | document
```

Here, it is apparent that we are already using the prefixes `WINDOW_` and `FILE_` as a kind of parameterisation of the phrase types `VERB` and `NOUN`: the problem is, however, that the parameterisation only exists at the level of documentation, in the names of the non-terminal symbols. We consequently need two different rules for combining a verb and a noun, one for each different type. Feature grammars let us make the parameterisation explicit, as follows:

```
COMMAND:[] --> VERB:[type=T] NOUN:[type=T]

VERB:[type=window] --> open | close | resize
VERB:[type=file] --> delete | copy | print

NOUN:[type=window] --> window | browser
NOUN:[type=file] --> file | document
```

Instead of treating the prefix as part of the category name, we break it out as the value of a *feature* called `type`, so that we can explicitly manipulate it. The payoff is that we are able to write the rule

```
COMMAND:[] --> VERB:[type=T] NOUN:[type=T]
```

which uses the *variable* `T` to indicate that the value of `type` in the noun and the verb has to be the same; we are thus able to collapse two rules into one. Complex feature grammars typically have dozens or even hundreds of different features, with correspondingly larger savings in compactness. There is an extensive literature on feature grammars; a good place to start is Chapter 11 of Jurafsky and Martin (2000). Although, strictly speaking, the two terms do not have exactly the same meaning, we will in this book also use the phrase "unification grammar" (UG) more or less as a synonym for "feature grammar". We will say a little about unification in Section 4.4.

1.3.1 Linguistically motivated feature grammars and grammar specialisation

Moving from CFG to feature grammars is in fact just the first of two steps in which Regulus raises the level of abstraction. The second is to generalise over feature grammars for different applications. Experience shows that complex natural language grammars tend to have a great deal of common structure, since they ultimately have to model general linguistic facts about English and other natural languages. There are consequently good reasons for wanting to save effort by implementing a *single* domain-independent core grammar, and deriving domain-independent grammars from it using some systematic process.

The central idea of the Regulus project is to realise this approach to implementation of domain-specific unification grammars. The starting point is a general English feature grammar, based on linguistic principles, which has been developed under a series of about ten projects and is available from the project website. This grammar can be adapted to a specific domain by adding domain-specific lexical entries. The resulting extended version of the general grammar is, however, too complex to be capable of compilation into CFG form. We solve the problem by extracting out an appropriate subset of the large grammar; we call this extraction process *grammar specialisation*. The point of the grammar specialisation process is to reduce the size and the ambiguity of the general grammar to a manageable level.

The version of grammar specialisation implemented in Regulus uses the EBL ("Explanation Based Learning") algorithm; this takes as input the original general feature grammar, a small corpus of training examples, and a set of declarations ("operationality criteria") which specify how the specialisation process is to be carried out. Basically, each example in the training set picks out a set of rules from the general grammar, and the operationality criteria criteria define how to combine these into new rules. The specialised feature grammar is compiled first into CFG form, then optionally into PCFG form, and finally into a recogniser. The relationships between the various knowledge sources and processing steps are illustrated in Figure 7.

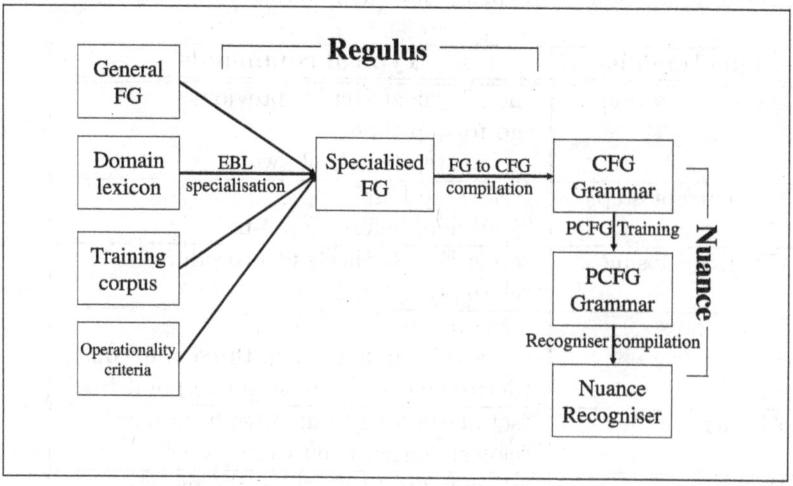

FIGURE 7 The Regulus processing path: the general feature grammar (FG) is successively transformed into a specialised FG, a CFG, a PCFG and a Nuance recogniser.

The methodology we have just outlined combines aspects of both the rule-based and the data-driven approaches; we end up with a rule-based language model, but we use a data-driven method to define it. A large part of the rest of the book is concerned with the details of this process. In particular, we describe the general English grammar and the two main Regulus compilation steps: grammar specialisation and feature grammar to CFG compilation.

1.4 Clarissa and MedSLT

In the following chapters, we will make frequent reference to the Clarissa and MedSLT applications. This section presents a brief overview of the two projects.

1.4.1 Clarissa

Clarissa (Rayner et al., 2005d,e) is an experimental speech enabled procedure navigator, designed for use on the International Space Station

(ISS), and developed at NASA Ames Research Center in a project that started in 2002. Astronauts on the ISS spend a large part of their time carrying out complex procedures, and at present have do this while simultaneously following written instructions on a PDF display, or sometimes even on a printed paper version. Since the tasks in question are often hands- and eyes-busy, and objects also float away in microgravity if not fastened down, this poses obvious practical problems.

Functionality	**Typical commands**
Basic navigation	"next", "next step", "previous" "go to step three" "go to step ten point two"
Non-current steps	"read step four" "read note before step nine"
Opening/closing	"open E M U checkout procedure" "close procedure"
Voice notes	"record voice note" "play voice note on step three point one" "delete voice note on step two point five"
Alarms	"set alarm for five minutes from now" "cancel alarm at ten twenty one"
Pictures	"show figure two", "hide the picture"
Output volume	"increase volume", "quieter"
Querying status	"where are we", "list voice notes" "list alarms", "what is the time"
Numerical values	"zero", "eleven", "ten point three" "eight thousand two hundred four" "no value"
Undoing/correcting	"undo", "go back" "no i said increase volume" "i mean step three point one"

TABLE 2 Examples of Clarissa functionality and commands

The Clarissa system, which was developed in close collaboration with several members of the astronaut corps[7], aims to offer a more ergonomically efficient solution. Astronaut users can navigate through procedures using only spoken commands, and have the system read steps to them aloud. The application can be run in a completely hands-

[7]In this connection, we would particularly like to mention T.J. Creamer and Mike Fincke.

and eyes-free mode, using "open mic", as opposed to "push-to-talk" recognition; the machine is always listening, and must decide for each recognised utterance whether the user is addressing it, or else possibly talking to a collegue or to Mission Control. There is also a conventional GUI display, which the user can refer to if appropriate.

The voice interface offers a total of about 75 different commands, which can be accessed using a vocabulary of about 260 words. Some typical examples are shown in Table 2. The initial version of the system is equipped with five XML-encoded procedures, three for testing water quality and two for space suit maintenance, and was first tested on the ISS on June 27, 2005.

The system contains five main modules: the speech processing module, the recognition filter, the semantic analyser, the dialogue manager and the visual display. Communication between modules is carried out using the Open Agent Architecture (OAA) protocol (Martin et al., 1998). The flow of information is as follows. Spoken input goes to the speech processing module, which produces a string of surface words, a set of confidence scores, and a meaning representation. The recognition filter uses the surface words and the confidence scores to decide whether to accept or reject the utterances. Its decisions support the "open-mic" behavior. After this, the semantic analyser converts the meaning representation into a form that can be used directly by the dialogue manager. The dialogue manager decides how to respond, and will in general both update the visual display and produce spoken output.

Regulus was used to build the grammar-based language model for the speech processing module, using the methods sketched in Section 1.3.1. Our starting point was the general Regulus feature-grammar for English, to which we added a Clarissa-specific lexicon with about 300 entries. The corpus of examples used to drive the specialisation process contained about 3300 utterances. We will present more details later, in Chapter 12. In particular, we will describe experiments there which show that Clarissa's Regulus-derived recogniser substantially outperforms a recogniser based on a standard class trigram language model trained on the same data.

1.4.2 MedSLT

MedSLT is a speech to speech translation system for emergency medical diagnosis (Bouillon et al., 2005). It translates standard examination questions about intensity, location, duration, quality of the pain, factors that increase/decrease the pain, medical/therapeutic processes and family antecedents of the patient, in subdomains based on symptom-types (for example, headaches, chest pain, etc). In the current version[8], translation is only one-way in the doctor to patient direction, which means that most communication is in the form of yes-no questions that can be answered non-verbally. In order to compensate for this restriction, the system has however a limited notion of dialogue context; it is then possible for the user to ask elliptical follow-on questions, for example: "is the pain in the front of the head?", followed by: "the back of the head?", "the left side?", "the right side?". Table 3 gives examples of MedSLT coverage, taken from the English headache subdomain.

Type	Examples
Where?	"is the pain above your eye" "is the pain always in the left side" "do you experience the pain in your jaw" "does the pain spread to the shoulder"
When?	"have you had the pain for more than a month" "do the headaches ever occur in the morning"
How long?	"does the pain typically last a few minutes" "does the pain ever last more than two hours"
How often?	"do you get headaches several times a week" "are the headaches occurring more often"
How?	"is it a stabbing pain" "is the pain usually severe"
Associated symptoms?	"do you vomit when you get the headaches" "is the pain accompanied by blurred vision"
Why?	"does bright light make the pain worse" "does drinking coffee give you headaches" "do you often get headaches when you eat cheese"
What helps?	"does sleep make the pain better" "does massage help"
Background?	"do you have a history of sinus disease" "have you had an e c g"

TABLE 3 Examples of English MedSLT coverage

The translation architecture is interlingua-based, and includes multiple processing engines, back-translation, context-dependent translation and a simple context-sensitive help module, that helps the user to learn the coverage of the system. The flow of processing is as follows. In order to take advantage of the robustness of data-driven methods and

[8]March 2006

the precision of rule-based language modelling, input speech is recognised using both a language model compiled by Regulus and a class N-gram model built using the Nuance SayAnything© package. The former produces a source semantic representation which is passed to the translation module; the latter produces a plain recognition string, that will be the input to the help module.

Translation is performed in several different steps. The source language semantic representation produced by Regulus is first passed to a discourse processing module, which interprets it in the context of the previous dialogue, in order to resolve possible ellipsis. The resolved representation is then transformed into its interlingual counterpart (Rayner et al., 2005b). The interlingual form is first translated back into the source language and shown to the user, who has the option to abort further processing if they decide that the system has failed to understand what they said. If the user approves the back-translation, the interlingual form is transferred into a target language representation. This is then transformed into a target language surface string using a generation grammar, and finally passed to a speech synthesis unit. The generation grammar is also compiled using Regulus.

If the system is unable to produce any translation, the user can consult the help component (Starlander et al., 2005), which uses the result of data-driven recognition to display a list of in-coverage example sentences. Examples are selected from a predefined list, using a heuristic that prioritises sentences maximizing the number of bigrams and unigrams shared with those extracted from the recognition result. In case of bad recognition, these examples can either include a similar sentence or paraphrase that can be directly selected by the user, or simply suggest possible alternative structures or vocabulary.

The current MedSLT demonstration system offers speech-to-speech translation from English into French, Japanese, Finnish, Spanish and Catalan. Initial versions with Japanese and French input also exist (Rayner et al., 2005c, Bouillon et al., 2006). The demonstration system supports three separate medical diagnosis subdomains (headaches, chest pain and abdominal pain) well enough that the full range of routine examination questions for each sub-domains is covered. The vocabulary for each subdomain is between 400 and 600 words.

The MedSLT system is used for many of the experiments described in this book. Chapter 11 investigates how the performance of the MedSLT recogniser varies as we change various parameters, like coverage and vocabulary size. Chapter 12 uses the same system to carry out a systematic comparison between Regulus-based speech understanding and a mainstream architecture based on a class N-gram language model and a set of phrase-spotting rules.

1.5 Related work

This section summarises related work on compilation of feature grammars into language models. An interesting early paper is (Chappelier et al., 1999), but this only described an isolated experiment in which a small feature grammar was transformed into a recogniser. The first general system capable of compiling a substantial class of feature grammars into language model form was the one developed by Moore and Gawron (Moore, 1998), which was implemented within the SRI Gemini system (Dowding et al., 1993). The Moore-Gawron method was used to build recognisers for several major projects, in particular SRI's CommandTalk (Stent et al., 1999), NASA Ames Research Center's Personal Satellite Assistant Simulator (Rayner et al., 2000b), and Stanford University's WITAS (Lemon et al., 2001). (Rayner et al., 2000c) describes work applying the Moore-Gawron algorithm to linguistically motivated feature grammars.

(Kiefer and Krieger, 2000) describes the *HPSG2CFG* algorithm and system, which was used to compile a substantial domain-independent HPSG grammar into CFG form; the resulting CFG grammars were not, however, used for speech recognition. The Moore-Gawron and Kiefer-Krieger approaches are compared in (Dowding et al., 2001), which also describes use of the Kiefer-Krieger method in the context of building concrete speech recognisers. UNIANCE, which has several points of contact with Regulus, is described in (Bos, 2002); a system built using UNIANCE is described in (Bos et al., 2003).

1.6 Plan of the book

The rest of the book is divided into two parts. Part I (Chapters 2 to 7) provides a practical tutorial introduction to Regulus. If you are only interested in the theory, you may prefer to skip this part. We start in Chapter 2 with the basics: software prerequisites, downloading and installation, writing an initial toy grammar, and compiling it into a functioning speech recogniser. Chapter 3 then explains how to integrate the recogniser into a minimal Prolog or Java-based speech application. The next three chapters describe how to use Regulus to build less trivial applications; Chapter 4 presents more detail on how to develop Regulus grammars, Chapter 5 describes command and control applications, and Chapter 6 speech translation applications. So far, we have only used small hand-coded Regulus grammars. Chapter 7 introduces the full system, and explains how to derive domain-specific Regulus grammars from the general linguistically motivated Open Source grammar for English that has been developed under the project. In particular, we provide detailed documentation showing how to add domain-specific lexicon entries compatible with the general grammar's structure. This concludes the tutorial half of the book.

Part II (Chapters 8 to 12) covers the theory behind Regulus. Chapter 8 describes the methods used to compile feature grammars into CFG-based language models, Chapter 9 the general feature grammar for English, and Chapter 10 the example-based grammar specialisation tools used to derive domain-specific feature grammars from the general ones. The next two chapters focus on empirical questions: Chapter 11 looks at scalability issues for Regulus derived grammars, and Chapter 12 compares Regulus with mainstream statistical/robust approaches to speech understanding. Chapter 13 concludes.

1.7 Summary

- There are two main types of dialogue strategy, "system-initiative" and "mixed-initiative".
- A recogniser needs two main types of information, an "acoustic model" and a "language model". The acoustic model relates sounds to words. The language model constrains the search space by specifying which sequences of words are permitted, and perhaps also their relative probabilities.
- There are two main approaches to building language models, "data-driven" ("corpus-based", "statistical") and "rule-based" ("grammar-based").
- The most common approach to data-driven language modelling is the class N-gram model. Typically $N = 2$ (bigram) or $N = 3$ (trigram).
- The most common approach to rule-based language modelling is Context Free Grammar (CFG).
- Data-driven approachs are conceptually simple and can produce excellent results, but require large quantities of training data, and can have problems modelling non-local constraints.
- Rule-based approaches are less dependent on training data and can model non-local constraints, but writing CFG grammars for complex domains is very challenging.
- Feature grammars are a way to raise the level of abstraction, by making it possible to write parameterised CFG grammars.
- Regulus further raises the level of abstraction when specifying a language model. General (domain-independent) feature grammars

are first compiled to domain-specific feature grammars, which are then compiled to CFG language models.

Exercises

1. Find a commercial telephone-based spoken dialogue system. Call it up and talk to it. How much freedom do you have in what you are allowed to say at various points in the dialogue?
2. Sketch a system-initiative dialogue for controlling a simple robot. What problems do you encounter?
3. If you know IPA, write down the pronunciations of some words. How much do they vary between different dialects and contexts of use?
4. Write a program to extract a bigram grammar from a text file. Run it on some online texts. What problems do you notice?
5. Extend the CFG in Figure 5 to cover numbers of up to six figures, e.g. "eighteen thousand two hundred and five" or "two hundred and twelve thousand six hundred".
6. Extend the toy feature grammar in Section 1.3 to cover a few more types of command.

Part I

Using Regulus

2

Getting started

Manny Rayner and Nikos Chatzichrisafis

2.1 Getting set up

The previous chapter explained the conceptual motivation behind Regulus. In this chapter, we will introduce the concrete system. We will start with the practical details of how to obtain and install the software you need in order to run Nuance and Regulus. Next, we explain how to build and run a toy Nuance recogniser based on a CFG grammar. Finally, we describe how to rewrite the CFG as a Regulus feature grammar, and compile that grammar into a Nuance recognition package. We show how the higher level of abstraction in the Regulus grammar lets us remove redundancy in the Nuance CFG grammar, by introducing features to parameterise the rules.

2.1.1 Hardware requirements

We recommend running on a machine with at least 256 MB of memory and a 1 GHz Pentium 4 processor. This should be enough that everything described here will actually work, though performance will sometimes be rather painfully slow. 1 GB memory and a 2 GHz processor should give comfortable performance.

2.1.2 UNIX, Windows and Cygwin

Many of the examples in this book assume that you are running a UNIX shell, like bash. Most readers, however, will probably be using some version of Windows. If you are, and if you haven't done so already, we recommend you to download Cygwin from `http://www.cygwin.com/`. This will give you a free UNIX-like environment, which will be almost indispensible for many of the things we're going to do. Of course, if you're already using UNIX, you can skip this step. When you download Cygwin, be certain to include the 'make' , 'cvs', and 'openssh' modules.

For the Windows users without 'bash' and 'make' support, there are 'bat' scripts in the Regulus distribution, which let you compile and run the examples under discussion.

2.1.3 Prolog

Regulus is implemented in SICStus Prolog. If you don't already have this, you can obtain it from `http://www.sics.se`. At the time of going to press, an academic single-user license cost about 130 Euros.

You should make sure that the environment variable `PATH` is set to include the SICStus `bin` directory. In Windows, you do this by opening the Control Panel, clicking on System, and then choosing the Advanced tab and the Environment Variables button. You can then edit the value of `PATH`.

You don't necessarily have to know Prolog to be able to use Regulus, though some previous familiarity will be useful. In particular, as we shall soon see, Regulus grammar syntax is based on Prolog syntax. It is somewhat easier to write Regulus applications in Prolog than in other languages, since the datastructures in the grammar are originally encoded in Prolog, but it is also perfectly possible to write them in Java (other languages will probably also be supported soon). We will discuss this further in Chapter 3.

2.1.4 Nuance

Next, you need to get hold of the Nuance Toolkit. Nuance is a commercial product, but they are fairly accommodating towards people who want to use it for research purposes. We expect that most readers will be academic researchers: if that describes you, please send a mail to `support@nuance.com`, briefly describing your project and explaining that you want a Nuance license. You should get one within a couple of weeks. If you want to use Nuance for commercial purposes, you should contact a local sales representative to obtain a standard development license. The Nuance website will advise you about how to do this.

When you've been given your Nuance license, you'll also have an account at Nuance that will allow you to download software. Follow the instructions to download and install a recent version of the Nuance Toolkit. If you want to develop recognisers for anything apart from American English, which comes with the basic toolkit, you should also download "Language Modules" for the languages you're interested in. Nuance supports about twenty different languages, including Arabic, Chinese, English, French, German, Italian, Japanese, Korean, Portugese and Spanish. In several cases, including Chinese, English and Spanish, there is support for multiple dialects.

You should also download and install Nuance's Vocalizer Text-To-Speech (TTS) engine. In order to use Vocalizer, you also need to obtain "Voice Packs" for the synthesised voices you will be using. In this book, we'll assume that you are going to use the "Laurie Woods" voice for English, and the "Julie Deschamps" voice for French. If you prefer to use different voices, the necessary changes to the scripts should be obvious. Note by the way that no extra licence code is required to install Vocalizer; when you reach the stage in the installation procedure where you are asked for a license code, just hit "return".

You are strongly advised to read at least some of the online Nuance documentation, in order to familiarise yourself with the basic operation of the Nuance Toolkit. You will find this material in the "doc" folder of the Nuance release. Look in particular at "Introduction to the Nuance System" and "Nuance Grammar Developer's Guide".

In the rest of the book, we are going to assume that you will always be running the Nuance license manager and any possible Vocalizer process on your own machine. To declare to Nuance that you are doing this, you need to edit the file `$NUANCE/data/nuance-resources.site` to include the lines

```
lm.Addresses=localhost
client.TTSAddresses=localhost:32323
```

IMPORTANT: Edit this file as described. If you do not do so, Nuance applications will not be able to find the license manager and will not run.

2.1.5 Why don't we use free software platforms?

We are frequently asked why Regulus needs to use commercial software like Nuance and SICStus. Ideally, we would prefer to run on free Open Source platforms. Right now, however, commercial systems offer considerably better performance than the free alternatives — this is why the companies that make them are able to charge money for their products. At some point, we may introduce a lower-performance version of Regulus which is compatible with free platforms.

2.1.6 Downloading and installing Regulus

Regulus is available from the SourceForge website at

```
http://sourceforge.net/projects/regulus/
```

There are two ways to install Regulus from the SourceForge site: downloading a release version, or using CVS to get the current version. Downloading a release is more likely to give you a stable version of the system, but you may need to update directly from CVS sometimes if you want a version containing a recent feature or fix.

You can download a release version as a zipfile by following the directions on the SourceForge site. You then need to unpack this zipfile to some suitable directory. Alternately, you can update directly from CVS by opening a UNIX or Cygwin window, going to the directory where you wish to install Regulus, and using the following invocation:

```
cvs -d:pserver:anonymous@cvs.sf.net:/cvsroot/regulus\
  co -P Regulus
```

In either case, you then need to set the value of the environment variable `REGULUS` to point to the Regulus root directory. Suppose for example you are running under Windows, and that you installed Regulus under `C:/Speech`. You should then set the value of `REGULUS` to `C:/Speech/Regulus`. It is important to use forward slashes rather than backslashes.

If you just want to browse the Regulus files without downloading them, you can do this directly on the SourceForge website. The root directory is at

```
http://cvs.sourceforge.net/viewcvs.py/regulus/
```

You can find other files and directories by following links in the obvious way.

2.2 A toy grammar in GSL

Before we actually start using Regulus, we will first review some of the background. As we have already said in the previous chapter, Regulus is a tool for building complex speech recognition grammars; it lets you write the grammars in a high-level formalism, and then compiles them down into the Nuance Grammar Specification Language (GSL) formalism, which is basically a version of CFG extended to allow construction of semantic values. If you don't know anything about GSL, you may want to look through some of the "Nuance Grammar Developer's Guide", included in the Nuance documentation folder, before you read further.

What we are going to do in this section is show you how to build, compile and test a very simple toy grammar directly in GSL; in Section 2.3, we are then going to do the same thing again, using Regulus. The point of the exercise is to illustrate how use of a high-level formalism can make the grammar cleaner and easier to understand.

Our first toy grammar will just use six words: the numbers "one" and "two", the singular nouns "cat" and "dog" and the plural nouns

```
.MAIN
[
  ( SINGULAR_NP:np ) { < value $np > }
  ( PLURAL_NP:np ) { < value $np > }
]

SINGULAR_NP
( SINGULAR_SPEC:s SINGULAR_NOUN:n )
    {return( ( ( spec $s ) ( noun $n ) ) )}

PLURAL_NP
( PLURAL_SPEC:s PLURAL_NOUN:n )
    {return( ( ( spec $s ) ( noun $n ) ) )}

SINGULAR_NOUN
[ dog {return( canis_domesticus )}
  cat {return( felis_domesticus )}
]

PLURAL_NOUN
[ dogs {return( canis_domesticus )}
  cats {return( felis_domesticus )}
]

SINGULAR_SPEC one {return( 1 )}

PLURAL_SPEC two {return( 2 )}
```

FIGURE 8 Hand-coded Toy0 grammar in Nuance GSL.
(**$REGULUS/Examples/Toy0/Nuance/hand_coded_toy0.grammar**)

"cats" and "dogs". It will allow two-word utterances consisting of a number followed by a noun. We will require singular numbers to go with singular nouns, and plural numbers with plural nouns: so we want to allow "one cat" or "two dogs", but not "*one cats" or "*two dog". An utterance will produce an associated semantic representation of the form

```
((spec <number>) (noun <animal>))
```

where `<number>` is a representation of the number, and `<animal>` is a representation of the animal: so for example "two dogs" will be represented as

```
((spec 2) (noun canis_domesticus))
```

Figure 8 shows the grammar. Using the Nuance `nuance-compile` utility, we can compile it into a Nuance recognition package, which is the form required by the underlying recognition engine and other Nuance tools, as follows:

```
$ cd $REGULUS/Examples/Toy0/Nuance
$ nuance-compile hand_coded_toy0 English.America
```

Here, the first argument (`hand_coded_toy0`) is the name of the grammar to be compiled, and the second (`English.America`) is the name of the Nuance "Language Module" (acoustic model) to use. If you prefer, and if you have installed the relevant Language Module, you could equally well compile the grammar for British English or some other Nuance-supported English dialect. After invoking `nuance_compile`, you should get several lines of trace output, starting with something like

```
Processing grammars.
```

and ending with

```
Done.
```

The Nuance compiler should also have created a new subdirectory of `$REGULUS/Examples/Toy0/Nuance` called `hand_coded_toy0`, which will be the recognition package. We can now test the grammar in text mode, using the Nuance `nl-tool` utility. A typical short session with `nl-tool` under UNIX or Cygwin might look like this:

```
$ cd $REGULUS/Examples/Toy0/Nuance
$ nl-tool -package hand_coded_toy0 -grammar .MAIN
Ready

one cat
Number of Interpretations: 1

{<value ((spec 1) (noun felis_domesticus))>}

two dogs
Number of Interpretations: 1

{<value ((spec 2) (noun canis_domesticus))>}

one cats
Number of Interpretations: 0

two dog
Number of Interpretations: 0
```

It is also easy to run the package as a speech recogniser. Once again, open a Cygwin window and connect to the relevant directory:

```
$ cd $REGULUS/Examples/Toy0/Nuance
```

Next, start the Nuance licence manager in the background:

```
$ nlm <your-Nuance-license-code> &
```

This should produce trace output ending in something like

```
Nuance License Manager ready to accept requests on
port 8470.
```

When the license manager is running, start a Nuance recognition server in the background, using the Toy0 recognition package we have just compiled:

```
$ recserver -package hand_coded_toy0 &
```

You should now get trace output something like

```
Nuance Recognition Server
All debug information is currently logged into
./logs/recserver_log_current
```

Finally, start a Nuance Xapp process, using the same Toy0 recognition package.

```
$ Xapp -package hand_coded_toy0
```

A Nuance Xapp recogniser-testing window should come up. Connect your microphone, click on the "Listen" button, and say "one cat". You should get the values "one cat" in the "Recognised String" pane, and

```
{<value ((spec 1)(noun felix_domesticus))>}
```

in the "Natural Language" pane. We encourage you to try these operations yourself.

Let's now go back and look at the structure of the grammar in Figure 8. The first rule (`.MAIN`) says that an utterance is either a singular noun phrase (`SINGULAR_NP`) or a plural noun phrase (`PLURAL_NP`). Since the grammar identifier `.MAIN` starts with a period, the rules of GSL syntax say that this is a "top-level grammar"; a top-level grammar is one that an application can pass to the recogniser as part of a recognition request (cf. Section 3.2).

The second rule says that a `SINGULAR_NP` is composed of a `SINGULAR_SPEC` followed by a `SINGULAR_NOUN`, and the third one says that `PLURAL_NP` is composed of a `PLURAL_SPEC` followed by a `PLURAL_NOUN`. The remaining rules consist of lexical entries for SINGULAR_NOUN, PLURAL_-NOUN, SINGULAR_SPEC and PLURAL_SPEC.

There is clearly something rather unsatisfying about this grammar; every rule seems to occur in two versions, one for SINGULAR and one for PLURAL. Although the problem does not seem particularly important when we only have the singular/plural distinction to consider, it acts combinatorially. If we had two such distinctions, we would get four copies of each rule; with three distinctions, we would have eight. This is exactly the kind of issue which can be addressed by moving to the more expressive Regulus feature-grammar formalism.

2.3 Rewriting Toy0 in Regulus

In this section, we will show how to use Regulus to rewrite the Toy0 grammar, in a way that lets us merge the "singular" and "plural" versions into single parameterised objects. We'll do this a piece at a time, and finally present the complete grammar. We start with the lexical rules, since they are the simplest ones. For example, consider the GSL rule

```
SINGULAR_SPEC one {return( 1 )}
```

which says that the word one is a SINGULAR_SPEC with associated semantic value 1. In Regulus, we will write the same rule like this:

```
spec:[sem=1, singplur=sing] --> one.
```

A term like spec is a *category symbol.* It functions as a generalisation of the two GSL grammar names SINGULAR_SPEC and PLURAL_SPEC. Similarly, noun will be a generalisation of SINGULAR_NOUN and PLURAL_NOUN and np will be a generalisation of SINGULAR_NP and PLURAL_NP. We distinguish between the "singular" and "plural" versions using the *feature* singplur. This can take the values sing ("singular") and plur ("plural"). There are two special features called sem and gsem, which we will get to shortly. We assign values to features using an equality sign, e.g.

```
singplur=sing
sem=1
```

We can create a list of feature-value pairs by enclosing it in square brackets, e.g.

```
[sem=1, singplur=sing]
```

and attach it to a category symbol, using a colon, to make a *category,* e.g.

```
spec:[sem=1, singplur=sing]
```

Finally, we can combine categories into *rules*, using the --> symbol. There has to be exactly one category on the left-hand side of the rule. The right hand side consists of a list that can contain either categories or surface words. In our first Regulus rule,

```
spec:[sem=1, singplur=sing] --> one.
```

we have the category spec:[sem=1, singplur=sing] on the left hand side, and the word one on the right-hand side. Here, the combination of the category symbol spec and the feature-value pair singplur=sing corresponds to the grammar name SINGULAR_SPEC in the GSL version. The feature-value pair sem=1 on the left-hand side corresponds to the return value 1 in the GSL rule.

If the GSL rule contains several entries in the body, the Regulus version will consist of several rules. For example, the GSL rule

```
SINGULAR_NOUN
[ dog {return( canis_domesticus )}
  cat {return( felis_domesticus )}
]
```

has two items in the body; the Regulus version will be the two rules

```
noun:[sem=canis_domesticus, singplur=sing] --> dog.
noun:[sem=felis_domesticus, singplur=sing] --> cat.
```

As mentioned earlier in Section 1.3, the strength of feature grammars comes from the fact that the values of features can be variables as well as constants. We can see this in the two GSL rules

```
SINGULAR_NP
( SINGULAR_SPEC:s SINGULAR_NOUN:n )
     {return( ( ( spec $s ) ( noun $n ) ) )}

PLURAL_NP
( PLURAL_SPEC:s PLURAL_NOUN:n )
     {return( ( ( spec $s ) ( noun $n ) ) )}
```

Both rules have exactly the same structure except for the systematic alternation of SINGULAR and PLURAL, so we can merge them into the single Regulus rule

```
np:[sem=[[spec,S], [noun,N]], singplur=Singplur] -->
   spec:[sem=S, singplur=Singplur],
   noun:[sem=N, singplur=Singplur].
```

Here, the values of the feature singplur on both the left and the right hand sides are the same variable, Singplur. (Regulus notation is built on top of Prolog; constants start with lower-case, variables with upper case). The feature singplur can either take the value sing, giving the first GSL rule, or plur, giving the second. Note also how the sem feature is used. The variable values S and N on the right hand side are doing the same work as the variables $s and $n in the GSL. The value

```
[[spec,S], [noun,N]]
```

in the left hand side corresponds to the GSL return value

```
( ( spec $s ) ( noun $n ) )
```

This points to a general principle: as the name suggests, the sem feature encodes the semantic value that is passed upwards in the grammar. When sem occurs in the right hand side, the semantic value is passed to the left hand side, as with the GSL "dollar variables". When sem occurs in the left hand side, the semantic value is passed to the rule above (the "calling" rule), in the same way that the GSL return construction passes back a value.

The sem feature, used in the left hand side, corresponds to the GSL return construction. The gsem feature maps into the GSL global slot-filling construction. We can see an example of this in the first rule from the Toy0 grammar. The GSL version is

```
.MAIN
[
   ( SINGULAR_NP:np ) { < value $np > }
   ( PLURAL_NP:np ) { < value $np > }
]
```

in which the angle brackets say that the global slot value is to be filled with the value of the variable $np. The Regulus version uses the gsem feature, as follows:

```
'.MAIN':[gsem=[value=NP]] -->
   np:[sem=NP].
```

As we have already seen, the sem feature on the right hand side means that the variable NP gets passed to the left hand side. The feature-value declaration

```
gsem=[value=NP]
```

translates into the GSL slot-filling declaration

```
< value $np >
```

In general, the value of the gsem feature must be a list of key-value pairs. For each such pair, the "key" is the name of a global slot, and the "value" is the value assigned to that slot. Unlike the sem feature, which can occur either on the left hand side or the right hand side of the rule, the gsem feature can *only* occur on the left hand side.

A final point that may need some explanation is why the Regulus version of the grammar contains a single rule for .MAIN, while the GSL version has two rules, one for SINGULAR_NP and one for PLURAL_NP. This is because the np category on the right hand side fails to specify any value for the feature singplur; Regulus interprets the *lack* of a value as equivalent to permitting *any* value. We could have made this explicit, by instead writing the rule as

```
'.MAIN':[gsem=[value=NP]] -->
  np:[sem=NP, singplur=Any].
```

Here, Any is a variable that does not occur elsewhere in the rule (an "anonymous" variable), and which consequently is free to take any possible value. Yet another equivalent way to write the rule is

```
'.MAIN':[gsem=[value=NP]] -->
  np:[sem=NP, singplur=sing\/plur].
```

In this version, the feature disjunction symbol \/ indicates that the value of the feature singplur can be either sing or plur. The choice between these different ways of writing the rule is a matter of taste.

2.3.1 Declarations

We have described the rules in the Regulus version of the grammar, but we aren't done yet. We need to specify various pieces of information that we have so far only mentioned informally, such as the fact that the spec, noun and np categories all have exactly one feature, singplur, and that the possible values for singplur are sing and plur. We do this using Regulus declarations. There are four different kinds:

feature_value_space Defines possible ranges of values that can be assigned to features.

feature Defines the features used in the various categories.

category Defines the category symbols used in the grammar.

top_level_category Defines which category symbols correspond to GSL "top level grammars".

We'll look at these one at a time.

feature_value_space declarations

A given feature is only allowed to take one of a finite predefined set of possible values. Here, the singplur feature is allowed to take the values

sing and **plur**. Typically, there will be several features, all of which can take values in the same range. A **feature_value_space** declaration lists a set of possible values, and associates an identifier with that range.

For the Toy0 grammar, we define a value space which contains the values **sing** and **plur**, and call it **singplur_value**. The declaration looks like this:

```
feature_value_space(singplur_value, [[sing, plur]]).
```

Note the double brackets around the list of possible values.

feature declarations

Once we have defined our value spaces, we can define the features too. A feature declaration associates a feature with its value space. For the Toy0 grammar, we have the single feature **singplur**, which will take values in **singplur_value**. The declaration is as follows:

```
feature(singplur, singplur_value).
```

It is not necessary to add declarations for the predefined semantic features **sem** and **gsem**.

category declarations

Now that we have features, we can also define category symbols. A **category** declaration associates a category with the set of features it can take.

The Toy0 grammar contains the four categories **.MAIN**, **np**, **spec** and **noun**. The first of these can only take the feature **gsem**; all the other take both a **sem** feature and a **singplur** feature. The declarations are:

```
category('.MAIN', [gsem]).
category(np, [sem, singplur]).
category(spec, [sem, singplur]).
category(noun, [sem, singplur]).
```

The list of possible features is enclosed in brackets. The features can be listed in any order.

top_level_category declarations

We need at least one GSL "top-level grammar". We specify the corresponding category symbol using the **top_level_category** declaration.

In the Toy0 grammar, the single top-level category is **.MAIN**. The relevant declaration is:

```
top_level_category('.MAIN').
```

The single quotes around **'.MAIN'** are required because Regulus syntax is based on Prolog syntax: **.MAIN** is a Prolog constant, but constants

```
% Declarations
feature_value_space(singplur_value, [[sing, plur]]).

feature(singplur, singplur_value).

category('.MAIN', [gsem]).
category(np, [sem, singplur]).
category(spec, [sem, singplur]).
category(noun, [sem, singplur]).

top_level_category('.MAIN').

% Grammar rules
'.MAIN':[gsem=[value=NP]] -->
   np:[sem=NP].

np:[sem=[[spec,S], [noun,N]], singplur=Singplur] -->
   spec:[sem=S, singplur=Singplur],
   noun:[sem=N, singplur=Singplur].

% Lexicon rules
spec:[sem=1, singplur=sing] --> one.
spec:[sem=2, singplur=plur] --> two.

noun:[sem=felis_domesticus, singplur=sing] --> cat.
noun:[sem=canis_domesticus, singplur=sing] --> dog.
noun:[sem=felis_domesticus, singplur=plur] --> cats.
noun:[sem=canis_domesticus, singplur=plur] --> dogs.
```

FIGURE 9 Toy0 Regulus grammar.
(`$REGULUS/Examples/Toy0/Regulus/toy0.grammar`)

normally have to start with a lower-case alphabetical character. If they start with anything else, the Prolog reader requires that the whole constant must be enclosed in quotes. The quotes are not part of the constant's name.

The complete Toy0 grammar consists of the rules together with the declarations, and is shown in Figure 9. Comments are written Prolog-style using an initial % sign.

2.4 Regulus configuration files

We're almost at the point where we can compile the Toy0 Regulus grammar into a Nuance recogniser, but there's one more thing left to

```
regulus_config(
   regulus_grammar,
   '$REGULUS/Examples/Toy0/Regulus/toy0.regulus').

regulus_config(
   top_level_cat,
   '.MAIN').

regulus_config(
   nuance_grammar,
   '$REGULUS/Examples/Toy0/Generated/recogniser').

regulus_config(
   working_file_prefix,
   '$REGULUS/Examples/Toy0/Generated/toy0').
```

FIGURE 10 Toy0 configuration file.
(**$REGULUS/Examples/Toy0/scripts/toy0.cfg**)

do: we need to write a Regulus configuration file, which will define the relevant files, directories and other objects associated with Toy0. The configuration file is shown in Figure 10.

The first entry in this file says that the Regulus grammar consists of the single file

```
$REGULUS/Examples/Toy0/Regulus/toy0.regulus
```

Note that once again the name of the file needs to be enclosed inside quotes, since it is a Prolog constant that doesn't start with a lower-case character[9]. It is possible to make the second argument a comma-separated list of files enclosed in square brackets, i.e.

```
regulus_config(
   regulus_grammar,
   [<file1>, <file2>, ...]).
```

if the grammar has been split into more than one file.

The second entry states that the grammar's top-level category is `.MAIN`. The third entry says that the base name for the generated Nuance grammar files is

```
$REGULUS/Examples/Toy0/Generated/recogniser
```

[9]If you are uncertain about the rules for Prolog syntax, it never actually does any harm to enclose a constant inside quotes.

The Regulus compiler will generate two files. The first of these is the main GSL grammar file and has a `.grammar` extension. The second one is a short file with a `slot_definitions` extension, which lists the slot names one per line. The Nuance documentation contains more information about the slot definition file.

Finally, the fourth entry defines where Regulus working files are to be placed. Here, they will all start with the prefix

```
$REGULUS/Examples/Toy0/Generated/toy0
```

2.5 Using Regulus

We can now use our sample grammar in the interactive Regulus development environment. First, we open a SICStus window. At the Prolog prompt, we load the development environment by typing

```
?- ['$REGULUS/Prolog/load'].
```

This should result in trace output as Prolog files are loaded, finishing with a "yes". The next step is to start Regulus using the Toy0 config file, as follows:

```
?- regulus('$REGULUS/Examples/Toy0/scripts/toy0.cfg'
  ).
```

This should produce a response something like

```
Loading settings from Regulus config file
c:/regulus/examples/toy0/scripts/toy0.cfg

>>
```

Here, >> is the Regulus prompt. We can compile the Regulus grammar into Nuance GSL form by entering the command

```
>> NUANCE
```

We should get a lot of trace output, ending with something like

```
-- Writing out rules...
   -- Nuance slot names written to file
      c:/regulus/examples/toy0/generatedfiles/
recogniser.slot_definitions
   -- Nuance rules written to file
      c:/regulus/examples/toy0/generatedfiles/
recogniser.grammar
0.0 secs

Compilation finished, 0.04 secs
```

At this point, we suggest that you look at the generated Nuance GSL grammar in

```
$REGULUS/Examples/Toy0/Generated/recogniser.grammar
```

You'll find that it's very similar to, but not quite the same as, the hand-coded GSL grammar in Figure 8.

Just as we did with the hand-coded GSL grammar, we can compile the Regulus-generated version of the grammar into a Nuance recogniser, and test it in text mode. The commands to compile the grammar are

```
$ cd $REGULUS/Examples/Toy0/Generated
$ nuance-compile recogniser English.America
```

and we can then run `nl-tool` in the way shown on page 30. Even though the hand-coded and Regulus-generated versions of the grammar are slightly different, we should still get the same behaviour as we did with the hand-coded grammar.

We can also run the recogniser in speech mode in the same way as we did with the hand-coded version (cf. page 31). The only difference is that here we start by going to the directory containing the Regulus-derived version, i.e.

```
$REGULUS/Examples/Toy0/Generated
```

before invoking the Nuance license manager and the `recserver` and `Xapp` utilities.

2.6 Summary

- Before you can use Regulus, you need to download Cygwin (if you're working on Windows), the Nuance Toolkit, Nuance Vocalizer and SICStus.
- You should read at least some of the Nuance documentation, in particular the "Nuance Grammar Developer's Guide".
- You can download Regulus from SourceForge, either as a zipfile (recent stable version) or through CVS (current version).
- If you try to build complex GSL grammars by hand, they often contain a lot of redundancy.
- Regulus is a tool that lets you write GSL grammars in a compact, parameterised form. The notation is a kind of feature-value based unification grammar.
- A Regulus category consists of a category symbol together with a list of feature-value pairs. A Regulus lexical item consists of a Prolog atom. A rule has one category symbol on the left, and a list of categories and/or lexical items on the right.

- The `sem` feature in Regulus translates into the `return` construction in GSL. The `sem` feature translates into the GSL global slot-filling construction.
- Regulus requires you to declare the grammar constants that you will use. In particular, you need to declare the features, sets of values that can be assigned to features, and categories.
- The Regulus config file declares the files associated with a given Regulus application. In particular, it declares the source grammar, the generated GSL grammar and the working directory.
- You can compile a Regulus grammar into GSL form by entering the Regulus development environment and using the `NUANCE` command.
- You can compile a GSL grammar into a recognition package using the Nuance `nuance-compile` utility.
- You can test a recognition package using the Nuance Xapp utility. You need to start three processes: a license manager, a recserver, and Xapp itself.

Exercises

1. Compile the hand-coded GSL grammar into a Nuance recognition package and run it in text mode, as shown on page 30.
2. Run the recogniser you have just built in speech mode, as shown on page 31. What happens when you say things like "one dogs" or "two cat"?
3. Compile the Regulus grammar into a Nuance GSL grammar. Compare the resulting GSL grammar with the hand-coded version. Are any of the differences interesting?
4. Compile the Regulus-derived GSL grammar into a Nuance recognition package and run it in text mode.
5. Run the second recogniser in speech mode. Does it behave in the same way as the first one? Look at the Nuance documentation for the `batchrec` utility, and see if you can come up with a way to test this systematically.
6. Try adding some more numbers and animals to the Regulus grammar, so that you can for example cover "three pigs" or "seven seals". Make sure that you can still compile and run it. Test that the new functionality you have added does what you want.
7. Try to extend the Regulus grammar so that you can optionally put an adjective between the number and the noun, e.g. "three little pigs" or "one hungry wolf". What new declarations do you need? What new rules?

8. Try writing a version of the Toy0 grammar for a different language, e.g. Spanish or French. (You will need to obtain the appropriate Language Pack from the downloads area on the Nuance site, and install it). Do you need to add new features? Why?

3

Simple applications

Manny Rayner and Nikos Chatzichrisafis

3.1 Introduction

In Chapter 2, we showed you how to write a simple Regulus grammar and compile it into a Nuance speech recognition package. In this chapter, we'll show you how to include these recognition packages in simple spoken dialogue and speech translation applications. Chapters 5 and 6 will describe how to build more elaborate applications.

Our first application will use the Toy0 recognition grammar from Chapter 2, which can recognise the utterances "one dog", "one cat", "two dogs" and "two cats". We record two sound-files, for a bark and a miaow. The user invokes recognition by pressing the return key, and then speaking a system utterance. If the system hears "one dog", it will play the bark file; "one cat" will get the miaow file; "two dogs" will get the bark file twice; and "two cats" will get the miaow file twice. If the user says something else, or if the system isn't able to recognise what they say, it will speak an error message using the Vocalizer text to speech engine.

We first show how to implement a SICStus Prolog-based version of the system. The advantage of doing things in Prolog is that processing meshes cleanly with the Prolog-based Regulus formalism, and we will see that this makes the code extremely simple and transparent. We then go on to show how to build a speech translation version of the system, in which the system's response is a spoken French translation of the input phrase. For readers who are unhappy with Prolog, the final section describes a Java based version of the Toy0 application.

All three versions of the application are implemented using the Regulus SpeechServer ("Regserver"), a utility that is included in the Regulus release. The Regserver provides a simple Regulus-compatible API to the main Nuance runtime system, that makes it possible to invoke speech recognition, produce spoken output using TTS or recorded audio files, and perform other speech-related tasks. The core of each version of the system is a small program consisting of a few dozen lines of Prolog or Java; this carries out speech-related tasks by invoking the Regserver. The Regserver in turn routes these requests to other processes, which are responsible for providing the low-level Nuance functionality. In all, we have the following five processes:

Application program The application program handles the top-level logic.

Regulus Speech Server ("Regserver") The Regserver process mediates requests between the application program, the Recserver process and the Vocalizer process, and is described in Section 3.2.

Nuance recserver The Nuance recserver process is loaded with the compiled Nuance recognition package, and is responsible for performing the actual speech recognition.

Nuance Vocalizer TTS The Nuance Vocalizer process (equipped with an English voice) performs text to speech conversion.

Nuance license manager As usual, we need to have a license manager process running.

Before describing the applications themselves, we introduce the Regulus Speech Server and its associated client library.

3.2 The Regulus Speech Server

The Regserver is a Nuance application built on top of the C++ RecEngine API, which provides a socket-based interface to the simpler kinds of Nuance functionalities. These functionalities include performing speech recognition, producing output speech using TTS, and playing recorded audio files. There is a Prolog client library[10], which can be used to interface Prolog programs to the Regserver. From the application programmer's point of view, this infrastructure in effect makes it possible to perform speech recognition and other operations in a pure Prolog framework. Compiled binary versions of the Regserver, for Windows and Solaris, can be found in

```
$REGULUS/RegulusSpeechServer/runtime/win32
```

and

```
$REGULUS/RegulusSpeechServer/runtime/sparc-solaris
```

[10]We will postpone discussion of the Java client library until Section 3.5.1

The source code is in the directory

```
$REGULUS/RegulusSpeechServer/C_src/socketServer
```

In Section 3.3.1, we explain how to invoke the Regserver binary to run an application.

The Regserver Prolog client library is in

```
$REGULUS/RegulusSpeechServer/Prolog/
  regulus_sockettalk.pl
```

The most important predicates are the following[11].

3.2.1 regulus_sockettalk_init(+PortNumber, +RecognitionPackage, +NuanceParameters)

This predicate starts a Regserver, using the specified recognition package, and a list of zero or more Nuance parameters encoded as a Prolog atom; it then initialises the client library, and opens a socket connection to the Regserver on port number `PortNumber`. You must call this before invoking any of the other predicates. Sample call:

```
regulus_sockettalk_init(
   4321,
   '$REGULUS/Examples/Toy0/Generated/recogniser',
   'audio.OutputVolume=220')
```

3.2.2 regulus_sockettalk_exit_client

Closes the socket connection to the Regserver. Sample call:

```
regulus_sockettalk_exit_client
```

3.2.3 regulus_sockettalk_say_file(+File)

`File` is a Prolog atom whose print name is the name of a recorded .wav file. The audio file is appended to the Nuance prompt queue. Sample call:

```
regulus_sockettalk_say_file(
   '$REGULUS/Examples/Toy0/wavfiles/woof.wav')
```

3.2.4 regulus_sockettalk_say_tts(+String)

`String` is a Prolog string. A request to say `String` using TTS is appended to the Nuance prompt queue. Sample call:

```
regulus_sockettalk_say_tts("Ready␣to␣start")
```

[11]We use the standard Prolog convention of marking input arguments with a `+` and output arguments with a `-`.

3.2.5 regulus_sockettalk_recognise(+Grammar, –Result)

`Grammar` is a Prolog atom representing a Nuance top-level grammar. A request to recognise speech using the top-level grammar `Grammar` is sent to the server. If recognition is successful, `Result` is unified with a term of the form

```
recognition_succeeded(Confidence, RecString, LF)
```

where

- `Confidence` is the Nuance recognition confidence score, an integer between 1 and 100.
- `RecString` is the recognition string (i.e. the surface words recognised by Nuance), encoded as a Prolog atom.
- LF is the logical form (semantic representation of `RecString`), encoded as a Prolog term.

A `Result` term after a successful recognition could look like this:

```
recognition_succeeded(
  77,
  'two␣dogs',
  [value=[[spec, 2],
          [noun, canis_domesticus]]])
```

If recognition is unsuccessful, `Result` is unified with the term

```
recognition_failed(Reason)
```

where `Reason` is a Prolog atom describing the type of failure, for example `'no or empty result'`. Sample call:

```
regulus_sockettalk_recognise('.MAIN', Result)
```

3.3 A toy dialogue system in Prolog

The Toy0 spoken dialogue application in Figures 11 and 12 illustrates use of the Regserver Prolog client library. The application consists of three parts: the start predicate `toy0_app/1` (top of Figure 11), the generic top loop predicate `top_loop/5` (Figure 12), and the main application predicate `process_recogniser_output/3` (bottom of Figure 11).

`toy0_app/1` (Figure 11) calls `top_loop/5` (Figure 12) with appropriate arguments; it passes the number of the `Port` on which the application is to talk to the Regserver, the recognition `Package` to use, an optional parameter string, the `StartMessage` to play when initialisation has finished, the `InitialState` (not used here), and the name of the

```
:- use_module(
  '$REGULUS/RegulusSpeechServer/Prolog/
   regulus_sockettalk').

:- ensure_loaded(
  '$REGULUS/Examples/Generic/Prolog/top_loop.pl').

toy0_app(Port) :-
  RecognitionPackage =
    '$REGULUS/Examples/Toy0/Generated/recogniser',
  top_loop(Port,
           RecognitionPackage,
           'audio.OutputVolume=200',
           "Ready␣to␣start",
           no_state,
           process_recogniser_output).

process_recogniser_output(Result, _InSt, _OutSt) :-
  Result = recognition_succeeded(_Confidence,
                                 _Words,
                                 [value=LF]),
  LF = [[spec, Number], [noun, Noun]],
  wavfile_for_noun(Noun, Wavfile),
  (   Number = 1 ->
      regulus_sockettalk_say_file(Wavfile) ;

      Number = 2 ->
      regulus_sockettalk_say_file(Wavfile),
      regulus_sockettalk_say_file(Wavfile)
  ),
  !.
process_recogniser_output(_Result, _InSt, _OutSt) :-
  regulus_sockettalk_say_tts(
      "Something␣went␣wrong"),
  !.

wavfile_for_noun(
  felis_domesticus,
  '$REGULUS/Examples/Toy0/wavfiles/miaow.wav').
wavfile_for_noun(
  canis_domesticus,
  '$REGULUS/Examples/Toy0/wavfiles/woof.wav').
```

FIGURE 11 The Toy0 application in Prolog.
(`$REGULUS/Examples/Toy0/Prolog/toy0_app.pl`)

```
:- use_module(
   '$REGULUS/RegulusSpeechServer/Prolog/
    regulus_sockettalk').

:- use_module('$REGULUS/PrologLib/utilities').

top_loop(Port, RecPackage, NuanceParams,
         StartMessage, InitialState, MainPred) :-
   absolute_file_name(RecPackage, AbsRecPackage),
   regulus_sockettalk_init(Port, AbsPackage,
                           NuanceParams),
   regulus_sockettalk_say_tts(StartMessage),
   loop(MainPred, InitialState).

loop(Pred, InState) :-
  format(
   '~NPRESS␣RETURN␣TO␣RECOGNISE,␣"EXIT"␣TO␣END␣>>␣',
   []),
  read_line(Line),
  (   Line = "EXIT" ->
      regulus_sockettalk_exit_client ;

      regulus_sockettalk_recognise('.MAIN',
                                   Result),
      format('~N~nRecognised:␣~w~n~n',
             [Result]),
      Call =.. [Pred, Result, InState, OutState],
      (   call(Call) ->
          true ;
          format('~NSomething␣went␣wrong.~n', []),
          InState = OutState
      ),
      !,
      loop(Pred, OutState)
   ).
```

FIGURE 12 Generic top loop for simple Prolog-based speech applications. (**$REGULUS/Examples/Generic/Prolog/top_loop.pl**)

MainPred that will process the result returned by speech recognition. Here, MainPred will be the predicate process_recogniser_output/3.

The initialisation code in the predicate top_loop/1 (top of Figure 12) starts by finding the absolute name of the recognition package, and then makes the call

```
regulus_sockettalk_init(Port, AbsPackage,
                        NuanceParams)
```

which starts a Regserver and opens a socket to it on Port. Next, we call regulus_sockettalk_say_tts/1 to speak the opening prompt using TTS. Recall that the argument to regulus_sockettalk_say_tts/1 is a Prolog string. Having finished initialisation, we enter the main loop, the predicate loop/2 in the lower half of Figure 12.

Inside loop/2, we first print a written prompt, and wait for the user to input a text line, terminated with a return character. If the line consists of the word "EXIT", we call regulus_sockettalk_exit_client/0 to terminate. Otherwise, we call regulus_sockettalk_recognise/2 to initiate a recognition request. Here, the first argument, the grammar name, is a Prolog atom. The recognition result is placed in the variable RecogniserOutput. We construct a call to the main processing Pred, where we pass in the recognition result and the InState, and get back the OutState. In this simple application, we don't use InState and OutState; in the more complicated applications shown in Chapter 5, dialogue state will become very important. Finally, we repeat the top loop.

In the Toy0 application, the main predicate is process_recogniser_output/3 (bottom of Figure 11). Here we first try to unify the recogniser output against the structure

```
recognition_succeeded(
      Confidence, Words, [value=LF])
```

to instantiate the variable LF to the logical form, and then unify LF with the structure

```
[[spec, Number], [noun, Noun]]
```

to get the Number and Noun values. The code can be kept very simple, since the the Prolog representation of the logical form is exactly the same as that in the original Toy0 Regulus grammar from Figure 9 in the previous chapter. We invoke the predicate wavfile_for_noun/2 to find the recorded file giving the sound associated with the animal, and then call regulus_sockettalk_say_file/1 either once or twice, depending on the value of Number. If any of this fails, we enter the second clause of process_recogniser_output/3, where we use TTS to produce a spoken error message.

3.3.1 Running the Toy0 application

To run the Toy0 application, start by opening two Cygwin/UNIX command windows. In the first one, start a Nuance license manager in the background, as follows:

```
$ cd $REGULUS/Examples/Toy0/Generated
$ nlm <nuance-license-code> &
```

You should get some trace output, to show that it has started up. Next, start a Nuance recognition server in the background, using the Toy0 recognition package:

```
$ recserver -package recogniser &
```

You should get more trace output. Finally, start a Nuance Vocalizer TTS process, also in the background:

```
$ vocalizer -num_channels 1 -voices_from_disk -voice
   lauriewoods &
```

We now have all three support processes up and running. In the second window, you can start the application process as follows:

```
$ cd $REGULUS/Examples/Toy0/scripts
$ sicstus -l load_and_run_app.pl
```

You should get trace output, ending with:

```
--- Connected to Regserver on port 1975
PRESS RETURN TO RECOGNISE, "EXIT" TO END >>
```

Start recognition by pressing the return key, and say "one cat". The application should print something like

```
Recognised: recognition_succeeded(72,one cat,
        [value=[[spec,1],[noun,felis_domesticus]]])
```

and play the "miaow" sound. It should then print the loop prompt again.

3.4 A toy speech translation system in Prolog

We can easily adapt the Toy0 spoken dialogue application, to turn it into a minimal English to French speech translator; as before, spoken output is produced by the Nuance Vocalizer TTS, but this time with a French voice. The code is shown in Figure 13. The top-level predicate is almost exactly as in Figure 11, and we use the same generic

```
:- use_module(
  '$REGULUS/RegulusSpeechServer/Prolog/
    regulus_sockettalk').
:- use_module('$REGULUS/PrologLib/utilities').
:- ensure_loaded(
  '$REGULUS/Examples/Generic/Prolog/top_loop.pl').

toy0_slt_app(Port) :-
   RecognitionPackage =
     '$REGULUS/Examples/Toy0/Generated/recogniser',
   top_loop(Port, RecognitionPackage,
            'audio.OutputVolume=200', "Commencez!",
            no_state, process_recogniser_output).

process_recogniser_output(Result, _InState,
                          _OutState) :-
   Result =
     recognition_succeeded(
          Confidence, Words, [value=LF]),
   french_utterance(LF, TargetWords, []),
   join_with_spaces(TargetWords, TargetAtom),
   atom_chars(TargetAtom, TargetString),
   regulus_sockettalk_say_tts(TargetString),
   !.
process_recogniser_output(_RecogniserOutput) :-
   regulus_sockettalk_say_tts(
      "Je␣ne␣comprends␣pas.").

% Toy DCG grammar for French noun phrases
french_utterance([Number, Noun]) -->
   french_number(Number, SingPlur),
   french_noun(Noun, SingPlur).

french_number([spec, 1], sing) --> [un].
french_number([spec, 2], plur) --> [deux].

french_noun([noun, felis_domesticus], sing) -->
                                        [chat].
french_noun([noun, felis_domesticus], plur) -->
                                        [chats].
french_noun([noun, canis_domesticus], sing) -->
                                        [chien].
french_noun([noun, canis_domesticus], plur) -->
                                        [chiens].
```

FIGURE 13 The Toy0 speech translation application in Prolog
($REGULUS/Examples/Toy0/Prolog/toy0_slt_app.pl)

top loop, defined earlier in Figure 12. The differences are in the definition of `process_recogniser_output/3`. We again start by extracting the logical form `LF` from the recognition result. Next, we use a simple Definite Clause Grammar (DCG; (Pereira and Warren, 1980)) to generate the French translation `TargetWords`, expressed as a list of Prolog atoms. We first convert `TargetWords` first into the single Prolog atom `TargetAtom` and then into the Prolog string `TargetString`[12]. Finally, we invoke `regulus_sockettalk_say_tts/1` to convert `TargetString` into spoken French output.

The actual translation is being done by the DCG, whose top-level predicate is `french_utterance/3`. The structure of the relevant French phrases is very similar to that of the English ones: "one dog" is "un chien", and "two cats" is "deux chats". The toy French DCG generation grammar is consequently similar to the English Regulus grammar in Figure 9: we say that a `french_utterance` consists of `french_number` followed by a `french_noun`, and then list examples of each one.

It is inelegant to use two different but closely related grammar formalisms in the same system; an obvious question is whether we can use a Regulus grammar instead of a DCG. In Chapter 6, we will see how to compile a Regulus grammar into a generator, so that it can be used for this kind of purpose.

We can run the Toy0 speech translation system in almost the same way as the Toy0 spoken dialogue system. We modify the procedure described in Section 3.3.1 as follows. In the first window, we start the Vocalizer process with a French voice rather than an English one, using the invocation

```
$ vocalizer -num_channels 1 -voice juliedeschamps \
> -voices_from_disk &
```

In the second window, we start the speech translation application instead of the spoken dialogue application:

```
$ cd $REGULUS/Examples/Toy0/scripts
$ sicstus -l run_toy0_slt_app.pl
```

Interaction with the application is the same as before, except that the application's responses are French translations rather than animal sounds.

[12] `join_with_spaces/2`, used to convert a list of atoms into a single atom, is a utility predicate defined in the file `$REGULUS/PrologLib/utilities.pl`.

3.5 A toy dialogue system in Java

In this section, we will describe a Java version of the Toy0 application. The downside of working in Java is that the Regulus datastructures don't match up with the language as nicely as they did in the Prolog version, so we have to do more work to unpack them into a form we can use. The upside is that we have direct access to all the useful features that Java provides.

We have designed the example to illustrate both the positive and negative aspects. The code is a bit more complicated, but the user interface is structured as an attractive Swing-based GUI, instead of as a primitive command-line application. The user clicks a button on the GUI to start recognition, and speaks. The system prints the recognition string at the bottom of the screen, and displays an appropriate image.

Section 3.5.1 describes the Java client library, which is used by the Java demo to communicate with the Regserver, and Section 3.5.2 the `RegResult` class, which encodes recognition results. Section 3.5.3 describes the application iself, and Section 3.5.4 describes how to compile and run it.

3.5.1 The Java client library

The Java client library consists of the `RegClient` and `RegResult` classes. Full HTML Java documentation for these classes is in the directory `$REGULUS/doc/regClient`; this section will only present a conceptual overview of the functionality offered. In general, the Java client library offers functionality similar to that of the Prolog client library described earlier in Section 3.3.

The `RegClient` object provides a connection to the RegServer. The constructor is an exact Java counterpart of the Prolog predicate `regulus_sockettalk_init` defined in Section 3.2; when the `RegClient` object is created, the constructor code starts an instance of the Regserver, and then connects to it over a port. The arguments are as follows:

```
RegClient(int serverPort,
          String recognitionPackage,
          String nuanceParameters)
```

where

`serverPort` is the port on which the client and server will communicate;

`recognitionPackage` is the Nuance recognition package passed to the Regserver on start-up `nuanceParameters` contains the Nuance parameters we want to pass to the Regserver

Once the `RegClient` object has been created, communication with the Regserver is performed by invoking `RegClient` methods. For the JDemo application, we will only need the three methods `recognize`, `playList` and `shutdown`, which we will now describe; the online documentation contains information about the other methods.

```
RegResult recognize(java.lang.String grammar)
```

A recognition action is started using the top-level grammar `grammar`. The result is returned as a `RegResult` object.

```
void playList(java.lang.String[] fileOrTTSList)
```

The Regserver attempts to realise the string array `fileOrTTSList` as spoken output. If a string starts with `-tts_text:`, then the rest of it is treated as a request to use text to speech synthesis; otherwise, the string is treated as the name of a recorded wavfile. It is possible to mix requests for TTS with wavfiles.

```
void shutdown()
```

Exit regserver process, and release held resources.

3.5.2 The RegResult class

Recognition results from the Regserver are passed back to the Java client as instances of `RegResult`. You can find out whether recognition was successful by calling the method

```
void isActionSuccesfull()
```

If the answer is positive, you can extract the recognition string using the method

```
String getRecognition()
```

and a string representation of the interpretation using the method

```
String getInterpretation()
```

The interpretation object itself can be retrieved with the method

```
Object getInterpretationObject()
```

In the interpretation object, key-value lists are represented as `Hashtables`, and normal lists as `ArrayLists`. The top-level interpretation object is always an `ArrayList` which contains one object, a `Hashtable` whose keys correspond to the global slots in the Nuance grammar. In the next section, we will see how to unpack a `RegResult` to access the information returned.

3.5.3 The JDemo application

The JDemo application demonstrates the use of the regulus Java library in a Java application with a simple graphical user interface. The user interface consists of a button, which initiates recognition when pressed. When recognition completes, the result is shown as an image in the application window. The code for the application is presented in Figures 14 to 17, and is described in detail below. Figure 14 contains declarations and the `main` method. Figure 15 shows the `JDemo` constructor. Figure Figure 16 lists the `getJButtonStartRecognition` method, which associates the recognition button with the `recognitionButtonPressed` method. The `recognitionButtonPressed` method itself is shown in Figure 17.

The `JDemo` constructor

Figure 15 shows the `JDemo` constructor. This starts by creating a new `RegClient` instance called `regulusClient`:

```
regulusClient =
  new RegClient(regServerPort, pathToRecognitionPackage,
    nuanceParameters);
```

As described in Section 3.5.1, the call to the `RegClient` constructor creates the Regserver process on the given port, with the specified package and parameters. Most of the rest of the `JDemo` constructor is concerned with defining the Swing window which constitutes the JDemo GUI. The key line is the following:

```
appPanel.add(new
   JPanel().add(getJButtonStartRecognition()));
```

which calls the `getJButtonStartRecognition` method to create the button which will start recognition. The code for `getJButtonStartRecognition` appears in Figure 16; the result is a new `JButton` object, carrying the text "Start Recognition". At the end of initialization the application plays a welcome message:

```
regulusClient.play("+tts␣Ready␣to␣start.");
```

The `recognitionButtonPressed` method

The central method in the example is `recognitionButtonPressed` (Figure 17), which is associated with the recognition button when `getJButtonStartRecognition` is first called. This function of this method is to initiate a recognition action, and then process the result. The line

```
RegResult regResult =
   regulusClient.recognize(appGrammar);
```

```
import java.io.*;

import java.net.*;
import java.util.*;

import java.awt.*;
import java.awt.event.*;

import javax.swing.*;
import javax.swing.border.*;

import net.sf.regulus.RegClient;
import net.sf.regulus.RegResult;

public class JDemo extends JFrame {
  RegClient regulusClient = null;

  final int regServerPort = 1975;
  final String pathToRecognitionPackage =
    "../Generated/recogniser";
  final String nuanceParameters =
    "audio.OutputVolume=120";

  JButton jButtonStartRecognition = null;
  ImageIcon appImage = null;
  JLabel statusBar = null;
  JLabel imageLabel = null;

  String appGrammar = ".MAIN";
  String pathToAudioFilesDirectory =
    "../java/audio";

  public static void main(String[] args) {
      try {
          JDemo app = new JDemo();
          app.show();
      }
      catch (Exception ex) {
          System.err.println("Exception:" + ex);
      }
  }

  <... other methods ...>

}
```

FIGURE 14 The Toy0 application in Java: top level (`$REGULUS/Examples/Toy0/Java/JDemo.java`)

```
public JDemo() throws Exception {
  super("Regulus␣Demo");


  // initialize recognition client
  regulusClient = new RegClient(regServerPort,
    pathToRecognitionPackage, nuanceParameters);

  // initialize display components
  appImage = JDemo.createImageIcon("img/unk.jpg",
                                   "unknown");
  imageLabel = new JLabel();
  imageLabel.setIcon(appImage);

  statusBar = new JLabel();
  statusBar.setBorder(
    BorderFactory.createEtchedBorder(EtchedBorder.RAISED)
  );
  statusBar.setText("Ready.");

  JPanel appPanel = new JPanel();
  BoxLayout bl =
    new BoxLayout(appPanel, BoxLayout.Y_AXIS);

  appPanel.setLayout(bl);
  appPanel.add(
    new JPanel().add(getJButtonStartRecognition()));
  appPanel.add(Box.createHorizontalStrut(3), null);

  appPanel.add(imageLabel);
  appPanel.add(Box.createHorizontalStrut(3), null);

  getContentPane().add(appPanel, BorderLayout.NORTH);
  getContentPane().add(statusBar, BorderLayout.SOUTH);

  // shut down speech server when window is closed
  this.setDefaultCloseOperation(JFrame.DISPOSE_ON_CLOSE);
  this.addWindowListener(new WindowAdapter() {
      public void windowClosed(WindowEvent arg0) {
        try {
            regulusClient.shutdown();
        }
        catch (IOException e) {
            e.printStackTrace();
        }
      }
  });

  pack();
  // play welcome message
  regulusClient.play("+tts␣Ready␣to␣start.");
}
```

FIGURE 15 The Toy0 application in Java: JDemo method ($REGULUS/Examples/Toy0/Java/JDemo.java)

```
/**
 * @return Returns the recognition button.
 *     When pressed, the recognitionButtonPressed()
 *     method is called
 */
private JButton getJButtonStartRecognition() {
  if (jButtonStartRec == null) {
      jButtonStartRec = new javax.swing.JButton();
      jButtonStartRec.setText("Start␣Recognition");

      jButtonStartRec.addActionListener(
                            new ActionListener() {
        public void actionPerformed(ActionEvent e) {
            recognitionButtonPressed(e);
        }
      });
  }
  return jButtonStartRec;
}

/** Returns an ImageIcon, or null if invalid path.*/
public final static ImageIcon createImageIcon(
  String path, String description) {
  URL imgURL = null;
  ImageIcon result = null;

  try {
      imgURL =
        JDemo.class.getClassLoader().getResource(path);

      if (imgURL == null) {
          imgURL = (new File(path)).toURL();
      }

      if (imgURL != null) {
         result = new ImageIcon(imgURL, description);
      }
      else {
          result = null;
      }
  }
  catch (MalformedURLException e) {
  }
  return result;
}
```

FIGURE 16 The Toy0 application in Java: `getJButtonStartRecognition` and `createImageIcon` methods (`$REGULUS/Examples/Toy0/Java/JDemo.java`)

starts recognition, and stores the result in `regResult`. We then invoke the `isActionSuccesfull` method on `regResult` to find out whether anything actually got recognised. If so, the lines

```
Object interpretationObject =
        regResult.getInterpretationObject();
```

retrieve the interpretation object. This will be a Java data structure which in Prolog would be something like

```
[value = [[spec, 1], [noun, canis_domesticus]]]
```

As described earlier in Section 3.5.2, the Java client library represents key-value lists as Java `Hashtable` objects and regular Prolog lists as `ArrayList` objects. We want to unpack the interpretation object to extract the values associated with `spec` and `noun`, which we do in the following steps. First, we cast `interpretationObject` to an `ArrayList`, and extract its zeroth element, which will be the `Hashtable`:

```
Hashtable h =
   (Hashtable)
   ((ArrayList) interpretationObject).get(0);
```

Next, we retrieve the value corresponding to the key `value` (this should be the only key):

```
ArrayList a = (ArrayList) h.get("value");
```

In our running example, the value of `a` will be an `ArrayList` representing the Prolog structure

```
[[spec, 1], [noun, canis_domesticus]]
```

We now extract the two elements of the list:

```
ArrayList specList = (ArrayList) a.get(0);
ArrayList nounList = (ArrayList) a.get(1);
```

After this step, the contents of `specList` will be an `ArrayList` representing the Prolog structure

```
[spec, 1]
```

and the contents of `nounList` will be an `ArrayList` representing the Prolog structure

```
[noun, canis_domesticus]
```

Finally, we extract the values corresponding to the keys `spec` and `noun`, here `1` and `canis_domesticus`. Note that we want both a `String` and an `int` representation of the value of `spec`:

```
String spec = (String) specList.get(1);
int iSpec = Integer.parseInt(spec);
String noun = (String) nounList.get(1);
```

We use noun and spec to construct the name of the JPG file we are going to display, and a description:

```
String imageToShow =
                "img/" + noun + "-" + spec + ".jpg";
String imageDescription = spec + "␣" + noun;
appImage =
  JDemo.createImageIcon(imageToShow, imageDescription);
```

after which we display the information:

```
imageLabel.setIcon(appImage);
```

We also display the recognised words in the status bar:

```
statusBar.setText(regResult.getRecognition());
```

Finally, we want to play noun's sound iSpec times. We do this by constructing a suitable String array with iSpec entries, each of which is the name of the recorded wavfile for the sound in question:

```
String[] playbackFiles = new String[iSpec];
for( int i=0 ; i < iSpec ; i ++ ){
    playbackFiles[i] =
    pathToAudioFiles + "/" + noun + ".wav";
}
```

and then playing the sounds by calling playList on the playbackFiles:

```
regulusClient.playList(playbackFiles);
```

If we failed to get a recognition result, we display the "unknown" icon and write an appropriate message to the status bar:

```
appImage =
        JDemo.createImageIcon("img/unk.jpg", "???");
imageLabel.setIcon(appImage);
statusBar.setText("No␣recognition");
```

Summary of JDemo application

Although relatively simple, JDemo illustrates many of the key techniques needed to build a Java-based Regulus application. In particular, it shows how to create a Swing window with a button that triggers recognition, how to initiate recognition, how to unpack the result, and how to perform a spoken response. In the exercises, we suggest ways to adapt the code in order to build considerably more complex applications.

3.5.4 Compiling and running the JDemo application

To compile the JDemo application, UNIX or Cygwin users should do the following:

```
private void recognitionButtonPressed(ActionEvent e)
{
  try {
    jButtonStartRec.setEnabled(false);
    RegResult result =
        regulusClient.recognize(appGrammar);

    if (result.isActionSuccesfull()) {
  // retrieve interpretation object
      Object interpretation =
        result.getInterpretationObject();
      System.out.println(interpretation);
  // retrieve the 'value' Hashtable
      Hashtable h = (Hashtable)
              ((ArrayList) interpretation).get(0);
  // retrieve the arraylist and the objects
      ArrayList a = (ArrayList) h.get("value");
      ArrayList specList = (ArrayList)a.get(0);
      ArrayList nounList = (ArrayList)a.get(1);
  // get values of "spec" and "noun"
      String spec = (String) specList.get(1);
      int iSpec = Integer.parseInt(spec);
      String noun = (String) nounList.get(1);
  // show img icon and display rec result
      String img =
        "img/" + noun + "-" + spec + ".jpg";
      String label = spec + "␣" + noun;
      appImage = JDemo.createImageIcon(img, label);
      imgLabel.setIcon(appImage);
      statusBar.setText(result.getRecognition());
  // play sound of the animals
      String[] playbackFiles = new String[iSpec];
      for( int i=0 ; i < iSpec ; i ++ ){
          playbackFiles[i] =
            pathToAudioFiles + "/" + noun + ".wav";
      }
      regulusClient.playList(playbackFiles);
    }
    else {
      appImage =
        JDemo.createImageIcon("img/unk.jpg", "???");
      imgLabel.setIcon(appImage);
      statusBar.setText("No␣recognition");
    }
    pack();
    jButtonStartRec.setEnabled(true);
  }
  catch (Exception err) {
      err.printStackTrace();
  }
}
```

FIGURE 17 The Toy0 application in Java: `recognitionButtonPressed` method (`$REGULUS/Examples/Toy0/Java/JDemo.java`)

1. Edit `Makefile.in` in `$REGULUS/Examples/Toy0/scripts` and set the `JAVA_HOME` variable to reflect your local settings.
2. Open a Cygwin shell and type

```
cd $REGULUS/Examples/Toy0/scripts
make jdemo
```

Windows users may run `compile_jdemo.bat` after editing the `JAVA_HOME` variable in `java_settings.bat`.

To run the JDemo application, do the following:

1. Start a Nuance license manager, as described in Section 3.3.1.
2. Start a Nuance recognition server with the Toy0 recognition package, as described in Section 3.3.1.
3. Open a Cygwin window, and type

```
cd $REGULUS/Examples/Toy0/scripts
make run_jdemo
```

   Window users can run `run_jdemo.bat` from the same directory[13].

You should get a Swing window, with a button marked "Start Recognition". Push the button, and say a phrase within the coverage of the Toy0 grammar, e.g. "one dog". The application should display a picture and make a spoken comment.

3.6 Summary

- The Regulus SpeechServer gives you an easy way to build Regulus-based applications. There are client libraries in Prolog and Java. The client and server communicate over a socket.
- To run a Regserver application, you need to start at least the following processes: a Nuance license manager, a Nuance recognition server, and the application itself. You may also need to start a TTS server and the Regserver itself.
- The client library contains primitives to carry out basic speech operations, including recognition and speech output using TTS or recorded wavfiles.
- The Prolog client library is simpler to use (if you know Prolog), because Regulus datastructures are originally Prolog-based.
- The Java client library requires more work in order to unpack the recognition output, but is easier to use if you want to build an application which combines speech and GUI-based interaction. There

[13] Note that, in order to let the Java platform know where Regulus has been installed, the calls to the Java command line in the scripts pass the Regulus path using the switch `-Dregulus=$REGULUS`.

is full Javadoc documentation for the library in the Regulus `doc` directory.

- In the Java client libary, communication with the Regserver is carried out using the `RegClient` class. The `RegClient` constructor starts a Regserver, and initiates contact with it. Recognition results are passed back as instances of the `RegResult` class.
- In the `RegResult` class, Prolog lists are represented as Java `Array-Lists`, and Prolog key/value lists are represented as Java `Hashtables`.

Exercises

1. Run the Prolog Toy0 spoken dialogue application.
2. Run the Prolog Toy0 speech translation application.
3. Run the Java Toy0 spoken dialogue application.
4. Extend the (Prolog or Java) spoken dialogue application to handle a larger set of numbers and animals.
5. If you are a Prolog programmer, extend the Prolog speech translation application to handle a larger set of numbers and animals.
6. If you are a Prolog programmer, and you know another language, port the Prolog speech translation application to translate into a different language.
7. Extend the (Prolog or Java) spoken dialogue application so that it has a notion of context. First extend the grammar so that it will accept plain numbers ("one", "two") and plain nouns ("dog", "cats"). Then extend the application code so that for example "one" spoken after "two dogs" will the treated as meaning "one dog", and "cats" after "two dogs" will be treated as meaning "two cats".
8. If you are a Java programmer, extend the `JDemo` application to allow input to be either in speech or in text mode.
9. If you are a Java programmer, try to write a Java version of the Toy0 speech translation application. Display the translated output in a separate pane of the window.

4

Developing grammars

Manny Rayner, Pierrette Bouillon

4.1 Introduction

Chapters 2 and 3 showed how to build a minimal grammar, compile it into a recogniser, and integrate it into an application. In this chapter, we will go on to describe methods for building larger grammars.

We start in Section 4.2 by explaining how to debug grammars interactively in the Regulus development environment. In Section 4.3, we then present a second example grammar, which has considerably more structure than the Toy0 grammar from Chapter 2. This grammar, which will also feature extensively in Chapters 5 and 6, is first used here to illustrate several new elements of the Regulus formalism. In particular, Section 4.4 introduces the idea of unification, and Section 4.5 describes Regulus macros, which are a powerful device for structuring grammars and other Regulus rule-sets. Finally, Section 4.6 describes how to compile and run the grammar, and Section 4.7 describes how to perform offline testing of Regulus-derived recognisers.

4.2 Using the Regulus development environment

It was possible to debug the very simple Toy0 grammar by running the derived Nuance recognition package, but readers who attempted the exercises have probably already discovered that this is not an ideal way to do things; every time we make a change, we are unable to test the modified Regulus grammar without compiling it first into a GSL form and then into a recognition package. A better approach is to debug the grammar first, *as* a feature grammar, in the Regulus development environment, and only then compile it into a recogniser. Figure 18 shows an example of a short session.

As in Section 2.5, we begin by loading the development environment

```
| ?- ['$REGULUS/Prolog/load'].

<trace output>

| ?- regulus('$REGULUS/Examples/Toy0/scripts/toy0.
  cfg').
Loading settings from Regulus config file
c:/regulus/examples/toy0/scripts/toy0.cfg

>> LOAD
(Load current Regulus grammar in DCG and left-corner
form)

<trace output>

>> one cat
(Parsing with left-corner parser)

Analysis time: 0.00 seconds

Return value: [[spec,1],[noun,felis_domesticus]]

Global value: []

Syn features: []

Parse tree:

.MAIN [TOY0:21-23]
   np [TOY0:24-28]
   /  spec lex(one) [TOY0:29-33]
   \  noun lex(cat) [TOY0:36-39]

------------- FILES ---------------

TOY0: c:/regulus/examples/toy0/regulus/toy0.regulus

>> three cats

Words not in current vocabulary: [three]
```

FIGURE 18 Short example session with Toy0 grammar in Regulus development environment

into SICStus, and starting Regulus with the Toy0 config file. We then use the LOAD command to load the current Regulus grammar into the development environment. We can now parse utterances interactively. When we type in the utterance "one cat", we get the semantic return value

```
[[spec , 1], [noun , felis_domesticus]]
```

and a parse tree

```
.MAIN [TOY0:21-23]
   np [TOY0:24-28]
   /  spec lex(one) [TOY0:29-33]
   \  noun lex(cat) [TOY0:36-39]
```

showing the derivation of the utterance. Each line in the tree corresponds to the use of a Regulus rule or lexicon entry; the tree shows the category symbol on the left hand side, and by default also displays the relevant file and line number. Printing of this extra information can be toggled using the commands LINE_INFO_ON and LINE_INFO_OFF. If we try the out-of-coverage utterance "three cats", we get a failure message warning us that the word "three" is not in the current grammar's vocabulary. At this point, you might want to try loading up the development environment, and experimenting for a few minutes with Toy0. In the next section, we will introduce a more complex grammar.

4.3 The Toy1 example grammar

Figures 20 to 23 present Toy1, a considerably more complex grammar than Toy0. Toy1 provides basic coverage for a home automation domain. We have two kinds of devices, lights and fans, and two rooms, the living room and the kitchen. There are three kinds of operations: switching on, switching off, and dimming. We can switch anything on or off, but it only makes sense to dim a light. We can also ask whether devices are on or off.

As in the Toy0 grammar, semantic representations are lists of key/-value pairs. So for example, the representation of "switch on the fan" is

```
[[utterance_type , command], [action , switch],
 [onoff , on], [device , fan]]
```

the representation of "switch off the light in the kitchen" is

```
[[utterance_type , command], [action , switch],
 [onoff , off], [device , light], [location , kitchen]]
```

and the representation of "is the light switched on" is

```
[[utterance_type, query], [state, be],
 [onoff, on], [device, light]]
```

It is worth pausing a moment at this point to discuss why the representations above only make reference to the main content words ("switch", "light", "on"), and fail to represent articles ("the"). The main reason is very simple, but may not be obvious to readers with limited experience in speech recognition. Recognisers have great difficulty hearing articles, which are typically unstressed and phonetically reduced. The consequence is that "a" and "the" easily get confused, and any application which relies on being able to distinguish them will perform poorly. It is more realistic to design the representations from the start so as not to represent articles; if it really is impossible to do this, the task may well be too difficult for the recognition technology we are describing in this book. In our experience, most simple speech-enabled applications do not in fact require representation of articles.

In the next two sections, we go on to describe the config file (Section 4.3.1), and then the grammar itself (Section 4.3.2).

4.3.1 Config file

The config file for the Toy1 grammar is shown in Figure 19. It is similar to the Toy0 config file (Figure 10, p. 38), but we have added several refinements, showing how to make both the config file and the grammar more modular.

First, rather than write out the full pathname for each file, as we did in the Toy0 config file, we declare the relevant directories using the `file_search_path` declarations shown in Figure 20. Each `file_search_path` associates a directory with an identifier. For example, the declaration

```
file_search_path(
        toy1_grammars,
        '$REGULUS/Examples/Toy1/Regulus').
```

lets us use `toy1_grammars` as an identifier for

```
$REGULUS/Examples/Toy1/Regulus
```

We could have placed the `file_search_path` declarations directly in the config file, but we chose to put them in the separate file

```
$REGULUS/Examples/Toy1/scripts/file_search_paths.cfg
```

and access them using the statement

```
include(
'$REGULUS/Examples/Toy1/scripts/file_search_paths.
  cfg').
```

```
include(
'$REGULUS/Examples/Toy1/scripts/file_search_paths.
  cfg').

regulus_config(regulus_grammar,
               [toy1_grammars(toy1_declarations),
                toy1_grammars(toy1_rules),
                toy1_grammars(toy1_lexicon)]).

regulus_config(top_level_cat,
               '.MAIN').

regulus_config(nuance_grammar,
               toy1_runtime(recogniser)).

regulus_config(working_file_prefix,
               toy1_runtime(toy1)).

regulus_config(working_directory,
               toy1_runtime('')).
```

FIGURE 19 Toy1 grammar: config file
(**$REGULUS/Examples/Toy1/scripts/toy1.cfg**)

(Note the Prolog-based syntax). Using **include** statements has the usual advantages: files become more modular, and one can include the same set of declarations in multiple config files. It is possible to split up config files using **include** statements in any way you want, and **includes** can be nested to any required depth.

Finally, we split the grammar into three separate files, respectively holding declarations, rules, and lexicon entries. We do this using the declaration

```
regulus_config(
   regulus_grammar,
   [toy1_grammars(toy1_declarations),
    toy1_grammars(toy1_rules),
    toy1_grammars(toy1_lexicon)]).
```

where the value of the **regulus_grammar** config entry is a three-element list. All three grammar files come from the same directory,

```
$REGULUS/Examples/Toy1/Regulus
```

and we use the **file_search_path** declaration above to write the path-

```
file_search_path(
        toy1_grammars,
        '$REGULUS/Examples/Toy1/Regulus').
file_search_path(
        toy1_prolog,
        '$REGULUS/Examples/Toy1/Prolog').
file_search_path(
        toy1_runtime,
        '$REGULUS/Examples/Toy1/GeneratedFiles').

file_search_path(tmp,'C:/Temp').
```

FIGURE 20 Toy1 grammar: file search paths
(**$REGULUS/Examples/Toy1/scripts/file_search_paths.cfg**)

names more compactly.

4.3.2 Grammar

We continue with the grammar rule file, which is shown in Figure 21. It defines the following main types of phrases:

np Noun phrases, e.g. “the kitchen” or “the light in the living room”.

location_pp Location prepositional phrases, e.g. “in the kitchen”.

command Imperative sentences, e.g. “switch on the light”.

yn_question Yes/no questions, e.g. “is the fan on”.

For convenience, we add the top-level category `utterance`, which generalises over `commands` and `yn_questions`. There are also three categories which can only be lexical:

verb (“switch”, “turn”, “dim”)

noun (“light”, “fan”, “kitchen” “living room”)

onoff (“on”, “off”, “switched on”, “switched off”)

Let's look first at the `utterance` rule

```
utterance:[sem=S] -->
        (   command:[sem=S] ;
            yn_question:[sem=S]
        ).
```

This introduces the useful constituent disjunction operator, which is written Prolog-style using a semi-colon. In general, the construction

```
( <A> ; <B> )
```

```
'.MAIN':[gsem=[value=S]] -->
        utterance:[sem=S].

utterance:[sem=S] -->
        (    command:[sem=S] ;
             yn_question:[sem=S]
        ).

command:[sem= concat([[utterance_type, command]],
                      concat(Op,
                             concat(OnOff, Np)))] -->
        verb:[sem=Op, vform=imperative,
              vtype=switch,
              obj_sem_np_type=ObjType],
        onoff:[sem=OnOff],
        np:[sem=Np, sem_np_type=ObjType].

command:[sem=concat([[utterance_type, command]],
                     concat(Op, Np))] -->
        verb:[sem=Op, vform=imperative,
              vtype=transitive,
              obj_sem_np_type=ObjType],
        np:[sem=Np, sem_np_type=ObjType].

yn_question:[sem=concat([[utterance_type, query]],
                         concat(Verb,
                                concat(OnOff,
                                       concat(Np, Loc
                                        ))))]
        -->
        verb:[sem=Verb, vform=finite, vtype=be,
              singplur=N, obj_sem_np_type=n],
        np:[sem=Np, singplur=N,
            sem_np_type=switchable],
        onoff:[sem=OnOff],
        ?location_pp:[sem=Loc].

np:[sem=concat(Noun, Loc),
    singplur=N, sem_np_type=SemType] -->
        the,
        noun:[sem=Noun, singplur=N,
              sem_np_type=SemType],
        ?location_pp:[sem=Loc].

location_pp:[sem=Loc] -->
        in,
        np:[sem=Loc, sem_np_type=location].
```

FIGURE 21 Toy1 grammar: rules
($REGULUS/Examples/Toy1/Regulus/toy1_rules.regulus)

should be read as "either <A> or <B>". The constituent disjunction operator is never strictly necessary, since it can always be expanded out, but one can often use it to write rules in a more compact and modular form. Here, it lets us collapse the two similar rules

```
utterance:[sem=S] --> command:[sem=S].

utterance:[sem=S] --> yn_question:[sem=S].
```

into a single rule. Next, we turn to the `np` rule

```
np:[sem=concat(Noun, Loc),
    singplur=N, sem_np_type=SemType] -->
        the,
        noun:[sem=Noun, singplur=N,
              sem_np_type=SemType],
        ?location_pp:[sem=Loc].
```

This contains two more constructions that didn't appear in the Toy0 grammar. First, we have an *optional* constituent,

```
?location_pp:[sem=Loc]
```

on the right-hand side: as in Nuance GSL, optionality is marked with the question-mark operator. Second, we build up the semantic value of the NP on the left-hand side by applying the `concat` operator to the semantic values of the `noun` and the optional `location_pp` on the right-hand side.

The semantics of Regulus `concat` are the same as those of the `concat` operator in GSL[14]: it takes two arguments, both of which must be lists, and returns a list consisting of their concatenation. For example, if the `np` is "the light in the kitchen", then the `noun` is "light", with semantics

```
[[device, light]]
```

the `location_pp` is "in the kitchen", with semantics

```
[[location, kitchen]]
```

and the semantics of "the light in the kitchen" are the concatenation of these two lists, i.e.

```
[[device, light], [location, kitchen]]
```

Throughout the grammar, you can see that in general we have applied the same principle of using `concat` to build up semantic representations. In the third and fourth rules, we concatenate the semantic

[14]Refer to the Nuance documentation for more details about the GSL concat operator, in particular Chapter 4 of "Nuance Grammar Developer's Guide".

values from the right-hand side, and also add an extra piece of structure to mark the semantic type of the utterance. Note the rule syntax used for doing this: for example, in the second command rule,

```
command:[sem=concat([[utterance_type, command]],
                     concat(Op, Np))] -->
        verb:[sem=Op, vform=imperative,
              vtype=transitive,
              obj_sem_np_type=ObjType],
        np:[sem=Np, sem_np_type=ObjType].
```

we want to add the extra key/value pair

```
[utterance_type, command]
```

to the list that makes up the semantic value of the left-hand side, so we enclose it in an extra pair of square brackets to make it into a one-element list.

Some clarification is required concerning how the concat operator interacts with optional constituents. In the np rule discussed above, the semantic value on the left-hand side is specified as

```
concat(Noun, Loc)
```

but the Loc contribution comes from an optional location_pp constituent. If the location_pp is omitted, then the convention employed by Regulus is that its associated semantic value Loc is set to the empty list. In this case, the semantic value of the left-hand side becomes simply

```
Noun
```

We have discussed the use of the sem feature in the grammar: let's now look at the other features. We'll start with those occurring in np, namely singplur and sem_np_type. singplur is the same feature that we saw in Toy0, and distinguishes singular from plural. The relevant declarations in Figure 22 are the same as those in Figure 9 on page 37:

```
feature_value_space(
      singplur_value, [[sing, plur]]).

feature(singplur, singplur_value).
```

sem_np_type is used to distinguish between different sortal types of NP. In this simple grammar, we have three types. The nouns "kitchen" and "living room" are of type location; "light" and "fan" are of type switchable, meaning that we can use them as objects of verbs like "switch on"; and "light" is also of type dimmable, meaning that we can

```
feature_value_space(
        singplur_value,
        [[sing, plur]]).
feature_value_space(
        vform_value,
        [[imperative, finite]]).
feature_value_space(
        vtype_value,
        [[transitive, switch, be]]).
feature_value_space(
        sem_np_type_value,
        [[n, location, switchable, dimmable]]).

feature(singplur, singplur_value).
feature(vform, vform_value).
feature(vtype, vtype_value).
feature(sem_np_type, sem_np_type_value).
feature(obj_sem_np_type, sem_np_type_value).

top_level_category('.MAIN').

category('.MAIN', [gsem]).
category(utterance, [sem]).
category(command, [sem]).
category(yn_question, [sem]).
category(np, [sem, singplur, sem_np_type]).
category(location_pp, [sem]).
category(noun, [sem, singplur, sem_np_type]).
category(verb,
        [sem, singplur,
         vform, vtype, obj_sem_np_type]).
category(onoff, [sem]).
```

FIGURE 22 Toy1 grammar: declarations
(`$REGULUS/Examples/Toy1/Regulus/toy1_declarations.regulus`)

```
verb:[sem=[[state, be]],
      vform=finite, vtype=be, singplur=sing,
      obj_sem_np_type=n] --> is.
verb:[sem=[[state, be]],
      vform=finite, vtype=be, singplur=plur,
      obj_sem_np_type=n] --> are.

verb:[sem=[[action, switch]],
      vform=imperative, vtype=switch, singplur=sing,
      obj_sem_np_type=switchable] --> switch.
verb:[sem=[[action, switch]],
      vform=imperative, vtype=switch, singplur=sing,
      obj_sem_np_type=switchable] --> turn.

verb:[sem=[[action, dim]],
      vform=imperative, vtype=transitive,
      singplur=sing,
      obj_sem_np_type=dimmable] --> dim.

noun:[sem=[[device, light]],
      sem_np_type=switchable\/dimmable,
      singplur=sing] --> light.
noun:[sem=[[device, light]],
      sem_np_type=switchable\/dimmable,
      singplur=plur] --> lights.
noun:[sem=[[device, fan]],
      sem_np_type=switchable,
      singplur=sing] --> fan.
noun:[sem=[[device, fan]],
      sem_np_type=switchable,
      singplur=plur] --> fans.

noun:[sem=[[location, kitchen]],
      sem_np_type=location,
      singplur=sing] --> kitchen.
noun:[sem=[[location, living_room]],
      sem_np_type=location,
      singplur=sing] --> living, room.

onoff:[sem=[[onoff, on]]] --> ?switched, on.
onoff:[sem=[[onoff, off]]] --> ?switched, off.
```

FIGURE 23 Toy1 grammar: lexicon
($REGULUS/Examples/Toy1/Regulus/toy1_lexicon.regulus)

use it as the object of the verb "dim". For reasons we'll see a bit later, we also want to allow a null value for sem_np_type, which we'll call n. The associated declarations in Figure 22 are:

```
feature_value_space(
        sem_np_type_value,
        [[n, location, switchable, dimmable]]).

  feature(sem_np_type, sem_np_type_value).
```

You may be wondering how it's possible to allow "light" to have two possible values for sem_np_type. To see how this works, we'll look at some of the lexicon entries in Figure 23. The entries for "living room" and "fan" are

```
noun:[sem=[[location, living_room]],
      sem_np_type=location,
      singplur=sing] --> living, room.

noun:[sem=[[device, fan]],
      sem_np_type=switchable,
      singplur=sing] --> fan.
```

(Note by the way that the fact that "living room" consists of two words doesn't pose a problem). The entry for "light" looks like this:

```
noun:[sem=[[device, light]],
      sem_np_type=switchable\/dimmable,
      singplur=sing] --> light.
```

The feature disjunction operator \/ (cf. also page 35) says that the feature's value can be either switchable *or* dimmable.

If we now go back and look at the rules in Figure 21, we can see how sem_np_type is used to constrain the grammar. For example, in the location_pp rule:

```
location_pp:[sem=Loc] -->
        in,
        np:[sem=Loc, sem_np_type=location].
```

we use the feature to make sure that only location NPs can be used in location PP phrases. The rules for command and yn_question show a more complicated way to use sem_np_type. The rule

```
command:[sem=concat([[utterance_type, command]],
                     concat(Op,
                            concat(OnOff, Np)))] -->
        verb:[sem=Op, vform=imperative,
```

```
                vtype=switch,
                obj_sem_np_type=ObjType],
            onoff:[sem=OnOff],
            np:[sem=Np, sem_np_type=ObjType].
```

covers imperative constructions with "on" and "off", e.g. "switch on the light". Here, the verb has a feature `obj_sem_np_type`, which has the same value as the `sem_np_type` feature on the NP. Looking at the entry for "switch" in Figure 23,

```
verb:[sem=[[action, switch]],
      vform=imperative, vtype=switch, singplur=sing,
      obj_sem_np_type=switchable] --> switch.
```

we see that if the verb in the `command` rule is "switch", then the value of `obj_sem_np_type` will be instantiated to `switchable`. This means that the value of `sem_np_type` in the NP must also be `switchable`.

This treatment is of course more elaborate than is really necessary in the very small Toy1 grammar. The only verbs of type `switch` are "switch" and "turn"; they both have `obj_sem_np_type` set to `switchable`, so we could have written the `command` rule and the entry for "switch" in the simpler forms

```
command:[sem=concat([[utterance_type, command]],
                     concat(Op,
                            concat(OnOff, Np)))] -->
            verb:[sem=Op, vform=imperative,
                  vtype=switch],
            onoff:[sem=OnOff],
            np:[sem=Np, sem_np_type=switchable].

verb:[sem=[[action, switch]],
      vform=imperative, vtype=switch,
      singplur=sing] --> switch.
```

The general construction we have used here is however scalable to more complex grammars, and we will use variants of it repeatedly in the large grammar described in Chapter 9.

4.4 Unification

When talking about feature grammars, we have so far only considered them as a compact notation for Context Free Grammars (CFGs). This is a perfectly adequate way to think about feature grammars as far as most of this book is concerned. However, there is an alternate view, based on the concept of *unification*, which we will briefly describe in this section. The unification view is often conceptually simpler, and we will in particular refer to it in Chapter 10. Let us start by considering the artifical example shown in Figure 24. Recall that the symbol \/ represents feature disjunction (cf. page 76):

```
p:[] --> q:[f=a\/b].            (Rule 1)

q:[f=X] --> r:[f=X, g=X].       (Rule 2)

r:[f=a\/c, g=a] --> word1.      (Rule 3)

r:[f=a, g=b] --> word2.         (Rule 4)
```

FIGURE 24 Artifical unification grammar example. The features `f` and `g` both take possible values from the set {`a, b, c`}. `p` is the top-level category.

```
p:[] --> q:[f=a].               (Rule 1a)
p:[] --> q:[f=b].               (Rule 1b)

q:[f=a] --> r:[f=a, g=a].       (Rule 2a)
q:[f=b] --> r:[f=b, g=b].       (Rule 2b)
q:[f=c] --> r:[f=c, g=c].       (Rule 2c)

r:[f=a, g=a] --> word1.         (Rule 3a)
r:[f=c, g=a] --> word1.         (Rule 3c)

r:[f=a, g=b] --> word2.         (Rule 4)
```

FIGURE 25 Artifical grammar from Figure 24, expanded into CFG form

We wish to show that it is possible to derive `word1`, but not `word2`, from the top-level category `p`. A straightforward way to do this would be to expand the grammar out to the CFG shown in Figure 25. It is clear from Figure 25 that

```
p:[]
```

can be rewritten, using Rule 1a, to

```
q:[f=a]
```

which can in turn be rewritten using Rule 2a to

```
r:[f=a, g=a]
```

and finally using Rule 3a to produce

```
word1
```

as required. There is however no such sequence of rewritings leading to `word2`.

We can also reason directly with the unexpanded rules in Figure 24. We start again with

```
p:[]
```

and use Rule 1 to rewrite this to

```
q:[f=Y]
```

with the condition that `Y` is a member of the set {`a, b`}. We then apply Rule 2, to rewrite this to

```
r:[f=Y, g=Y]
```

again with the condition that `Y` is a member of the set {`a, b`}. Finally, we match the new result against the left hand side of Rule 3, namely

```
r:[f=a\/c, g=a]
```

Matching the value of the feature `f`, we have that `Y` must be a member of the set {`a, c`}; matching the value of `g`, we have that `Y` must be exactly the value `a`. We already have that `Y` must be a member of the set {`a, b`}. All three conditions can be fulfilled if we have that `Y` equals `a`, allowing us to rewrite to

```
word1
```

as required. In contrast, if we wish to rewrite to `word2`, we must try to match

```
r:[f=Y, g=Y]
```

against the left hand side of Rule 4, namely

```
r:[f=a, g=b]
```

Matching the value of the feature `f`, we have that `Y` must have the value `a`; matching `g`, we have that `Y` must have the value `b`. Since `Y` cannot have both values simultaneously, Rule 4 cannot be applied, and we cannot produce `word2`.

This style of reasoning is called *unification*. Feature grammar rules contain variables, and we apply rewriting rules to categories that are partially underspecified, in the sense that they in general also contain variables. When we match a category against the left hand side of a rule, we obtain further conditions on the variables involved. A basic result in computer science (Robinson, 1965) says that the conditions resulting from a unification either have a unique solution, or else no solution; furthermore, if we perform several successive unifications, matching different pairs of categories against each other, it makes no difference in which order we perform the unifications. In this toy example, it was probably easier to understand the derivations by first expanding out to CFG form. For large grammars, containing many features, this is however usually impossible, and it is necessary to think about them at least some of the time in terms of unification.

The important thing to realise is that both views are actually equivalent, and that if you are unsure about a result in one view it often possible to clarify it by shifting to the other one. We illustrate with a an example that often confuses beginners, namely the case of a shared constrained variable. If we write a rule of the schematic form

```
p:[f=a\/b] --> q:[f=a\/b].
```

it is somehow easy to imagine that the value of `f` in mother and daughter has been constrained to be the same. We can immediately see that this is untrue if we expand the rule out into CFG form, as

```
p:[f=a] --> q:[f=a].
p:[f=a] --> q:[f=b].
p:[f=b] --> q:[f=a].
p:[f=b] --> q:[f=b].
```

If we do want the two values of `f` to be the same, we must instead write the rule in a form like

```
p:[f=a\/b, f=X] --> q:[f=X].
```

(The Regulus feature grammar formalism allows a feature to be specified any number of times, as long as the specifications are internally consistent). This time, the CFG expansion is

```
p:[f=a] --> q:[f=a].
p:[f=b] --> q:[f=b].
```

which as desired both constrains the value of `f` in mother and daughter to be the same, and restricts them to having a value that is either `a` or `b`.

There is an extensive literature on unification and unification grammars, and this section has merely touched on some of the most basic aspects. For further information, Chapter 11 of Jurafsky and Martin (2000) is a good first stop.

4.5 Macros

Going back to the Toy1 grammar, the next topic we will address is that of macros. When we look at the entries in Figure 23, it is clear that even this tiny lexicon contains a great deal of unnecessary repetition. For example, the entries for "is" and "are",

```
verb:[sem=[[state, be]],
      vform=finite, vtype=be, singplur=sing,
      obj_sem_np_type=n] --> is.

verb:[sem=[[state, be]],
      vform=finite, vtype=be, singplur=plur,
      obj_sem_np_type=n] --> are.
```

are almost exactly the same. The only differences are in the value of the `singplur` feature (`sing` versus `plur`), and in the surface form (`is` versus `are`). It would be nice to capture the common structure in some way.

Regulus provides a simple but quite powerful *macro* mechanism, which makes it possible to address this kind of problem. A *macro definition* is of the form

```
macro(<Name>(<Arg_1>, ... <Arg_n>), <Body>).
```

where `<Name>` is a Prolog functor, `<Arg_1>` to `<Arg_n>` are zero or more Prolog terms and `<Body>` is a Prolog term. (If `n` is equal to zero, the normal conventions of Prolog syntax mean that we actually write `<Name>` and not `<Name>()`). A *macro invocation* is a term of the form

```
@<Name>(<CallArg_1>, ... <CallArg_n>)
```

where `<CallArg_1>` to `<CallArg_n>` are arbitrary Prolog terms. The compiler attempts to unify `<CallArg_1>` to `<CallArg_n>` with `<Arg_1>` to `<Arg_n>`. If it can do so, it replaces `@<Term>` with `<Body>` which will typically have been instantiated by the process of unifying the arguments. This may sound rather abstract and complicated, so let's immediately show how we can use macros to tidy up the lexicon entries for "is" and "are" that we've just seen. We define a macro `form_of_be` as follows:

```
macro(form_of_be(Word, Singplur),
      (  verb:[sem=[[state, be]],
               vform=finite, vtype=be,
               singplur=Singplur, obj_sem_np_type=n]
         --> Word )).
```

Here, the body,

```
verb:[sem=[[state, be]],
      vform=finite, vtype=be,
      singplur=Singplur, obj_sem_np_type=n]
--> Word
```

encodes the common structure, and is parameterised by the values of the surface form (the variable `Word`) and `singplur` feature (the variable `Singplur`). The head,

```
form_of_be(Word, Singplur)
```

contains the two parameters `Word` and `Singplur`, which will be instantiated when the macro is invoked. With the definition in place, we can now write the entries themselves in the compact form

```
@form_of_be(is, sing).
@form_of_be(are, plur).
```

Figure 26 shows how we can rewrite most of the whole Toy1 lexicon in the same style. You may at this point find it useful to spend a few minutes comparing the original version from Figure 23 with the "macrotised" version.

4.5.1 Multiple expansions of macros

Most of the macros and entries in Figure 26 just repeat the basic patterns we've already discussed with the `form_of_be` macro, but the `device_noun` shows a new possibility: we have two definitions, rather than just one. This illustrates a basic principle with Regulus macros. If a macro invocation can be expanded in more than one way, the compiler produces *all* the different expansions, which generally means that multiple entries are created. In the case of `device_noun`, we have two macro definitions, for the singular and plural forms of the noun respectively:

```
macro(dev_noun([SingForm, PlurForm], Sem, NPType),
      (   noun:[sem=[[device, Sem]],
                sem_np_type=NPType, singplur=sing]
          --> SingForm )).
macro(dev_noun([SingForm, PlurForm], Sem, NPType),
      (   noun:[sem=[[device, Sem]],
                sem_np_type=NPType, singplur=plur]
          --> PlurForm )).
```

Consider now how we expand the macro invocation

```
@dev_noun([fan, fans], fan, switchable).
```

The invocation matches both macro definitions. If we use the first definition, we instantiate `SingForm` to `fan`, `PlurForm` to `fans`, `Sem` to `fan`

```
macro(form_of_be(Word, Singplur),
      (  verb:[sem=[[state, be]],
               vform=finite, vtype=be,
               singplur=Singplur, obj_sem_np_type=n]
         --> Word )).

@form_of_be(is, sing).
@form_of_be(are, plur).

macro(switch_verb(Word, Sem),
      (  verb:[sem=[[action, Sem]],
               vform=imperative, vtype=switch,
               singplur=sing,
               obj_sem_np_type=switchable]
         --> Word )).

@switch_verb(switch, switch).
@switch_verb(turn, switch).

macro(dev_noun([SingForm, PlurForm], Sem, NPType),
      (   noun:[sem=[[device, Sem]],
                sem_np_type=NPType, singplur=sing]
          --> SingForm )).
macro(dev_noun([SingForm, PlurForm], Sem, NPType),
      (   noun:[sem=[[device, Sem]],
                sem_np_type=NPType, singplur=plur]
          --> PlurForm )).

@dev_noun([light, lights], light, switchable\/
  dimmable).
@dev_noun([fan, fans], fan, switchable).

macro(loc_noun(SingForm, Sem),
      (   noun:[sem=[[location, Sem]],
                sem_np_type=location, singplur=sing]
          --> SingForm )).

@loc_noun(kitchen, kitchen).
@loc_noun((living, room), living_room).

macro(onoff_word(Word, OnOff),
      ( onoff:[sem=[[onoff, OnOff]]] --> Word )).

@onoff_word((?switched, on), on).
@onoff_word((?switched, off), off).
```

FIGURE 26 Using macros to rewrite entries in the Toy1 lexicon which share common structure
(**$REGULUS/Examples/Toy1/Regulus/toy1_lexicon_with_macros.regulus**)

and NPType to switchable. Of these, PlurForm is irrelevant since it doesn't appear in the body of the definition. Filling in the other values, the result is as follows:

```
noun:[sem=[[device, fan]],
      sem_np_type=switchable,
      singplur=sing] --> fan.
```

Using the second definition is similar: again, we instantiate SingForm to fan, PlurForm to fans, Sem to fan and NPType to switchable. This time, SingForm is irrelevant, and the result is

```
noun:[sem=[[device, fan]],
      sem_np_type=switchable, singplur=plur] -->
        fans.
```

The type of solution we have outlined above is generally useful for writing lexical entries in a compact form: we will examine this in more detail in Chapter 7.

4.5.2 Using macros inside rules

The macros we have so far seen expand out to whole rules. Macros can also be used to capture common structure inside rules. For example, the value of the sem feature in all the lexicon macros from Figure 26 is the same, a list of the form

```
[[<Tag>, <Sem>]]
```

where <Tag> is a tag like action, location or onoff, and <Sem> is a constant like switch, kitchen or off. We could enforce this common structure by defining a macro sem_value as follows:

```
macro(sem_value(Tag, Sem),
      [[Tag, Sem]]).
```

Since we are free to place macro invocations inside macro definitions, we could then for example rewrite the loc_noun macro in a more abstract way:

```
macro(loc_noun(SingForm, Sem),
      (   noun:[sem= @sem_value(location, Sem),
                sem_np_type=location, singplur=sing]
          --> SingForm )).
```

If we want to, we can take the process a step further, and make the sem feature part of a larger macro. We define the macro sem as follows:

```
macro(sem(Tag, Sem),
      [sem= @sem_value(Tag, Sem)]).
```

The loc_noun macro will now look like this:

```
macro(loc_noun(SingForm, Sem),
      (   noun:[ @sem(location, Sem),
                 sem_np_type=location, singplur=sing]
          --> SingForm )).
```

The sem macro illustrates an important point: when the body of the macro, as here, is a list of feature-value pairs, the expanded value is treated specially. If the value were treated in the standard way, the result of expanding the invocation

```
@loc_noun(kitchen, kitchen).
```

would be

```
noun:[[sem=[[location, Sem]]],
      sem_np_type=location, singplur=sing] -->
       kitchen.
```

Since it is not valid Regulus rule syntax, we would never want to create a rule like this one with a nested feature-value list. The Regulus compiler thus uses the convention that any nested feature-value lists resulting from macro-expansion are flattened to remove the nesting. In this case, the result of performing the macro expansion is consequently

```
noun:[sem=[[location, Sem]],
      sem_np_type=location, singplur=sing] -->
       kitchen.
```

where the extra layer of nesting resulting from expanding the sem macro has been removed.

4.6 Compiling the Toy1 recogniser

As described in Section 2.5, we can compile the Toy1 grammar into Nuance form using NUANCE command, and then invoke the nuance-compile utility to create a recognition package. There is however one important extra point that we need to take account of. Unlike the Toy0 grammar, the Toy1 grammar is *recursive*. More specifically, it is *right-recursive*, since the NP rule

```
np:[sem=concat(Noun, Loc),
    singplur=N, sem_np_type=SemType] -->
        the,
        noun:[sem=Noun, singplur=N,
              sem_np_type=SemType],
        ?location_pp:[sem=Loc].
```

ends in an optional location_pp, and the location_pp rule

```
location_pp:[sem=Loc] -->
        in,
        np:[sem=Loc, sem_np_type=location].
```

ends in an np. We can thus have an arbitrarily long chain of location_-pps at the end of an np, e.g. "switch on the light in the kitchen in the kitchen in the kitchen". Obviously this isn't a desirable feature of the grammar; we have only allowed it here so as to present an example of right-recursion. There are many grammars, however, where right-recursion is perfectly natural.

Right-recursion in Regulus translates into right-recursion in the generated GSL grammar, and is permitted by the Nuance compiler. However, when invoking nuance-compile on right-recursive grammars, you have to explicitly specify the parameter -dont_flatten. We thus compile the recogniser package as follows:

```
cd $REGULUS/Examples/Toy1/GeneratedFiles
nuance-compile recogniser English.America \
> -dont_flatten
```

4.6.1 Offline compilation of Regulus grammars

We have explained how to compile Regulus grammars interactively from within the Regulus development environment. In general, we will often prefer to perform the compilation offline using Makefiles or other scripts. Doing this requires three steps.

To start, we need to write a Prolog file, which loads the Regulus environment and then executes the required Regulus commands in offline mode using the predicate regulus_batch. regulus_batch takes two arguments: the first is the name of a Regulus config file, and the second is a list of Regulus commands, each expressed as a Prolog string. In this case, we just want to execute the NUANCE command, so the list will have a single entry. The Prolog file is shown in Figure 27.

The second step is to have a way to execute the Prolog file from the command-line. We do this using the SICStus -l option: the command

```
sicstus -l <File>
```

starts SICStus, and loads the contents of <File>. Finally, we package up the call to sicstus and the call to nuance-compile inside a normal Makefile, so that we can invoke the whole sequence using a single make command. The Makefile is shown in Figure 28. Other ways to do the packaging would be to use a shell script or Perl script.

```
% Compile the main Regulus code
:- compile('$REGULUS/Prolog/load').

% Compile Regulus grammar to Nuance
:- regulus_batch(
        '$REGULUS/Examples/Toy1/scripts/toy1.cfg',
        ["NUANCE"]).

:- halt.
```

FIGURE 27 Toy1 grammar: offline compilation to GSL form (**$REGULUS/Examples/Toy1/scripts/build_nuance_files.pl**)

```
default:
        ${MAKE} recogniser

recogniser:
        sicstus -l build_nuance_files.pl
        nuance-compile ../GeneratedFiles/recogniser\
          English.America -dont_flatten

clean:
        rm -R ../GeneratedFiles/*
```

FIGURE 28 Toy1 grammar: Makefile for offline compilation to GSL form (Relevant part of **$REGULUS/Examples/Toy1/scripts/Makefile.pl**)

4.7 Systematic testing of recognisers

Up to now, we have tested recognition packages in a completely *ad hoc* way, either through Nuance Xapp or by using them as part of a spoken dialogue system. Serious development, however, requires an ability to carry out systematic regression testing. This section will explain how we can perform regression testing on Regulus-derived recognisers. Most of the infrastructure we will use is part of the Nuance Toolkit, and readers are advised to consult the online Nuance documentation where appropriate.

There are three components involved in performing regression testing. First, we must log spoken input in a reusable form. Second, we have to be able to run recognition offline on logged speech data. Third, we want if possible to interpret the results of offline speech recognition in a way that is compatible with Prolog-based Regulus semantic representations.

4.7.1 Logging speech input

You can log input speech by using the Nuance parameter

```
client.RecordDirectory
```

in the call that starts the Regulus SpeechServer (regserver). For Prolog applications, this will involve modifying the value of `ServerParams` in the call to `regulus_sockettalk_init` (Section 3.2); for Java applications, you need to change the value of `serverArguments` in the `RegClient` constructor (Section 3.5.1). The names of recorded wavfiles are by default of the form `uttNN.wav`.

4.7.2 Doing offline speech recognition using batchrec

Once you have created the recorded wavfiles that you will use for offline testing, the next step is to create two reference files which point to them. The first (the "testset file") lists all the wavfiles, in a format of one file per line. The second (the "transcriptions file") again lists one wavfile per line, but this time also gives a text representation (transcription) of the words spoken. The transcription should be written in a way that is compatible with the output of speech recognition. In particular, it should be all lower-case, and should use the same orthographic conventions as the recognition grammar.

You can now perform offline recognition using the Nuance `batchrec` utility. An invocation of `batchrec` should specify a testset file, a transcriptions file, a recognition package, and a top-level grammar. A typical call is thus of the form:

```
batchrec -package <Package> -testset <Testset>
-transcriptions <Transcriptions> -grammar .MAIN
```

You can find more information about the `batchrec` utility in the online Nuance documentation.

4.7.3 Using the Regulus batchrec tool

The format of output from the `batchrec` utility is often inconvenient for Regulus-based applications: in particular, semantic values are given in GSL form, and are not easily analysable. The Regulus release includes the file

```
$REGULUS/PrologLib/batchrec_tools.pl
```

which defines a utility that sits on top of `batchrec` and reformats the output into a Prolog-based form directly compatible with Regulus syntax. The top-level predicate,

```
do_batchrec(+Wavfiles, +Transcriptions, +RecParams,
            +TraceFile, +PrologFile, +TmpDir)
```

performs a Nuance batchrec run and then converts the output into Prolog-readable form. The arguments are as follows:

`Wavfiles` The "testset" file

`Transcriptions` The "transcriptions" file

`RecParams` Nuance parameters to use (list of Prolog atoms: must include the recognition package and top-level grammar)

`TraceFile` File to hold raw text batchrec output

`PrologFile` File to hold Prolog-readable version of batchrec output

`TmpDir` Directory to hold temporary files

Figure 29 shows a typical call to `do_batchrec`. The resulting Prolog-readable output file contains one record for each wavfile processed during the run. The format is

```
batchrec_item([
    wavfile=<Wavfile>,
    transcription=<Transcription>,
    words=<Words>,
    confidence=<Confidence>,
    nl_confidence=<NLConfidence>,
    nl_value=<NLValue>
]).
```

Here, `<Wavfile>` is the name of the wavfile, `<Transcription>` and `<Words>` are the transcribed and recognised words, both represented as lists of Prolog atoms, `<Confidence>` and `<NLConfidence>` are the two Nuance confidence scores, and `<NLValue>` is the semantic value, formatted as a Prolog term. Figure 30 shows an example of a typical output record.

4.8 Summary

- You can use the Regulus development environment to debug grammars without compiling them into GSL form. This is usually the simplest alternative.
- Complex semantic values in Regulus grammars can be built up using the `concat` operator.
- Grammars can be made more readable by using the disjunction (`;`) and optionality (`?`) operators.
- Features can be constrained to take one of several possible values using the feature disjunction (`\/`) operator.

```
do_batchrec(
 '$REGULUS/Examples/Toy1/corpora/wavfiles.txt',
 '$REGULUS/Examples/Toy1/corpora/transcriptions.txt',
 [package=
  '$REGULUS/Examples/Toy1/Generated/recogniser',
  grammar='.MAIN'],
 '$REGULUS/Examples/Toy1/Generated/trace.txt',
 '$REGULUS/Examples/Toy1/Generated/trace.pl',
 '$REGULUS/Examples/Toy1/Generated').
```

FIGURE 29 Example call to run `do_batchrec` on Toy1 data. The example "testset" and "transcriptions" files are included in the release, as well as the sample wavfiles that they point to.

```
batchrec_item([
wavfile=
   'c:/regulus/examples/toy1/corpora/wavfiles/utt01.wav',
transcription=[switch,on,the,light],
words=[switch,on,the,lights],
confidence=49,
nl_confidence=47,
nl_value=[[utterance_type,command],[action,switch],
          [onoff,on],[device,light]]
]). %c:/regulus/examples/toy1/corpora/wavfiles/utt01.wav
```

FIGURE 30 Portion of output from `do_batchrec` run on Toy1 data

- A common grammar-writing technique is to assign sortal features to nouns, and give verbs corresponding features which constrain the types of the nouns they can combine with.
- A good way to make lexica more compact is to use Regulus macros.
- If a macro invocation matches more than one definition, it expands out to multiple entries. If a macro is used inside a Regulus grammar rule in such a way that the result is a nested list, then the list is automatically flattened.
- Right recursion is permitted in Regulus grammars, but you then have to compile the resulting GSL grammar using the `-dont_flatten` option.
- You can execute Regulus commands offline using the predicate `regulus_batch`. This makes it possible to invoke Regulus from inside shell scripts and Makefiles.

- You can log the input to a Regulus application by using the Nuance parameters `client.WriteWaveforms` and `client.RecordDirectory`.
- You can perform offline recognition on stored wavfile data using the Nuance `batchrec` utility. The Regulus `do_batchrec` predicate can be used to call `batchrec` and format its trace output in a Regulus-friendly Prolog-readable form.

Exercises

1. Run the Toy1 grammar interactively in the Regulus development environment. Convince yourself that the sentences which are supposed to be within coverage really are. Find some simple sentences which you would intuitively like to be within coverage, but aren't.
2. Extend the grammar to cover at least one of the new sentences you noted in item (1).
3. Add some new vocabulary to the original version of the Toy1 lexicon, as shown in Figure 23. Load the modified grammar into the development environment and check that it works correctly.
4. Do the same thing, using the macrotised version of the lexicon in Figure 26.
5. As noted in Section 4.6, it would really be better if the Toy1 grammar didn't permit right-recursion. Try to modify the grammar so as to block this possibility.
6. Compile the grammar into a recogniser, as described in Section 4.6. Test it using Xapp, as described on page 31.

5

A spoken dialogue system

Manny Rayner and Beth Ann Hockey

5.1 Introduction

In Chapter 3, we showed how to build a Prolog-based spoken dialogue application using the minimal Toy0 Regulus grammar, and in Chapter 4 we presented Toy1, a Regulus grammar for a small home automation domain. In this chapter, we will show how to build a less trivial spoken dialogue application using the Toy1 grammar. Figure 31 shows some examples of the kind of interactions we want the Toy1 application to support. We have a simulated home containing two rooms, the kitchen and the living room, and three devices: a light and fan in the kitchen, and a light in the living room. Even though the domain and the range

$\mathbf{U}_1$	switch on the light
$\mathbf{S}_1$	sorry, that's ambiguous
$\mathbf{U}_2$	switch on the light in the kitchen
$\mathbf{S}_2$	the light in the kitchen is on
$\mathbf{U}_3$	is the light switched on in the kitchen
$\mathbf{S}_3$	the light in the kitchen is on
$\mathbf{U}_4$	is the light switched on in the living room
$\mathbf{S}_4$	no
$\mathbf{U}_5$	switch on the fan in the living room
$\mathbf{S}_5$	sorry that doesn't make sense

FIGURE 31 Example interaction with Toy1 dialogue system

of supported language are very constrained, there are more problems to solve than might at first appear. When we issue a command or ask a question, the system may simply respond as expected, by carrying out a command (turns 2) or answering a question (turns 3 and 4).

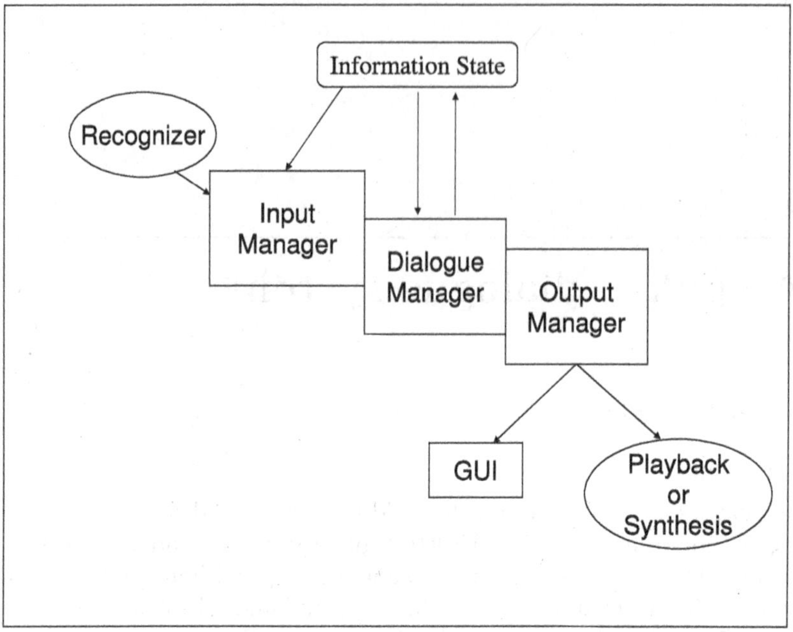

FIGURE 32 Generic spoken dialogue architecture

However, there are other possibilities to think about as well. In turn 1, the command is ambiguous, since there are two lights available. In turn 5, the command is inconsistent, since there is no fan in the living room. We want the system to respond sensibly in these kinds of situations.

Regulus provides some support for development of spoken dialogue applications, which we will use here to construct the Toy1 system. The basic framework, which is illustrated in Figure 32, implements a version of "update semantics" (Larsson and Traum, 2000), and assumes that all dialogue context is maintained as an object which we call the *information state*. We make no assumptions about what the information state contains. Typical content might include some or all of the current state of the application, the history of the dialogue, which participant is considered to hold the dialogue initiative, possible referents for anaphora, and so on. The core of the system is side-effect free, so that its operation can be conceptualised as an *update function* of the form

$$f : LF \times State \rightarrow Actions \times State$$

At each turn, the system receives a logical form *LF* from the speech recogniser, and also has available the previous *State*; the result of applying f to these two arguments is a list of *Actions* and a new *State*. We will have more to say later about exactly how we pass the *LF* to the application, and what we do with the *Actions*.

Raw logical forms and low-level descriptions of actions are usually hard to reason with directly; consequently, the central portion of the system, the dialogue manager, works with abstract representations of these two kinds of objects. We will refer to abstract representations of logical forms as *dialogue moves*, and abstract representations of actions as *abstract actions*. Following (Allen et al., 2000), we split the application into three modules, which we call the *input manager*, the *dialogue manager* and the *output manager*. The input manager takes as input a logical form and the current information state, and outputs a dialogue move. The dialogue manager takes as input a dialogue move and the current information state, and produces an abstract action and a new information state. Finally, the output manager takes an abstract action as input, and produces a concrete action. In the Regulus development environment, the input manager, dialogue manager and output manager are realised by supplying definitions for the three predicates `lf_to_dialogue_move/3`, `update_dialogue_state/4` and `abstract_action_to_action/2`; it is also necessary to define the predicate `initial_dialogue_state/1`, which specifies the initial information state.

The rest of the chapter will expand this brief sketch, using the Toy1 application as a running example. Section 5.2 presents an overview of the application, and in general explains how to develop dialogue applications in the Regulus environment. Sections 5.3, 5.4 and 5.5 describe the input manager, dialogue manager and output manager respectively. Section 5.6 explains how to integrate the dialogue management modules with recognition and spoken output. Finally, Section 5.7 describes a more elaborate version of the Toy1 application, which also handles incomplete utterances and corrections.

5.2 The Toy1 spoken dialogue system

In this section, we will describe in more detail the Regulus framework for developing spoken dialogue applications, and how it has been used to implement the Toy1 system. We have already, in Chapter 4, seen examples of logical forms produced by the Toy1 recogniser (cf. Section 4.3). We now need to define the other key data-structures we will use: information states, dialogue moves, abstract actions and concrete actions. We start with information states.

In the first version of the system, it will be sufficient for the information state to describe the current settings of the three devices in our simulated house. (Later, in Section 5.7, we will present a more elaborate version of the system which will require more state). For now, we need, for each device, to represent its type (`light` or `fan`), its location (`kitchen` or `living_room`), and whether or not it is switched on (`on` or `off`). Since lights can be dimmed, we also need to represent the intensity, which we will represent as a number between 0 and 100. Each device state will thus be represented as a Prolog record of the form

```
dev(<Type>, <Loc>, <OnOff>, <Intensity>)
```

For example, we will represent the fact that the kitchen light is currently dimmed to an intensity of 50% as

```
dev(light, kitchen, on, 50)
```

The full state will be a list of three such records. So for example the state

```
[dev(light, kitchen, on, 50),
 dev(light, living_room, on, 100),
 dev(fan, kitchen, off, 0)]
```

says that the kitchen light is on and dimmed to 50%, the living room light is fully on, and the fan is off.

We have two types of dialogue moves: queries, e.g. "is the fan switched on?" and commands, e.g. "switch on the fan". We will represent a dialogue move as a two-element list of the form

```
[<MoveType>, <Pattern>]
```

where `<MoveType>` is `command` or `query`, and `<Pattern>` is a (perhaps partially instantiated) term of the form

```
dev(<Type>, <Loc>, <OnOff>, <Intensity>)
```

In a query, the `<Pattern>` will be used to match against potentially relevant records in the information state; thus for example we will represent "is the fan switched on?" as

```
[query, dev(fan, _, on, _)]
```

where the "location" and "intensity" slots in the pattern are left uninstantiated. In a command, the `<Pattern>` shows the record we want to create, so we for example represent "dim the light in the kitchen" as

```
[command, dev(light, kitchen, on, 50)]
```

The only type of concrete action we will have is speaking, using the TTS engine. We will represent a request to speak a string using TTS as

```
tts(<String>)
```

We will represent speaking actions abstractly as terms of the form

```
say(<UtteranceRepresentation>)
```

where `<UtteranceRepresentation>` is a term representing the structure of the utterance. In particular, we will represent an utterance like "the light in the living room is off" as

```
say(dev(light, living_room, off, 0))
```

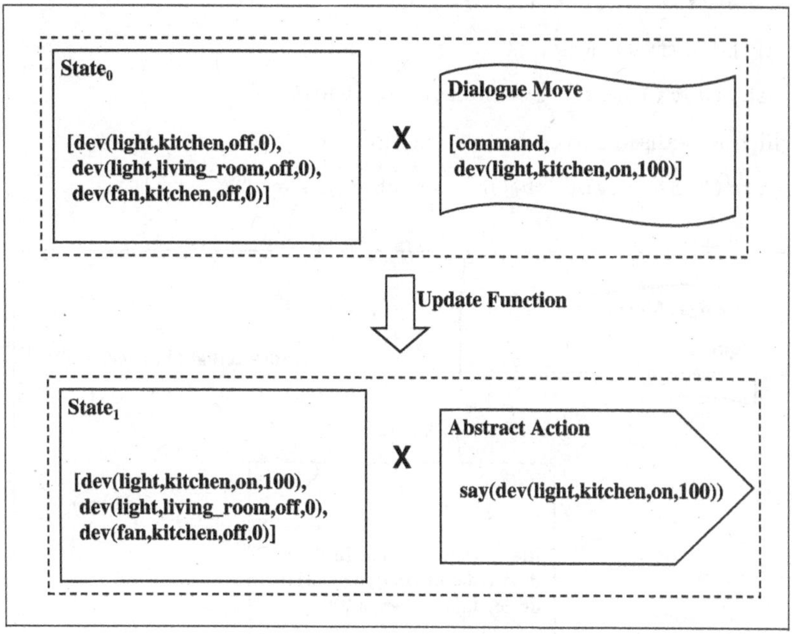

FIGURE 33 Updating the information state after a command

Figures 33 and 34 illustrate how the different data-structures interact in the context of commands and queries. At the top of Figure 33, everything is switched off, and the input information state State_0 is consequently

```
[dev(light, kitchen, off, 0),
 dev(light, living_room, off, 0),
 dev(fan, kitchen, off, 0)]
```

The input utterance is "switch on the light in the kitchen", which produces the LF

```
[[utterance_type, command], [action, switch],
 [onoff, on], [device, light], [location, kitchen]]
```

and the dialogue move

```
[command, dev(light, kitchen, on, 100)]
```

After the update, the output state State_1 at the bottom of the figure has the kitchen light switched on,

```
[dev(light, kitchen, on, 100),
 dev(light, living_room, off, 0),
 dev(fan, kitchen, off, 0)]
```

and the abstract action is

```
say(dev(light, kitchen, on, 100))
```

which is realised as the concrete action

```
tts("the␣light␣in␣the␣kitchen␣is␣on")
```

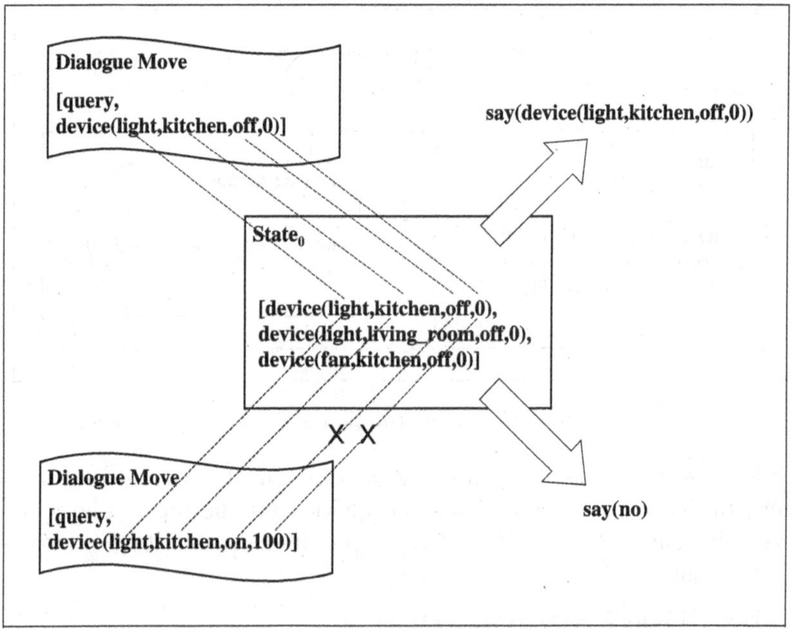

FIGURE 34 Testing the information state after a query

In Figure 34, we show processing of two queries on the same input dialogue state as in the previous figure, with everything switched off.

The question "is the light switched off in the kitchen" produces the dialogue move

```
[query, dev(light, kitchen, off, 0)]
```

Since the light actually is switched off, the resulting abstract action is

```
say(dev(light, kitchen, off, 0))
```

which is realised as the concrete action

```
tts("the␣light␣in␣the␣kitchen␣is␣off")
```

In contrast, the question "is the light switched *on* in the kitchen" gets the dialogue move

```
[query, dev(light, kitchen, on, 100)]
```

with abstract action

```
say(no)
```

and concrete action

```
tts("no")
```

We will now explain how to use the interactive Regulus environment to develop dialogue applications of this kind.

5.2.1 Developing dialogue applications

In order to develop and test Prolog-based dialogue applications in the interactive Regulus environment, it is necessary to supply definitions for the four predicates listed below, which specify the top-level dialogue management functionalities. The files defining them are declared in the applications's config file, using the **dialogue_files** declaration. Figure 35 shows how this has been done for the Toy1 application. We have chosen to split up the predicates into three files for modularity reasons, but it is equally possible to use a single file, or more files. The predicates to be defined are the following:

```
lf_to_dialogue_move(+LF, +InState, -DialogueMove)
```

Defines the input manager (cf. Section 5.3); takes a logical form and the current state as input, and returns a dialogue move.

```
update_dialogue_state(+DialogueMove, +InState,
                      -AbstractAction, -OutState)
```

Defines the dialogue manager (cf. Section 5.4); takes a dialogue move and the current state as input, and returns an abstract action and a new state.

```
abstract_action_to_action(+AbstractAction,
                          -ConcreteAction)
```

Defines the output manager (cf. Section 5.5); takes an abstract action as input, and returns a concrete action.

```
initial_dialogue_state(-State)
```

Defines the initial information state.

```
% Most declarations taken from generic file

include('$REGULUS/Examples/Toy1/scripts/toy1.cfg').

% Dialogue specific declarations:

% Dialogue processing code in these three files
regulus_config(dialogue_files,
               [toy1_prolog('input_manager.pl'),
                toy1_prolog('dialogue_manager.pl'),
                toy1_prolog('output_manager.pl')]).
```

FIGURE 35 Config file for Toy1 dialogue application.
(**$REGULUS/Examples/Toy1/scripts/toy1_dialogue.cfg**)

When you have written the config file and the files implementing the four dialogue processing predicates, you will be able to run dialogue applications in the interactive environment. Figure 36 shows a sample session, which illustrates use of two new commands:

```
LOAD_DIALOGUE
```

recompiles all the dialogue files, and

```
DIALOGUE
```

puts the development environment in a mode suitable for development of dialogue applications. When a sentence is typed in, the resulting logical form is passed through the dialogue processing predicates, starting with the input manager and ending with the output manager. The information state is stored between turns, so that each utterance is processed using the information state resulting from processing the previous utterance in the session. There is also a third command (not illustrated in the figure) called

```
INIT_DIALOGUE
```

```
$ cd $REGULUS/Examples
$ sicstus

| ?- ['$REGULUS/Prolog/load'].

(...)

yes
| ?- regulus('Toy1/scripts/toy1_dialogue.cfg').

(...)

>> LOAD
(Load current Regulus grammar)

(...)

>> LOAD_DIALOGUE
(Load dialogue-related files)

(...)

>> DIALOGUE
(Do dialogue-style processing on input sentences)

>> switch on the light in the kitchen

      Old state: [dev(light,kitchen,off,0),
                  dev(light,living_room,off,0),
                  dev(fan,kitchen,off,0)]
             LF: [[utterance_type,command],
                  [action,switch],[onoff,on],
                  [device,light],[location,kitchen]]
  Dialogue move: [command,dev(light,kitchen,on,100)].
Abstract action: say(dev(light,kitchen,on,100))
Concrete action: tts("the␣light␣in␣the␣kitchen␣is␣on"
  )
      New state: [dev(light,kitchen,on,100),
                  dev(light,living_room,off,0),
                  dev(fan,kitchen,off,0)]

Dialogue processing time: 0.00 seconds
```

FIGURE 36 Dialogue processing in the basic version of the Toy1 Prolog-based dialogue application.

This resets the dialogue state to the state defined by the predicate `initial_dialogue_state/1`.

In the next three sections, we describe how the Toy1 dialogue processing modules are implemented.

5.3 The input manager

The input manager's task is to transform the input LF (the representation produced by the recogniser) into a dialogue move (the representation required by the dialogue manager). In the basic Toy1 application, this processing step is straightforward. We will briefly describe a more elaborate version in Section 5.7, which in particular will be able to handle incomplete utterances.

To recapitulate, the Toy1 grammar accepts two kinds of utterances, queries and commands. A typical query might be "is the light switched on in the kitchen?". This will receive the LF

```
[[utterance_type, query], [state, be], [onoff, on],
 [device, light], [location, kitchen]]
```

We want to produce the dialogue move

```
[query, dev(light, kitchen, on, _)]
```

The uninstantiated fourth slot is for the intensity; we want the pattern in the dialogue move to match records representing both lights which are fully on (intensity = `100`) and lights which are on but dimmed (intensity = `50`). Similarly, a typical command is "dim the light in the living room", with LF

```
[[utterance_type, command], [action, dim],
 [device, light], [location, living_room]]
```

Here, we want the dialogue move

```
[command, dev(light, living_room, on, 50)]
```

The Prolog code for the input manager is shown in Figure 37. The top-level predicate is `lf_to_dialogue_move/3`, with three arguments; the second argument (the current information state) is formally required, but not used in this simple version of the input manager.

`lf_to_dialogue_move/3` needs to obtain the values of the five variables `DoOrQuery`, `Device`, `Location`, `OnOff` and `Intensity`, which are used to instantiate the generic dialogue move

```
[DoOrQuery,
 dev(Device, Location, OnOff, Intensity)]
```

```
lf_to_dialogue_move(LF, _PreviousState, Move) :-
    get_do_or_query(LF, DoOrQuery),
    get_device_type(LF, Device),
    get_location(LF, Location),
    get_onoff(LF, OnOff),
    get_intensity(LF, DoOrQuery, Intensity),
    Move =
      [DoOrQuery,
       dev(Device, Location, OnOff, Intensity)],
    !.
lf_to_dialogue_move(_LF, _DialogueMove) :-
    format('~N~nLF␣to␣dialogue␣move␣failed~n', []),
    fail.

get_do_or_query(LF, DoOrQuery) :-
    member([utterance_type, DoOrQuery], LF), !.

get_device_type(LF, Device) :-
    member([device, Device], LF), !.

% Location is optional
get_location(LF, Location) :-
    member([location, Location], LF), !.
get_location(_LF, _Location).

get_onoff(LF, OnOff) :-
    member([onoff, OnOff], LF), !.
get_onoff(LF, OnOff) :-
    member([action, dim], LF),
    OnOff = on, !.

% For a command, "on" means 100
get_intensity(LF, command, Intensity) :-
    member([onoff, on], LF),
    Intensity = 100, !.
% But for a query, any value is OK
get_intensity(LF, query, Intensity) :-
    member([onoff, on], LF),
    Intensity = _, !.
get_intensity(LF, _DoOrQuery, Intensity) :-
    member([onoff, off], LF),
    Intensity = 0, !.
get_intensity(LF, _DoOrQuery, Intensity) :-
    member([action, dim], LF),
    Intensity = 50, !.
```

FIGURE 37 Simple Toy1 Input Manager code.
(**$REGULUS/Examples/Toy1/Prolog/input_manager.pl**)

These values are obtained by calling the predicates `get_do_or_query/2`, `get_device_type/2`, `get_location/2`, `get_onoff/2` and `get_intensity/3`, to extract the respective pieces of information from the input LF. The structure of each of these predicates is more or less the same; the idea is just to call `member/2` to match an appropriate key/value pair in the LF. For example, `get_do_or_query/2` extracts the value associated with the key `utterance_type`, and is defined by the clause

```
get_do_or_query(LF, DoOrQuery) :-
      member([utterance_type, DoOrQuery], LF), !.
```

Despite the minimal nature of the application, there are a few non-obvious points. The predicates `get_do_or_query/2` and `get_device_type/2` both consist of a single clause, calling `member/2`, since we require the dialogue move to specify the move type (`command` or `query`) and the device type. However, there is no obligation to specify the location (a query like "is the fan switched on?" makes good sense). Consequently, the definition of `get_location/2` contains a second clause; if the call to `member/2` in the first clause fails to find a key/value pair with key `location`, the location field is left uninstantiated.

There is also a slight complication with the `Intensity` field. As noted above, it is reasonable to interpret "on" in a query as referring to any intensity. In a command, however, it seems correct to interpret "on" as meaning "fully on", implying an intensity of 100. The definition of `get_intensity/2` is written to reflect this distinction.

In general, experience shows that the task of converting between logical forms and dialogue moves is usually more complicated than one would intuitively expect. The underlying reason seems to be that language is inherently vague, while software applications such as command and control systems require precise interpretations; this means that vague concepts must somehow be turned into precise ones, a process which may require making additional assumptions. The issues involved here are explored further in (Rayner, 1993).

In the next section, we move on to the dialogue manager.

5.4 The dialogue manager

The dialogue manager implements the predicates `initial_dialogue_state/1`, which specifies the initial state, and `update_dialogue_state/4`, which defines how the system responds to a new dialogue move. The input to `update_dialogue_state/4` consists of the dialogue move and the current information state; the output is an abstract action and a new information state. The code for the Toy0 dialogue manager is shown in Figures 38 and 39.

```
:- module(dialogue_manager,
     [initial_dialogue_state/1,
      update_dialogue_state/4]
    ).

:- use_module(library(lists)).

initial_dialogue_state([
     % Light in kitchen, off
     dev(light, kitchen, off, 0),

     % Light in living room, off
     dev(light, living_room, off, 0),

     % Fan in kitchen, off
     dev(fan, kitchen, off, 0)]).

update_dialogue_state(Move, InS, AbsAct, OutS) :-
     findall([SomeAbsAct, SomeOutS],
             possible_update(Move, InS,
                             SomeAbsAct, SomeOutS),
             Pairs),
     update_state1(Move, Pairs, InS, AbsAct, OutS),
     !.
update_dialogue_state(_Move, _InS, _AbsAct, _OutS)
  :-
     format('~N~nUnable to update.~n', []),
     fail.
```

FIGURE 38 Simple Toy1 Dialogue Manager code, top level. (**$REGULUS/Examples/Toy1/Prolog/dialogue_manager.pl**)

First, in the upper half of Figure 38, `initial_dialogue_state/1`. specifies a start state, which we have arbitrarily chosen to be one in which all the devices are turned off. Next, in the lower half of the same figure, we have the top level of `update_dialogue_state/4`. This performs a `findall` to list all possible ways to perform a "normal" update (a direct response to a command or a query); the predicate defining "normal" updates is `possible_update/4`. The list of possible update results, stored as pairs of the form

```
[<AbstractAction>, <NewState>]
```

are placed in the variable `Pairs`. When the `findall` has completed,

```
% Query, no possible match. Say 'no'.
update_state1(Move, Pairs, InS, AbsAct, OutS) :-
     Move = [query, _Pattern],
     Pairs = [],
     AbsAct = say(no),
     InS = OutS,
     !.
% Command, no possible match. Say you can't do it.
update_state1(Move, Pairs, InS, AbsAct, OutS) :-
     Move = [command, _Pattern],
     Pairs = [],
     AbsAct = say(unable_to_interpret),
     InS = OutS,
     !.
% One possible match. Choose it.
update_state1(_Move, Pairs, _InS, AbsAct, OutS) :-
     Pairs = [[SingleAbsAct, SingleOutS]],
     AbsAct = SingleAbsAct,
     OutS = SingleOutS,
     !.
% Several possible matches. Say it's ambiguous.
update_state1(_Move, Pairs, InS, AbsAct, OutS) :-
     length(Pairs, NPossibleAbsActs),
     NPossibleAbsActs > 1,
     AbsAct = say(ambiguous),
     InS = OutS,
     !.

possible_update([query, Pat], InS, AbsAct, OutS) :-
     member(Pat, InS),
     AbsAct = say(Pat),
     OutS = InS.
possible_update([command, Pat], InS, AbsAct, OutS)
  :-
     apply_pattern(InS, Pat, AbsAct, OutS).

apply_pattern([dev(Dev, Loc, OnOff0, Int0) | R],
              dev(Dev, Loc, OnOff, Int), AbsAct,
              [dev(Dev, Loc, OnOff, Int) | R]) :-
     dif([OnOff0, Int0], [OnOff, Int]),
     AbsAct = say(dev(Dev, Loc, OnOff, Int)).
apply_pattern([F | OldR], Pat, AbsAct, [F | NewR])
  :-
     apply_pattern(OldR, Pat, AbsAct, NewR).
```

FIGURE 39 Simple Toy1 Dialogue Manager code, main processing. (**$REGULUS/Examples/Toy1/Prolog/dialogue_manager.pl**)

we call update_state1/5 to decide on the specific response, which, as described below, will depend on how many elements Pairs contains.

The predicate possible_update/4 is shown in the lower half of Figure 39, and defines "normal" updates for queries (first clause) and commands (second clause). For queries, a "normal" update after the dialogue move

```
[query, Pat]
```

consists of finding a record in the information state that matches Pat; if there is one, the resulting abstract action is

```
say(Pat)
```

(speak a description of the matching record) and the new information state is the same as the old one. For example, suppose the spoken query was "is the fan on?" and the information state is

```
[dev(light, kitchen, on, 100),
 dev(light, living_room, off, 0),
 dev(fan, kitchen, on, 100)]
```

Then the dialogue move is

```
[query, dev(fan, _, on, _)]
```

and this matches the third record in the information state, yielding the abstract action

```
say(dev(fan, kitchen, on, 100))
```

Similarly, the second clause of possible_update/4 handles commands, using the predicate apply_pattern/4 defined at the bottom of Figure 39. Given an input dialogue move of the form

```
[command, dev(Dev, Loc, OnOff, Int)]
```

apply_pattern/4 searches through the state to find a device record with the same values of Dev and Loc, but different values on at least one out of OnOff and Int. If it finds such a record, it updates the state with the new values. The resulting abstract action is again

```
say(Pat)
```

The predicate update_state1/5, defined in the upper half of Figure 39, counts the number of solutions found by possible_update/4 and formulates a response. In this minimal system, we only distinguish four possible cases, corresponding to the four clauses in the definition of the predicate:

1. There are no possible updates, and the dialogue move is a query. The response is simply to answer "no".
2. There are no possible updates, and the dialogue move is a command. The response is to say that the command makes no sense.
3. There is exactly one possible update; in other words, the dialogue move made sense, and was unambiguous. The update found by `possible_update/5` becomes the actual update.
4. There are several possible updates. The response is to say that the dialogue move is ambiguous.

In a more elaborate version of the dialogue manager, we could try to present more fine-grained responses in cases 1, 2 and 4. There are some suggestions about how to do this in the exercises at the end of the chapter.

5.5 The output manager

The output manager implements the predicate `abstract_action_to_action/2`, which converts abstract actions into concrete ones. In Toy0, this only involves converting abstract output requests, like

```
say(dev(light, kitchen, off, 0))
```

into concrete TTS calls, like

```
tts("the light in the kitchen is off")
```

Figure 40 presents the code for the Toy1 output manager, most of which consists of a straightforward DCG generation grammar. The predicate `perform_output_generation/2` calls the generation grammar to turn the abstract output representation into a list of words. It then converts the list into an atom by calling the Regulus utility `join_with_spaces/2`, and finally calls `atom_chars/2` to produce a Prolog string that can be used as an argument to the concrete action `tts`.

In more complex applications, the output manager might have to deal with other abstract actions too, such as updating the display on the screen, writing files, sending email, or accessing the Web.

5.6 Integrating dialogue management with recognition

We can easily adapt the methods from Chapter 3 to integrate the input manager, the dialogue manager, the output manager and the Toy1 recogniser into a functioning speech-enabled application. As before, we use the Regserver and the generic top-loop from Figure 12.

The code is presented in Figures 41 and 42, which should be compared with the corresponding code for Toy0 in Figure 11. In the Toy0

```
:- module(output_manager,
        [abstract_action_to_action/2]).

:- use_module(library(lists)).
:- use_module('$REGULUS/PrologLib/utilities').

abstract_action_to_action(say(AbstractResponse),
                          tts(String)) :-
     perform_output_generation(AbstractResponse,
                               String),
     !.

perform_output_generation(AbstractAction,
                          OutputString) :-
     generation_grammar(AbstractAction,
                        OutputWords, []),
     join_with_spaces(OutputWords, OutputAtom),
     atom_chars(OutputAtom, OutputString),
     !.
perform_output_generation(_AbsAct, _String) :-
     format('~N~nError␣in␣output␣manager.~n', []),
     fail.

generation_grammar(no) --> ['no'].
generation_grammar(unable_to_interpret) -->
     ['sorry␣that␣doesn\'t␣make␣sense'].
generation_grammar(ambiguous) -->
     ['sorry,␣that\'s␣ambiguous'].

generation_grammar(dev(Dev, Loc, _OnOff, Int)) -->
     generation_grammar(dev(Dev)),
     ['in'], generation_grammar(location(Loc)),
     ['is'], generation_grammar(intensity(Int)).

generation_grammar(dev(light)) --> ['the␣light'].
generation_grammar(dev(fan)) --> ['the␣fan'].

generation_grammar(location(kitchen)) -->
     ['the␣kitchen'].
generation_grammar(location(living_room)) -->
     ['the␣living␣room'].

generation_grammar(intensity(0)) --> ['off'].
generation_grammar(intensity(100)) --> ['on'].
generation_grammar(intensity(Other)) -->
     { number(Other), 0 < Other, Other < 100 },
     ['dimmed'].
```

FIGURE 40 Simple Toy1 Output Manager code. (**$REGULUS/Examples/Toy1/Prolog/output_manager.pl**)

```
:- use_module(
  '$REGULUS/Examples/Toy1/Prolog/input_manager').
:- use_module(
  '$REGULUS/Examples/Toy1/Prolog/dialogue_manager').
:- use_module(
  '$REGULUS/Examples/Toy1/Prolog/output_manager').

:- ensure_loaded(
  '$REGULUS/Examples/Generic/Prolog/top_loop.pl').

:- use_module('$REGULUS/PrologLib/utilities').
:- use_module(
     '$REGSERVER/Prolog/regulus_sockettalk').

toy1_app(Port) :-
      RecognitionPackage =
        '$REGULUS/Examples/Toy1/Generated/recogniser',
      initial_dialogue_state(InitialState),
      top_loop(Port, RecognitionPackage,
               'audio.OutputVolume=200',
               "Ready␣to␣start", InitialState,
               process_recogniser_output).
```

FIGURE 41 Toy1 dialogue application, top level
(`$REGULUS/Examples/Toy1/Prolog/toy1_app.pl`)

application, we never used the fourth argument of `top_loop/5`, and just left it uninstantiated. Here, we start in `toy1_app/1` (bottom of Figure 41) by calling `initial_dialogue_state/1`, and passing the result as the "state" argument of `top_loop/5`.

The main action happens in the predicate `process_recogniser_output/3` (top half of Figure 42). We extract the `LF` from the `RecogniserOutput`, and then in succession call the input manager (`lf_to_dialogue_move/3`), the dialogue manager (`update_dialogue_state/4`) and the output manager (`abstract_action_to_action/2`), printing trace output as we go. At the end, we call `perform_action/1` on the output concrete action. This just checks that the argument is a term of the form

```
tts(<String>)
```

and calls `regulus_sockettalk_say_tts/1` to send a TTS request to the Regserver.

```
process_recogniser_output(RecogniserOutput, InState,
                          OutState) :-
     format('~N~nOld␣state:␣~w', [InState]),
     RecogniserOutput =
       recognition_succeeded(
            Confidence, Words, [value=LF]),
     format('~N~nRecognised:␣"~w"␣(conf:␣~d)~n',
            [Words, Confidence]),
     format('~NLF:␣~w~n', [LF]),

     lf_to_dialogue_move(LF, InState, DialogueMove),
     format('~NDialogue␣move:␣', []),
     portray_clause(DialogueMove),

     update_dialogue_state(DialogueMove, InState,
                           AbsAction, OutState),
     format('~NAbstract␣action:␣~w', [AbsAction]),

     abstract_action_to_action(AbsAction, Action),
     convert_strings_to_quoted_atoms(Action,
                                     PrintAction),
     format('~NConcrete␣action:␣~w', [PrintAction]),
     perform_action(Action),

     format('~N~nNew␣state:␣~w~n', [OutState]),
     !.
process_recogniser_output(RecogniserOutput, InState,
                          OutState) :-
     format('~N~nCouldn\'t␣process:␣~w~n',
            [RecogniserOutput]),
     Action = tts("Sorry,␣something␣went␣wrong"),
     perform_action(Action),
     InState = OutState,
     !.

perform_action(Action) :-
     (    ( Action = tts(String),
            is_prolog_string(String) ) ->
          String1 = String ;
          String1 = "Sorry,␣something␣went␣wrong"
     ),
     regulus_sockettalk_say_tts(String1),
     !.
perform_action(Action) :-
     format('~N~nUnable␣to␣perform␣action:␣~w~n',
            [Action]),
      !.
```

FIGURE 42 Toy1 dialogue application, main processing ($REGULUS/Examples/Toy1/Prolog/toy1_app.pl)

5.6.1 Running the Toy1 dialogue application

The Toy1 dialogue application is run in the same way as the Toy0 application in Section 3.3.1. As before, we open two Cygwin/UNIX windows, and perform the following steps to run the basic version.

1. In the first window, start a Nuance license manager in the background:

   ```
   $ cd $REGULUS/Examples/Toy1/Generated
   $ nlm <... your Nuance license code ...> &
   ```

2. In the first window, start the Vocalizer process:

   ```
   $ vocalizer -num_channels 1 -voices_from_disk &
   ```

3. In the first window, start a Nuance recognition server in the background, using the Toy1 recognition package:

   ```
   $ recserver -package recogniser &
   ```

4. When the first three processes are running, start the dialogue application in the second window:

   ```
   $ cd $REGULUS/Examples/Toy1/scripts
   $ sicstus -l load_and_run_app.pl
   ```

Interaction with the Toy1 application is similar to that with the Toy0 application described earlier.

5.7 Dealing with ellipsis and corrections

In this last section, we will describe a more elaborate version of the Toy1 application, which is able to handle *ellipsis* and *corrections*. Figure 43 shows examples of the new functionality. We start with everything switched off, and in turn 1 switch on the light in the kitchen. In turn 2, we use the elliptical (incomplete) command "in the living room"; the system interprets this as equivalent to "switch on the light in the living room". In turn 3, we switch on the fan, but in turn 4 we change our minds and say "undo". This has the effect of returning us to the previous state. In turn 5, we switch off the light in the kitchen. Turn 6 shows a correction move, which also involves ellipsis processing. We say "no, i meant in the living room", and this has the effect of both undoing the previous command, and also carrying out the replacement command "switch off the light in the living room". In the rest of the section, we will outline how these new capabilities are implemented. We describe in turn the config file, the grammar, the information state, the input manager and the dialogue manager. The output manager is almost identical to the one in Section 5.5, and is not described.

(kitchen light off, living room light off, fan off)	
$\mathbf{U}_1$	switch on the light in the kitchen
$\mathbf{S}_1$	the light in the kitchen is on
(kitchen light on, living room light off, fan off)	
$\mathbf{U}_2$	in the living room
$\mathbf{S}_2$	the light in the living room is on
(kitchen light on, living room light on, fan off)	
$\mathbf{U}_3$	switch on the fan
$\mathbf{S}_3$	the fan in the kitchen is on
(kitchen light on, living room light on, fan on)	
$\mathbf{U}_4$	undo
$\mathbf{S}_4$	ok, undone
(kitchen light on, living room light on, fan off)	
$\mathbf{U}_5$	switch off the light in the kitchen
$\mathbf{S}_5$	the light in the kitchen is off
(kitchen light off, living room light on, fan off)	
$\mathbf{U}_6$	no i meant in the living room
$\mathbf{S}_6$	the light in the living room is off
(kitchen light on, living room light off, fan off)	

FIGURE 43 Ellipsis, undo and correction in extended version of Toy1

5.7.1 Config file and other files

All the files for the extended version of Toy1 are in the directory

```
$REGULUS/Examples/Toy1
```

The config file is

```
scripts/toy1_dialogue_corrections.cfg
```

and as usual points to all the other files. The additional grammar rules are in the files

```
Regulus/toy1_ellipsis.regulus
Regulus/toy1_corrections.regulus
```

and the input manager, dialogue manager and output manager are respectively in the files

```
Prolog/input_manager_corrections.pl
Prolog/dialogue_manager_corrections.pl
Prolog/output_manager_corrections.pl
```

The file

```
Prolog/dialogue_state.pl
```

contains code used by both the input manager and the dialogue manager to maintain the information state.

5.7.2 Grammar

The grammar contains four new rules, which cover ellipsis and correction utterances. The representations of elliptical utterances are marked with the tag

```
[utterance_type , phrase]
```

and correction utterances are marked

```
[control , correction]
```

Thus for example the representation of "in the kitchen" is

```
[[utterance_type , phrase], [location , kitchen]]
```

and that of "no i meant in the living room" is

```
[[control , correction],
 [utterance_type , phrase], [location , living_room]]
```

5.7.3 Information state

In order to be able to handle ellipsis and corrections, the information state needs to hold more information than just the current states of the devices. We add two new components: the most recent dialogue move (used for interpreting ellipsis), and a back-pointer to the previous information state (used for processing corrections). An information state in the extended version is thus conceptually a triple

```
<<Devices>, <PreviousMove>, <LastState>>
```

where `<Devices>` is the information state used in the simple version of the Toy0 application. It is worth noting that, since each information state contains a back-pointer to its predecessor, a state now implicitly contains the entire history of the dialogue.

The information state is manipulated using the two predicates `get_from_state/3` and `set_in_state/4`, defined in

```
$REGULUS/Examples/Toy1/Prolog/dialogue_state.pl
```

For example, the call

```
get_from_state(last_dialogue_move , S, Move)
```

says that `Move` is the `last_dialogue_move` component of state `S`. The call

```
set_in_state(last_dialogue_move , S1, Move , S2)
```

says that state S2 is the result of modifying state S1 so that the value of the last_dialogue_move component is Move.

5.7.4 Input manager

The input manager from Section 5.3 needs to be extended to handle ellipsis and correction moves. The processing consists of three phases. First, we construct a "plain" version of the dialogue move out of the input LF, using the methods of Section 5.3. Second, we look at the most recent dialogue move (stored in the information state, as mentioned above), and if appropriate use it to fill in uninstantiated slots in the "plain" dialogue move. Finally, if the LF is marked as a correction, we put a "correction" wrapper around the whole dialogue move.

We illustrate with an example. Assume that the most recent utterance was "switch off the light in the kitchen", with dialogue move

```
[command, dev(light, kitchen, off, 0)]
```

We now want to process "no i meant in the living room", with LF

```
[[control, correction],
 [utterance_type, phrase], [location, living_room]]
```

This first gives us the "plain" dialogue move

```
[_, dev(_, living_room, _, _)]
```

where the slots for utterance-type, device-type, on-or-off and intensity are all uninstantiated. The second phase of processing fills in the uninstantiated slots from the previous dialogue move, giving us

```
[command, dev(light, living_room, off, 0)]
```

Last, since the utterance is marked as a correction, we add a "correction" wrapper, giving us the final result

```
[correction,
  [command, dev(light, living_room, off, 0)]]
```

The code for carrying out the second and third processing phases is straightforward. In the next section, we describe how the extended version of the dialogue manager produces updates for correction moves.

5.7.5 Dialogue manager

Most of the code in the enhanced version of the dialogue manager is taken from the basic one described in Section 5.4. The differences are all concerned with handling of correction moves, and affect the definition of the predicate update_dialogue_state/4, the simple version of which

```
update_dialogue_state(undo, InS,
                      AbsAct, OutS) :-
     get_from_state(last_state, InS, OldS),
     OutS = OldS,
     AbsAct = say(reverted),
     !.
update_dialogue_state([correction, Move], InS,
                      AbsAct, OutS) :-
     get_from_state(last_state, InS, OldS),
     update_dialogue_state(Move, OldS, AbsAct, OutS),
     !.
update_dialogue_state(Move, InS, AbsAct, OutS) :-
     set_in_state(last_state, InS, InS, S1),
     set_in_state(last_dialogue_move, S1, Move, S2),
     findall([SomeAbsAct, SomeOutS],
             possible_update(Move, S2,
                             SomeAbsAct, SomeOutS),
             Pairs),
     update_state1(Move, Pairs, S2, AbsAct, OutS),
     !.
update_dialogue_state(_Move, _InS, _AbsAct, _OutS) :-
     format('~N~nUnable␣to␣update.~n', []),
     fail.
```

FIGURE 44 Toy1 Dialogue Manager code, enhanced to handle corrections: definition of predicate **update_dialogue_state/4**. (**$REGULUS/Examples/Toy1/Prolog/dialogue_manager.pl**)

was shown earlier in Figure 38. The enhanced definition is presented in Figure 44.

The two clauses in the original version of **update_dialogue_state/4** appear here as the third and fourth clauses in Figure 44. The second (failure) clause from the old version appears unchanged. The first clause from the old version handles normal (non-correction) moves, and is the same, except that two lines have been added at the beginning to save the current information state and the current dialogue move.

The first two clauses in Figure 44 are new, and deal with undo and correction moves. The first, which handles plain "undo" moves, says that the update for an "undo" is defined by reverting the information state to the stored previous state, and producing an abstract action to inform that an undo has been carried out. The second clause, which is for corrections proper ("No, I said/meant...") says that the update in the state `InS` for the move

```
[correction, Move]
```

is defined by first finding the preceding state `OldS`, and then carrying out the update for `Move` in `OldS`.

The treatment of undos and corrections described here is the one used in the Clarissa system (Rayner and Hockey, 2004), and has been extensively tested in that context. One of its pleasant features is that multiple corrections are handled correctly: for example, the reader can easily check that the sequence "switch on the light in the kitchen"... "no, i mean the light in the living room"... "no, i mean the fan" produces the expected result. A drawback, however, is that it is not possible to undo an undo: a sequence of two undos reverts to the state two utterances earlier, rather than first reverting to the previous state and then moving forward again to the current state. In one of the exercises, we suggest ways to address this problem.

5.8 Summary

- The Regulus development environment provides support for Prolog-based spoken dialogue applications.
- Dialogue management is assumed to be side-effect free, and is based on a version of update semantics. All context is kept in a Prolog object called the *information state*. The operation of the dialogue module is defined by an update function of the form

$$f : LF \times State \rightarrow Actions \times State$$

- The dialogue module is split into an *input manager*, a *dialogue manager* and an *output manager*. The dialogue manager operates on abstract descriptions of inputs and outputs, called *dialogue moves*, and *abstract actions*. The input manager and output manager translate between concrete and abstract representations.
- The three dialogue modules are realised by supplying definitions for the predicates `lf_to_dialogue_move/3`, `update_dialogue_state/4` and `abstract_action_to_action/2`. The files containing these predicates need to be defined in the config file.
- The interactive development environment contains three dialogue-related commands. The `LOAD_DIALOGUE` command loads the dialogue processing code. The `DIALOGUE` command puts the development environment into dialogue mode. The `INIT_DIALOGUE` command resets the dialogue to the initial state.
- Dialogue moves are typically fairly different from logical forms. Translating from logical forms into dialogue moves is not necessarily

a trivial task.

- The dialogue manager needs to be able to handle both normal and abnormal responses. In particular, it needs to be able to deal with *inconsistent* and *ambiguous* utterances.
- Abstract speaking actions typically use structured representions of the content to be spoken. One easy way to convert these into concrete words is to use a DCG generation grammar.
- It is often important to be able to handle *ellipsis* (incomplete utterances), and *corrections* (retracting or changing the previous utterance). Ellipsis is typically handled in the input manager, and corrections in the dialogue manager.

Exercises

1. Extend the plain Toy1 system to include a larger number of rooms. At a minimum, put a light in each room. Which modules do you need to alter?
2. Extend the plain Toy1 system to include at least one new kind of device. Which modules do you need to alter?
3. Extend the plain Toy1 system to give better answers when the dialogue move is ambiguous. For example, if both lights are off, the response to "switch on the light" might be "I don't know whether you mean 'switch on the light on the kitchen' or 'switch on the light in the living room"'.
4. Extend the plain Toy1 system to give better negative answers. For example, if the fan is on, and the query is "is the fan off?", the response could be something like "no, the fan in the kitchen is not off".
5. Extend the "corrections" version of the Toy1 system so as to give more informative responses when performing an "undo" move. A typical response could be something like "Undone. The light in the kitchen is now on again".
6. Extend the "corrections" version of the Toy1 system so as to make it possible to undo an undo move. You will probably want to add a new command to the grammar which is specifically for undoing undos, and enhance the dialogue state with appropriate extra information. Does your treatment create any new problems?
7. Suitably adapting the methods of Section 3.5, implement a Java version of the plain Toy1 system. You may find it helpful to start by thinking about how you will achieve the effect of the `findall` in `update_dialogue_state/4` using Java.

6

A speech translation system

Pierrette Bouillon and Manny Rayner

6.1 Introduction

In this chapter, we will show how to use Regulus to build speech to speech machine translation applications. Most of this part of the system has been developed under the Open Source MedSLT project, a speech to speech translation system for medical domains (cf. Section 1.4.2).

In a rule-based system, translation involves several different resources: a linguistic description of the source language (SL), a description of the target language (TL) and, in transfer-based systems, a set of contrastive translation rules ("transfer rules"; see (Arnold et al., 1994) for a good introduction to machine translation). In a **transfer-based** system, the translation process is performed in three main stages: analysis of the SL sentence into a SL representation, using the SL description; translation of this SL representation into a suitable TL representation, using the transfer rules; and finally generation of the target sentence from the TL representation, using the TL description. In an **interlingua-based** framework, the translation is done in two stages: analysis of the SL to the interlingua and then generation from the interlingua to the TL.

In the rest of the chapter, we continue the running example from Chapters 4 and 5. We first describe the Regulus translation process using the transfer-based framework (Section 6.2). We then present the details of how to use the interactive development environment for translation applications (Section 6.3), after which we introduce the interlingua framework (Section 6.4). Section 6.5 explains how to extend the system to translate elliptical expressions as well as full sentences. Section 6.6 describes tools available for supporting systematic regression testing of translation applications. Finally, Section 6.7 shows how to

```
>> switch on the light

Source: switch on the light
Target: allumez la lampe
Other info:
   n_parses=1
   source_representation=
              [[action,switch],[device,light],
               [onoff,on],[utterance_type,command]]
   target_representation=
              [[action,allumer],[device,lampe],
               [utterance_type,command]]
   n_generations=1
   other_translations=[]
```

FIGURE 45 Example session using transfer-based framework

integrate the translation engine into a full speech enabled system.

6.2 Transfer-based systems

The piece of Regulus trace in Figure 45 illustrates the three main translation steps in the transfer-based framework. In the first stage, the source sentence "switch on the light" is parsed by the Toy1 grammar. As explained in Chapter 4, the result is a flat representation, the one given in `source_representation`. This list of elements is then directly mapped into the corresponding target representation, from which the target French sentence, "allumez la lampe", is generated.

The config file that defines the SL and TL resources involved in this process is given in Figure 46. The line

```
include('$REGULUS/Examples/Toy1/scripts/toy1.cfg').
```

first specifies that all the SL declarations will be taken from the config file for Toy1 (Figure 19, page 69). After this, we have two more entries that specify the extra resources needed for the translation process:

1. The `transfer_rules` entry defines the rules that map the English representation into its French equivalent.
2. `generation_rules` points to the file containing the rules which generate surface words from the French representation. These rules are the compiled form of the French grammar, as explained in Section 6.3.1.

We will now describe these two new components.

```
% Most declarations taken from generic file
include('$REGULUS/Examples/Toy1/scripts/toy1.cfg').

% Translation specific declarations:

% Compiled generation grammar.
regulus_config(generation_rules,
               toy1_runtime('generator.pl')).

% Rules for translating source language
%  representations
% into target language representations
regulus_config(transfer_rules,
               toy1_prolog('eng_to_fre.pl')).
```

FIGURE 46 Config file for transfer-based translation version of Toy1 application. (`$REGULUS/Examples/Toy1/scripts/toy1_slt_transfer.cfg`)

6.2.1 Transfer rules

In order to translate the SL representation into the target representation, we need a set of transfer rules. These will map the list of SL attribute-values pairs, which are the output from analysis, into the TL pairs, which are the input to generation. The set of rules necessary for our Toy1 application is given in Figure 47.

As in most translation systems, we need to distinguish two types of rules. Entries of the type `transfer_lexicon` specify lexical correspondances. They are used for one-to-one mapping of attribute-value pairs, so for instance the `transfer_lexicon` entry

```
transfer_lexicon([action, dim], [action, baisser]).
```

says that we should replace the element

```
[action, dim]
```

in the English representation by

```
[action, baisser]
```

in the French one. In contrast, entries of the type `transfer_rule` are used for structural transfer, when one-to-one mapping cannot apply because of syntactic divergences between languages. For example, in Figure 47, the `transfer_rule` entry

```
transfer_rule([[action, switch], [onoff, on]],
              [[action, allumer]]).
```

```
transfer_rule([[action, switch], [onoff, on]],
              [[action, allumer]]).

transfer_rule([[action, switch], [onoff, off]],
              [[action, éteindre]]).

transfer_lexicon([utterance_type, command],
                 [utterance_type, command]).
transfer_lexicon([utterance_type, query],
                 [utterance_type, query]).
transfer_lexicon([state, be],
                 [state, être]).
transfer_lexicon([action, dim],
                 [action, baisser]).
transfer_lexicon([device, light],
                 [device, lampe]).
transfer_lexicon([device, fan],
                 [device, ventilateur]).
transfer_lexicon([location, kitchen],
                 [location, cuisine]).
transfer_lexicon([location, living_room],
                 [location, salon]).
transfer_lexicon([onoff, on],
                 [onoff, allumé]).
transfer_lexicon([onoff, off],
                 [onoff, éteint]).
```

FIGURE 47 Transfer rules for Toy1 application.
(**$REGULUS/Examples/Toy1/Prolog/eng_to_fre.pl**)

maps the two English attribute-value pairs

```
[[action, switch], [onoff, on]]
```

representing the combination of verb and particle "switch on" to the single French attribute-value pair

```
[[action, allumer]]
```

representing the verb "allumer".

In this simple example, there is never more than one way to use the rules to translate any given SL representation. In a more complex set of transfer rules, it is often possible to get situations where several rules, or sets of rules, are all potentially applicable. The basic principle used to resolve rule conflicts is that the *most specific* rule is chosen. For example, if the choice is between applying a single `transfer_rule` to a list of attribute-value pairs, or a different `transfer_lexicon` entry to each individual element, then the `transfer_rule` is used. If the choice is between two `transfer_rules`, then the one which translates the largest number of attribute-value pairs is chosen. (The idea here, which is common to many systems, is that a complex rule blocks word-to-word translation). Finally, if there is still more than one rule that can be applied, the run-time system selects the one which appears earliest in the source file.

6.2.2 Generation

The role of the generation grammar is to take as input the linear representation produced by the transfer rules, and return a surface string. Formally, a Regulus generation grammar is identical to a Regulus analysis grammar, as we can see in the small French generation grammar built for this application (see Figures 48 to 50).

Linguistically, however, a generation grammar poses different problems and makes different demands. The main problem for an analysis grammar is ambiguity: a single string can receive multiple interpretations. Conversely, the key problem for a generation grammar is overgeneration: the grammar must limit the set of possible paraphrases that can be generated from one represention, or else choose the best candidate from among them. The toy French generation grammar shown here has been carefully constructed so as not to overgenerate. In particular, NPs like *la cuisine* ("the kitchen") or *le ventilateur* ("the fan") are listed directly in the lexicon, rather than being constructed compositionally, as in the English grammar, from an article and a noun. Our reason for doing this is that the source and target representations are underspecified, and do not represent articles[15]. If the French grammar had the same structure as the English one, the representation

```
[device , ventilateur]
```

would for example generate not only *le ventilateur* ("the fan") but also *un ventilateur* ("a fan").

The grammar writer has two main ways to attack this kind of problem. The one that we have used here is to write an artificially constrained grammar; the problem is that the structure of this grammar easily becomes unnatural. Really, of course, it is much better to build up NPs compositionally from articles and nouns, and in practice we generally have to write the grammar first in the natural and linguisti-

[15]We discuss our reasons for not including articles in the representations on page 68.

```
feature_value_space(number_value, [[sing, plur]]).
feature_value_space(gender_value, [[masc, fem]]).
feature_value_space(vform_value,
                    [[imperative, finite]]).
feature_value_space(vtype_value,
                    [[transitive, être]]).
feature_value_space(sem_np_type_value,
                    [[n, location, device]]).

feature(number, number_value).
feature(gender, gender_value).
feature(vform, vform_value).
feature(vtype, vtype_value).
feature(sem_np_type, sem_np_type_value).
feature(obj_sem_np_type, sem_np_type_value).

top_level_category('.MAIN').

category('.MAIN', [gsem]).
category(utterance, [sem]).
category(command, [sem]).
category(yn_question, [sem]).
category(np, [sem, number, gender, sem_np_type]).
category(location_pp, [sem]).
category(verb, [sem, number, gender, vform, vtype,
                obj_sem_np_type]).
category(onoff, [sem, number, gender, sem_np_type]).
```

FIGURE 48 Toy1 French generation grammar (declarations). (From **$REGULUS/Examples/Toy1/Prolog/french.regulus**)

cally motivated style, and then transform it into the constrained one. This kind of transformation is tedious and unpleasant to do manually, but can be carried out efficiently using corpus-based grammar specialisation methods (cf. Section 10.3.4).

The second possibility is to let the grammar generate multiple strings, but define *preferences* which say that some strings are better or worse than others. The Regulus translation engine supports a simple generation preference mechanism. These are defined using declarations of the form

```
generation_preference(<WordList>, <Score>).
```

where `<WordList>` is a Prolog list of surface words, and `<Score>` is a

```
'.MAIN':[gsem=[value=S]] -->
  utterance:[sem=S].

utterance:[sem=S] -->
  (    command:[sem=S] ;
       yn_question:[sem=S]
  ).

command:[sem=concat([[utterance_type, command]],
                    concat(Verb,
                           concat(Np, Loc)))] -->
  verb:[sem=Verb, vform=imperative,
        vtype=transitive,
        obj_sem_np_type=ObjType],
  np:[sem=Np, sem_np_type=ObjType],
  ?location_pp:[sem=Loc].

yn_question:[sem=
             concat([[utterance_type, query]],
                    concat(Verb,
                           concat(Adj,
                                  concat(Np, Loc))))]
   -->
   np:[sem=Np, number=N, gender=Gen,
       sem_np_type=SubjType],
   verb:[sem=Verb, vform=finite, vtype=être,
         number=N, gender=Gen, obj_sem_np_type=n],
   onoff:[sem=Adj, sem_np_type=SubjType, number=N,
          gender=Gen],
   ?location_pp:[sem=Loc].

location_pp:[sem=Loc] -->
    dans,
    np:[sem=Loc, sem_np_type=location].
```

FIGURE 49 Toy1 French generation grammar, rules (From `$REGULUS/Examples/Toy1/Regulus/french.grammar`)

```
verb:[sem=[[state, être]],
     vform=finite, vtype=être, number=sing,
     gender=masc, obj_sem_np_type=n] --> 'est-il'.
verb:[sem=[[state, être]],
     vform=finite, vtype=être, number=plur,
     gender=masc, obj_sem_np_type=n] --> 'sont-ils'.
verb:[sem=[[state, être]],
     vform=finite, vtype=être, number=sing,
     gender=fem, obj_sem_np_type=n] --> 'est-elle'.
verb:[sem=[[state, être]],
     vform=finite, vtype=être, number=plur,
     gender=fem,
     obj_sem_np_type=n] --> 'sont-elles'.
verb:[sem=[[action, allumer]],
     vform=imperative, vtype=transitive,
     number=plur,
     obj_sem_np_type=device] --> allumez.
verb:[sem=[[action, baisser]],
     vform=imperative, vtype=transitive,
     number=plur,
     obj_sem_np_type=device] --> baissez.
verb:[sem=[[action, éteindre]],
     vform=imperative, vtype=transitive,
     number=plur,
     obj_sem_np_type=device] --> éteignez.

np:[sem=[[device, lampe]],
    sem_np_type=device, number=sing,
    gender=fem] --> la, lampe.
np:[sem=[[device, ventilateur]],
    sem_np_type=device, number=sing,
    gender=masc] --> le, ventilateur.
np:[sem=[[location, cuisine]],
    sem_np_type=location, number=sing,
    gender=fem] --> la, cuisine.
np:[sem=[[location, salon]],
    sem_np_type=location, number=sing,
    gender=masc] --> le, salon.

onoff:[sem=[[onoff, allumé]],
       number=sing, gender=masc] --> allumé.
onoff:[sem=[[onoff, allumé]],
       number=sing, gender=fem] --> allumée.
onoff:[sem=[[onoff, éteint]],
       number=sing, gender=masc] --> éteint.
onoff:[sem=[[onoff, éteint]],
       number=sing, gender=fem] --> éteinte.
```

FIGURE 50 Toy1 French generation grammar, lexicon (From `$REGULUS/Examples/Toy1/Regulus/french.grammar`)

positive or negative number. The effect of the generation preferences is to define a score on each generated string, calculated by summing the preference scores for all substrings. In the French example with definite and indefinite articles, we could for example allow the grammar to generate both variants, and then prefer *la cuisine* (definite) by adding the declaration

```
generation_preference([la, cuisine], 1).
```

or alternately disprefer *une cuisine* (indefinite) by adding the declaration

```
generation_preference([une, cuisine], -1).
```

We will now explain how to compile and load the new components which are required for translation applications.

6.3 Developing translation applications

In addition to the SL grammar, a translation application needs a TL grammar, compiled for generation, and a set of transfer rules. The Regulus development environment contains two modes specifically designed for developing these components. When developing a translation application, you will typically want to set up two Regulus windows. One window will be running in "generation mode" (Section 6.3.1), and will have the TL grammar loaded. The other window will be running in "translation mode" (Section 6.3.2), and will have loaded the SL grammar and all the resources needed for transfer and generation. It is important to understand that although the translation window also requires the TL grammar, it only uses it in its compiled form. If it is necessary to make a change in the TL generation grammar, it is first compiled in the generation mode window; the compiled form must then be reloaded in the translation window. We will explain shortly how to perform these various operations.

6.3.1 Developing generation grammars

As we have already said, a generation grammar is formally the same as any other Regulus grammar. To be able to use the generation grammar, we as usual need to write a config file. The config file for the Toy1 French grammar is given in Figure 51. Comparing it with the corresponding file for the English Toy1 grammar in Figure 19 (page 69), we can see that they are very similar. The differences specifically derive from the fact that one is being compiled into a recognition package, and the other into a generator.

In both files, we specify the source grammar (`regulus_grammar`), the top level category (`top_level_cat`) and where to put temporary files

```
include(
'$REGULUS/Examples/Toy1/scripts/file_search_paths.
  cfg').

  regulus_config(
     regulus_grammar,
     [toy1_grammars(french)]).

  regulus_config(
     top_level_cat,
     '.MAIN').

  regulus_config(
     generation_rules,
     toy1_runtime('generator.pl')).

  regulus_config(
     working_file_prefix,
     toy1_runtime(french_generation)).

  regulus_config(
     working_directory,
     toy1_runtime('')).
```

FIGURE 51 Toy1 French generation grammar, config file (`$REGULUS/Examples/Toy1/scripts/french.cfg`)

(`working_file_prefix`, `working_directory`). The difference is that, instead of specifying where to put the derived Nuance recognition grammar, we have the entry

```
regulus_config(generation_rules,
               toy1_runtime('generator.pl')).
```

which says where to store the compiled generation version of the grammar.

The process of building a generation grammar is also similar to that used to build a recognition grammar, described in Section 2.5. As before, we start by opening a SICStus window, and loading the development environment:

```
| ?- ['$REGULUS/Prolog/load'].
```

We then start Regulus using the config file for the French generation grammar:

```
| ?- regulus('$REGULUS/Examples/Toy1/scripts/french.
  cfg').
```

When the Regulus prompt comes up, we compile the Regulus grammar into generation form using the command

```
>> LOAD_GENERATION
```

This writes a compiled version of the grammar to the file

```
$REGULUS/Examples/Toy1/GeneratedFiles/generator.pl
```

Although the TL grammar is intended to be used for generation (producing a surface string from a representation), it would in practice be very inconvenient to test it using only the generation-compiled form; typing in a representation is typically slow and error-prone. For testing purposes, it is instead much easier to type in a surface string, parse it into a representation, and then generate from that representation. The development environment's "generation mode", invoked by the command

```
>> GENERATION
```

offers precisely the functionality we have just described. Figure 52 shows an example. We start Regulus, load the grammar in both analysis form (LOAD) and generation form (LOAD_GENERATION), and then put the system into generation mode (GENERATION). When we type in the utterance

```
allumez la lampe dans la cuisine
```

("switch-on the light in the kitchen"), the system first parses it using the analysis grammar and produces a representation. It then uses the generation grammar on this representation, and generates back the original string, showing that, at least in this case, the grammar works equally well in both directions.

6.3.2 Developing transfer rules

The generation mode is designed for developing generation grammars. There is also a "translation" mode, which is intended to support development of transfer rules; this time, input sentences are subjected to the operations of SL parsing, transfer and TL generation. Figure 53 illustrates interaction in translation mode. After compiling the SL grammar with LOAD and the translation-specific resources with LOAD_TRANSLATE, the Regulus top-level is put into translation mode with the TRANSLATE command. If necessary, it is possible to go back into analysis mode using the NORMAL_PROCESSING command. For switching between the transfer-based and interlingua framework, the commands are INTERLINGUA and

```
| ?- regulus(
      '$REGULUS/Examples/Toy1/scripts/french.cfg').

(...)

>> LOAD
(Load current Regulus grammar in DCG and left-corner
form)

(...)

>> LOAD_GENERATION
(Compile and load current generator grammar)

(...)

>> GENERATION
(Generate from parsed input sentences)

>> allumez la lampe dans la cuisine

Sem value: [[utterance_type,command],
             [action,allumer],[device,lampe],
             [location,cuisine]]

Syn features: []

Generating:

Generation time: 0.00 seconds

Words: allumez la lampe dans la cuisine

Generated tree:

.MAIN
   utterance
      command
      /  verb lex(allumez)
      |  np
      |  /  spec lex(la)
      |  \  noun lex(lampe)
      |  location_pp
      |  /  lex(dans)
      |  |  np
      |  |  /  spec lex(la)
      \  \  \  noun lex(cuisine)
```

FIGURE 52 Example session showing how to run the French Toy1 grammar in generation mode

```
>> LOAD
(Load current Regulus grammar in DCG and left-corner
form)

(...)

>> LOAD_TRANSLATE
(Load translation-related files)

(...)

>> NO_INTERLINGUA
(Perform translation directly, i.e. not through
interlingua)

>> TRANSLATE
(Do translation-style processing on input sentences)

>> switch on the light

Source: switch on the light
Target: allumez la lampe
Other info:
   n_parses=1
   source_representation=
               [[action,switch],[device,light],
                [onoff,on],[utterance_type,command]]
   target_representation=
               [[action,allumer],[device,lampe],
                [utterance_type,command]]
   n_generations=1
   other_translations=[]
```

FIGURE 53 Example session showing how to run the transfer-based version of Toy1 in translation mode

NO_INTERLINGUA. The default is the interlingua-based framework described in the next section.

6.4 Translation through interlingua

In Sections 6.2 and 6.3, we have shown how to use the transfer-based framework. In Regulus, translation can also be performed using the interlingua framework. Interlingua is a neutral representation that captures whatever is common between languages (Arnold et al., 1994). The advantage is that, provided the interlingua is well defined, it is not necessary to write contrastive rules (i.e. transfer rules); translation instead goes first from the source to the interlingua, and then from the interlingua to the target. In a multilingual project, this framework is quite attractive: it means that, if you want to add a new language as input, you only need to add rules that map between that language and the interlingua, without explicitly considering other languages. For a general domain, the task of defining the interlingua is extremely challenging. In speech applications, it is more feasible, since domains are usually very restricted.

Figure 54 illustrates processing in the interlingua-based version of Toy1. In this framework, SL representations are first mapped into the interlingua, which are then transformed into the TL representations, for which target sentences are generated. As in the transfer-based framework, **source_representation** indicates the result of analysis and **target_representation** the input for the generation. **interlingua** is the new, language independent, level of representation. In this small application, it is clear that the source representation and the interlingua will be quite similar. The only difference here is that the SL representation of the verb and preposition

```
[action, switch], [onoff, on]
```

have been combined into the interlingua representation

```
[action, switch_on]
```

since we can consider that they form only one concept; they are translated by one word in French.

In the transfer-based framework, we needed one set of rules for translating source representations into target representations. In the Interlingua-based framework, constrastive rules are not necessary any more. We need instead two sets of rules: one to go from the SL representation to the interlingua, and one to go from the interlingua to the TL. We also require that all the interlingua constants must be declared explicitly. For our Toy1 application, the two sets of rules are given in

```
>> INTERLINGUA
(Perform translation through interlingua)

>> switch on the light

Source: switch on the light
Target: allumez la lampe
Other info:
   n_parses=1
   source_representation=
              [[action,switch],[device,light],
               [onoff,on],[utterance_type,command]]
   source_discourse=
              [[utterance_type,command],
               [action,switch],[onoff,on],
               [device,light]]
   resolved_source_discourse=
              [[utterance_type,command],
               [action,switch],[onoff,on],
               [device,light]]
   resolution_processing=trivial
   interlingua=[[action,switch_on],[device,light],
               [utterance_type,command]]
   target_representation=
              [[action,allumer],[device,lampe],
               [utterance_type,command]]
   n_generations=1
   other_translations=[]
```

FIGURE 54 Example session showing how to run the interlingua-based version of Toy1 in translation mode

Figures 55 and Figure 56; the file defining the interlingua constants is in Figure 57

Both rule sets are implemented using the same formalism as for the transfer-based framework, and should hopefully be self-explanatory. They are declared respectively using the `from_interlingua_rules` and `to_interlingua_rules` entries in the config file shown in Figure 58. The interlingua declarations file is specified by the `interlingua_declarations` entry.

In the next section, we describe a simple treatment of ellipsis processing, which is also implemented as part of the Regulus translation engine.

```
transfer_rule([[action, switch], [onoff, on]],
              [[action, switch_on]]).

transfer_rule([[action, switch], [onoff, off]],
              [[action, switch_off]]).

transfer_lexicon([utterance_type, command],
                 [utterance_type, command]).
transfer_lexicon([utterance_type, query],
                 [utterance_type, query]).
transfer_lexicon([state, be], interlingua
                 [state, be]).
transfer_lexicon([action, dim],
                 [action, dim]).
transfer_lexicon([device, light],
                 [device, light]).
transfer_lexicon([device, fan],
                 [device, fan]).
transfer_lexicon([location, kitchen],
                 [location, kitchen]).
transfer_lexicon([location, living_room],
                 [location, living_room]).
transfer_lexicon([onoff, on],
                 [onoff, on]).
transfer_lexicon([onoff, off],
                 [onoff, off]).
```

FIGURE 55 Toy1 rules for translation to interlingua
(**$REGULUS/Examples/Toy1/Prolog/eng_to_interlingua.pl**)

6.5 Translation of ellipsis

Ellipsis is very common in normal speech. For example, in the Toy1 system, it is clumsy to follow the question "Is the light switched on in the living room?" with "Is the light switched on in the kitchen?"; it is much more natural to shorten the second question to the elliptical form "In the kitchen?" (cf. also Section 5.7). The difficulty is that translation now becomes context-dependent, with each sentence being translated in the context of the preceding ones. Regulus includes a mechanism for doing this in the interlingua framework. As in Section 5.7, the basic idea is to expand ("resolve") incomplete utterances in the context of the preceding dialogue, and use the expanded version as the interlingua representation. To continue the example, the Toy1 grammar represents

```
transfer_lexicon([utterance_type, command],
                 [utterance_type, command]).
transfer_lexicon([utterance_type, query],
                 [utterance_type, query]).
transfer_lexicon([state, be],
                 [state, être]).
transfer_lexicon([action, switch_on],
                 [action, allumer]).
transfer_lexicon([action, switch_off],
                 [action, éteindre]).
transfer_lexicon([action, dim],
                 [action, baisser]).
transfer_lexicon([device, light],
                 [device, lampe]).
transfer_lexicon([device, fan],
                 [device, ventilateur]).
transfer_lexicon([location, kitchen],
                 [location, cuisine]).
transfer_lexicon([location, living_room],
                 [location, salon]).
transfer_lexicon([action, switch_on],
                 [action, allumer]).
transfer_lexicon([action, switch_off],
                 [action, éteindre]).
transfer_lexicon([onoff, on],
                 [onoff, allumé]).
transfer_lexicon([onoff, off],
                 [onoff, éteint]).
```

FIGURE 56 Toy1 rules for translation from interlingua to French (**$REGULUS/Examples/Toy1/Prolog/interlingua_to_fre.pl**)

"Is the light switched on in the living room?" as

```
[[utterance_type, query], [state, be], [onoff, on],
 [device, light], [location, living_room]]
```

and "In the kitchen?" as

```
[[utterance_type, phrase], [location, kitchen]]
```

If "In the kitchen?" comes immediately after "Is the light switched on in the living room?", it is interpreted as though its representation were

```
[[utterance_type, query], [state, be], [onoff, on],
 [device, light], [location, kitchen]]
```

```
interlingua_constant([action, switch_on]).
interlingua_constant([action, switch_off]).
interlingua_constant([utterance_type, command]).
interlingua_constant([utterance_type, query]).
interlingua_constant([state, be]).
interlingua_constant([action, dim]).
interlingua_constant([device, light]).
interlingua_constant([device, fan]).
interlingua_constant([location, kitchen]).
interlingua_constant([location, living_room]).
interlingua_constant([onoff, on]).
interlingua_constant([onoff, off]).
```

FIGURE 57 Toy1 interlingua constants
(**$REGULUS/Examples/Toy1/Prolog/interlingua_declarations.pl**)

The resolved representation is produced by taking the main content of the second utterance,

```
[[location, kitchen]]
```

and substituting it for a similar element in the representation of the first utterance,

```
[[location, living_room]]
```

In the rest of the section, we explain how to configure the translation subsystem of Regulus to perform this kind of ellipsis resolution. The key point is how define the notion of "similar element", to determine which substitutions are possible. Rather than directly specifying the relevant patterns in the semantic representations, we write a corpus of examples for each class, consisting of types of inter-substitutable phrases. We then extract semantic representations from each class, and generalise them by stripping out the lexical tags. To continue the Toy1 example, we define a class called `location` containing the single example "in the living room". The ellipsis class compiler first converts "in the living room" into the semantic representation

```
[[location, living_room]]
```

and then generalises to the pattern

```
[[location, _]]
```

In general, there will be several classes, each one containing several patterns. When an incomplete utterance is submitted to ellipsis processing at run-time, these patterns are used to find if the utterance is a

```
% Most declarations taken from generic file
include('$REGULUS/Examples/Toy1/scripts/toy1.cfg').

% Translation specific declarations:

% Compiled generation grammar.
regulus_config(
     generation_rules,
     toy1_runtime('generator.pl')).

% File declaring permitted interlingual constants.
regulus_config(
     interlingua_declarations,
     toy1_prolog('interlingua_declarations.pl')).

% Rules for translating source language
% representations into interlingual representations
regulus_config(
     to_interlingua_rules,
     toy1_prolog('eng_to_interlingua.pl')).

% Rules for translating interlingual representations
% into target language representations
regulus_config(
     from_interlingua_rules,
     toy1_prolog('interlingua_to_fre.pl')).
```

FIGURE 58 Config file for interlingua-based version of Toy1 translation app ($REGULUS/Examples/Toy1/scripts/toy1_slt.cfg)

```
ellipsis_class(device, ['the␣light','the␣fan']).
ellipsis_class(location, ['in␣the␣living␣room']
```

FIGURE 59 Toy1 ellipsis class definitions ($REGULUS/Examples/Toy1/Prolog/ellipsis_classes.pl)

well formed ellipsis, and which class it matches. The run-time processor then attempts to find a sub-list of the stored previous representation which matches a pattern belonging to the same class, and performs the relevant substitution.

In order to do context dependent translation in the Toy1 application, three steps are therefore necessary. Firstly, we need to define the different ellipsis classes, containing the corresponding examples. This is done in an `ellipsis_class` file, which consists of a set of definitions of the form:

```
ellipsis_class(<Id>, <Examples>).
```

Figure 59 shows the very simple `ellipsis_class` file for Toy1; it defines two classes `device` and `location`, characterised respectively by "the light", "the fan" (`device`) and "in the kitchen" (`location`). The second step is to update the config file, to add an entry pointing to this file:

```
regulus_config(ellipsis_classes,
               toy1_prolog('ellipsis_classes.pl')).
```

Finally, we compile the declarations, in translation mode, using the command `COMPILE_ELLIPSIS_PATTERNS`.

It will now be possible to perform context dependent translation; for example if we first type in "switch off the light in the kitchen", producing *éteignez la lampe dans la cuisine*, and follow up with "in the living room", we get *éteignez la lampe dans le salon.*

When developing translation systems, it is important to be able to run standard test suites and check that changes made to the system have not invalidated examples that previously worked. In the following, we will describe how to use Regulus to perform systematic regression testing of a translation application.

6.6 Systematic development

The basic idea behind the regression testing module is the usual one: the developer defines a test suite, runs it, marks which results are correct, and store the judgements. To find out what effect a change has had, one re-runs the corpus and compares the result with the one you got previously. Regulus makes it possible to perform these operations on both text and speech corpora. We start with text corpora (as we will see in Section 6.6.1, speech corpora are only slightly more complicated), and continue to use the Toy1 application as our running example.

The first step is to add the necessary new entries to the config file. Figure 60 shows the relevant file for Toy1, which is built on top of the `toy1_slt` config file shown in Figure 58. The first entry, for `translation_corpus`, defines where the text translation corpus is found. The contents of this file are shown in Figure 61. Entries are formatted in Prolog form, with each utterance represented as a Prolog atom and a period at the end of each record. The second entry, for `translation_corpus_results`, defines where the output appears.

```
% Include main speech translation config file
include(
   '$REGULUS/Examples/Toy1/scripts/toy1_slt.cfg').

file_search_path(toy1_corpora,
   '$REGULUS/Examples/Toy1/corpora').

% Corpus for testing text translation
regulus_config(translation_corpus,
   toy1_corpora('toy1_corpus.pl')).

% Results of batch text translation
regulus_config(translation_corpus_results,
   toy1_runtime('toy1_translation_results.pl')).

% Translation judgements (permanent)
regulus_config(translation_corpus_judgements,
   toy1_corpora('toy1_translation_judgements.pl')).

% Recogniser parameters for speech recognition
regulus_config(translation_rec_params,
   [package=toy1_runtime(recogniser),
    grammar='.MAIN']).

% Corpus for testing speech translation
regulus_config(translation_speech_corpus,
   toy1_corpora('toy1_transcriptions.txt')).

% Results of batch speech translation
regulus_config(translation_speech_corpus_results,
   toy1_runtime(
        'toy1_speech_translation_results.pl')).

% Recognition judgements (to edit + permanent)
regulus_config(
   translation_corpus_tmp_recognition_judgements,
   toy1_runtime(
        'toy1_tmp_recognition_judgements.pl')).

regulus_config(
   translation_corpus_recognition_judgements,
   toy1_corpora('toy1_recognition_judgements.pl')).
```

FIGURE 60 Toy1 config file for batch translation
($REGULUS/Examples/Toy1/scripts/toy1_slt_batch.pl)

```
sent('switch␣on␣the␣light').
sent('switch␣on␣the␣light␣in␣the␣kitchen').
sent('switch␣the␣fan␣off').
sent('dim␣the␣light␣in␣the␣living␣room').
sent('is␣the␣light␣switched␣on').
sent('is␣the␣light␣in␣the␣kitchen␣switched␣off').
```

FIGURE 61 Toy1 corpus file for batch translation of text (`$REGULUS/Examples/Toy1/corpora/toy1_corpus.pl`)

We can now use the Regulus top-level command `TRANSLATE_CORPUS` to translate the material in the corpus file. The file is formatted to be Prolog-readable, and the material appears twice: first as a human-readable comment, and then as the Prolog-readable term

```
translation(
    'switch␣on␣the␣light',
    'allumez␣la␣lampe',
    (... more information ...)
    ?
  ).
```

Here, the first argument is the source utterance, the second is the target, and the third contains detailed trace information. The question mark appearing as the fourth argument indicates that there is so far no stored judgement as to whether the translation is correct or not. To create a judgement, the developer edits the file to replace the question marks by instances of either `good` (the translation was fully correct), `ok` (the translation is acceptable but not perfect), or `bad` (the translation is unacceptable). If ellipsis processing is switched on (cf. Section 6.5), the first (source) argument to the translation record will also indicate the most recent preceding successful translation, constituting the relevant context. The judgement should in this case reflect whether translation is appropriate or not with reference to this context.

There are no absolute criteria for distinguishing between the three categories: it is most productive to think of them as notes to oneself. If something is marked as `good`, the developer is saying that she doesn't need to worry about it; `bad` means that she definitely need to fix it; and `ok` means that she could leave it as it is, but ideally would like to improve it.

Once the file has been edited and saved, the top-level command `UPDATE_TRANSLATION_JUDGEMENTS` is invoked to store the judgements for future use. They are placed in the file defined by the `translation_-`

`corpus_judgements` config file entry, the third one in Figure 60. The next time the corpus is run, the stored judgements are checked, and Regulus will print the number of utterances known to belong to each of the three judgement categories.

6.6.1 Batch processing of speech corpora

Batch translation of speech data is similar, but the fact that speech recognition is involved as well means that more declarations are needed in the config file. We continue our example with Toy1. Looking once again at Figure 60, the entry for `translation_rec_params` tells Regulus how to invoke the compiled recognition package (cf. Section 2.5). At a minimum, it needs to specify where the package is, and which top-level grammar to use. Using the same format, it is also possible to specify other Nuance parameters, as described in the online Nuance documentation.

The entry after it, for `translation_speech_corpus`, specifies the file holding the speech corpus. This is formatted as a Nuance "transcriptions" file (cf. Section 4.7), where each line consists of an absolute pathname specifying a wavfile, followed by a list of space-separated words giving a transcription of the file's contents. If you want Nuance to produced accurate figures for Word Error Rate (WER), it is important to make sure that the transcriptions use the same conventions as the Regulus grammar. We also need to specify where the translation output will end up: this is the function of the `translation_speech_corpus_results` entry.

When we have the above resources defined, we can perform batch speech translation using the Regulus command

```
TRANSLATE_SPEECH_CORPUS
```

The format of the speech translation output file is almost identical to that for text translation, except that it contains both the transcription (i.e. what was really said), and the recognised words. If you want to create permanent judgements of translation correctness, you can edit this file in the same way as the batch text translation output file, replacing questions marks with judgements, and then use the command

```
UPDATE_TRANSLATION_JUDGEMENTS_SPEECH
```

to store these judgements. Note that the judgements should assume that the source utterance is the *transcription*, not the recognised words, which are an artefact internal to the translation system.

In a speech translation system, it is often useful to know whether errors are caused by speech recognition or by translation. In order to support this distinction in the batch process routines, it is also possible to judge spoken utterances as correctly or incorrectly recognised. The last two lines in the config file serve this purpose. The entry for

```
translation_corpus_tmp_recognition_judgements
```

defines the location of a temporary file which is written out after each invocation of batch speech translation, and contains one record for each utterance whose recognition string failed to match its transcription. Even if not all the words in the transcription and the recognised string match exactly, the user may still consider that recognition was essentially correct; the point of recognition judgement is to capture these cases, which may be fairly frequent[16]. The format of an entry in the temporary recognition judgement file is

```
judged_recognition(
     <transcription>,
     <recognition result>,
     ?
  ).
```

This time, the judge needs to replace the question mark with a simple `y` or `n`, depending on whether or not she considers that recognition was correct. The intent is to model a user interaction style where the user has the option of aborting processing after they have seen the recognition result; thus the only possibilities are to abort or not abort, and a binary classification is appropriate. When the temporary file has been edited, the judgements can be saved using the command

```
UPDATE_RECOGNITION_JUDGEMENTS
```

The stored judgements are saved in the permanent judgements file defined by the config file parameter

```
translation_corpus_recognition_judgements
```

6.7 Integrating translation with recognition

The treatment so far in this chapter has been almost entirely concerned with text translation. In this section, we will briefly describe how to combine the techniques we have presented here with those covered earlier in Chapter 3, and build speech translation systems (cf. also Section 5.6). A sample application is shown in Figures 62, 63 and 64. This comprises two files:

[16]In practice, the most common case is misrecognition of articles.

```
:- ['$REGULUS/Prolog/load'].

:- regulus_batch(
     '$REGULUS/Examples/Toy1/scripts/toy1_slt.cfg',
     ["LOAD_TRANSLATE"]).

:- compile(
      '$REGULUS/Examples/Toy1/Prolog/toy1_slt_app').

:- toy1_slt_app(1975).

:- halt.
```

FIGURE 62 Toy1 speech translation application, loading and invocation ($REGULUS/Examples/Toy1/scripts/load_and_run_slt_app.pl)

```
% This assumes that Regulus, the translation files
% and the target grammar have been loaded.

:- use_module('$REGULUS/Prolog/translate').
:- ensure_loaded(
   '$REGULUS/Examples/Generic/Prolog/top_loop.pl').
:- use_module('$REGULUS/PrologLib/utilities').
:- use_module(
   '$REGSERVER/Prolog/regulus_sockettalk').

toy1_slt_app(Port) :-
     RecognitionPackage =
       '$REGULUS/Examples/Toy1/Generated/recogniser',
     top_loop(Port,
              RecognitionPackage,
              'audio.OutputVolume=200',
              "Commencez!",
              no_state,
              process_recogniser_output).
```

FIGURE 63 Toy1 speech translation application, top level ($REGULUS/Examples/Toy1/Prolog/toy1_slt_app.pl)

```
$REGULUS/Examples/Toy1/scripts/
                          load_and_run_slt_app.pl
```

loads and runs the application, the main code for which is in

```
$REGULUS/Examples/Toy1/Prolog/toy1_slt_app.pl
```

Looking at Figure 62, we begin by loading the Regulus environment

```
:- ['$REGULUS/Prolog/load'].
```

and then the translation-related files for the Toy1 translation application:

```
:- regulus_batch(
     '$REGULUS/Examples/Toy1/scripts/toy1_slt.cfg',
     ["LOAD_TRANSLATE"]).
```

We then compile the application itself:

```
:- compile('$REGULUS/Examples/Toy1/Prolog/
   toy1_slt_app').
```

and start it on port 1975:

```
:- toy1_slt_app(1975).
```

The application top level is in Figure 63, and is very similar to the Toy0 speech translation application shown earlier in Figure 13; we use the generic top loop from Figure 12 and output the system response using TTS. Note however that we include the module declaration

```
:- use_module('$REGULUS/Prolog/translate').
```

which gives us access to the Regulus translation engine. This is used for the main translation processing, shown in Figure 64. The top-level translation predicate is `process_recogniser_output`, which converts the recogniser output `Rec` into `Response`, a string, and then speaks it. If recognition has been successful, `Rec` will be a term of the form

```
recognition_succeeded(Conf, Words, [value=SLRep])
```

where `SLRep` is the source language representation. This is first converted into the interlingual representation `IntRep` using the call

```
transfer_representation_to_interlingua(SLRep,
                                       IntRep)
```

Next, `IntRep` is translated into a target language representation `TLRep`:

```
transfer_representation_from_interlingua(IntRep,
                                         TLRep)
```

Finally, the target language generation grammar is invoked on `TLRep` using the call

```
generate_surface_words(TLRep, TLWords, _)
```

to produce the target language string `TLWords`. The three predicates `transfer_representation_to_interlingua/2`, `transfer_representation_from_interlingua/2` and `generate_surface_words/3` are all defined in `$REGULUS/Prolog/translate.pl`, and assume that suitable translation files have been loaded into the Regulus environment.

6.7.1 Running the Toy1 speech translation application

The Toy1 speech translation application is run in the same way as the Toy0 application in Section 3.4. As before, we open two Cygwin/UNIX windows, and perform the following steps.

1. In the first window, start a Nuance license manager in the background:

   ```
   $ cd $REGULUS/Examples/Toy1/GeneratedFiles
   $ nlm <... your Nuance license code ...> &
   ```

2. In the first window, start the Vocalizer process with a French voice:

   ```
   $ vocalizer -num_channels 1
   > -voice juliedeschamps -voices_from_disk &
   ```

3. In the first window, start a Nuance recognition server in the background, using the Toy1 recognition package:

   ```
   $ recserver -package recogniser &
   ```

4. When the first three processes are running, start the speech translation application in the second window:

   ```
   $ cd $REGULUS/Examples/Toy1/scripts
   $ sicstus -l load_and_run_slt_app.pl
   ```

Interaction with the Toy1 app is similar to that with the Toy0 app described earlier.

6.8 Summary

- Rule-based translation systems require a source language grammar, a target language grammar, and some way to convert source language representations into target language representations.

```
process_recogniser_output(Rec, Response) :-
    Rec = recognition_succeeded(Conf,
                                 Words,
                                 [value=SLRep]),
    format('~N~nSL␣words:␣"~w"␣(conf:␣~d)~n',
           [Words, Conf]),
    format('~N~nSL␣representation:␣~w~n', [SLRep]),
    translate_to_interlingua(SLRep, IntRep),
    translate_to_target_representation(IntRep,
                                        TLRep),
    output_generation(TLRep, Response),
    !.
process_recogniser_output(Rec, Response) :-
    format('~N~nUnable␣to␣process:␣~w~n', [Rec]),
    Response = "Je␣ne␣peux␣pas␣traduire.".

translate_to_interlingua(SLRep, IntRep) :-
    transfer_representation_to_interlingua(SLRep,
                                           IntRep),
    format('~N~nInterlingua␣representation:␣', []),
    portray_clause(IntRep),
    !.
translate_to_interlingua(_SL, _Int) :-
    format('~N~nCan\'t␣convert␣to␣interlingua~n',
           []),
    fail.

translate_to_target_representation(IntRep, TLRep) :-
    transfer_representation_from_interlingua(IntRep,
                                             TLRep),
    format('~N~nTL␣representation:␣', []),
    portray_clause(TLRep),
    !.
translate_to_target_representation(_Int, _TL) :-
    format('~N~nCan\'t␣convert␣to␣TL~n', []),
    fail.

output_generation(TLRep, TLString) :-
    generate_surface_words(TLRep, TLWords, _),
    join_with_spaces(TLWords, TLAtom),
    atom_chars(TLAtom, TLString),
    format('~N~nTarget␣string:␣"~w"~n', [TLAtom]),
    !.
output_generation(_TLRep, _TLString) :-
    format('~N~nCan\'t␣produce␣target␣string~n',
           []),
    fail.
```

FIGURE 64 Toy1 speech translation application, main processing (`$REGULUS/Examples/Toy1/Prolog/toy1_slt_app.pl`)

- In transfer-based systems, the source language representation is transformed directly into a target language representation. In interlingua systems, the source language representation is first transformed into an interlingual representation, which is then transformed into a target language representation.
- The Regulus translation engine supports both transfer-based and interlingua-based translation. It assumes a flat representation consisting of a list of attribute-value pairs.
- A `transfer_lexicon` entry maps an attribute-value pair to an attribute-value pair. A `transfer_rule` entry maps a list of attribute-value pairs to a list of attribute-value pairs.
- When there is more than one way to apply the rules, the most specific rule is chosen. This means that `transfer_rule` entries take precedence over `transfer_lexicon` entries, and that `transfer_rule` entries with longer left-hand sides take precedence over ones with shorter left-hand sides.
- The target language grammar needs to be compiled in generation form. The generation form is placed in a file specified by a config file entry.
- The key problem when developing a generation grammar is limiting over-generation.
- There are special modes in the Regulus development environment to support development of generation grammars and translation applications. The `GENERATION` command puts the environment in generation mode, and the `TRANSLATE` command puts it in translation mode.
- When using Regulus for translation, new entries need to be added to the config file. At a minimum, these must define sets of transfer rules and the compiled generation grammar for the target language.
- The translation engine supports a simple form of ellipsis resolution, to permit context-dependent translation. Ellipsis resolution works by substituting phrases which have been declared to belong to similar semantic types. The declarations are compiled using the `COMPILE_ELLIPSIS_PATTERNS` command.
- The development environment supports systematic regression testing of translation applications in both text and speech mode.
- The translation engine can be integrated into Prolog-based speech applications using predicates defined in the file `$REGULUS/Prolog/-translate`.

Exercises

1. Run the transfer-based version of the Toy1 application in the development environment.
2. Run the interlingua-based version of the Toy1 application in the development environment.
3. Run the speech-to-speech version of the Toy1 application.
4. Add some more vocabulary to the interlingua-based application, to include more devices and rooms. If you don't know French, look up translations in a dictionary. Try and find a French native speaker who can tell you whether the translations are correct.
5. Add some more examples to the test suite, and run it in text mode using the regression testing tools.
6. Use the methods described in Section 4.7 to record speech files as you test the speech-to-speech version. Transcribe them and add them to the speech corpus. Run this corpus using the regression testing tools.

7

Using grammar specialisation

Manny Rayner

7.1 Overview

In Chapters 2 to 6, we have described how to write small Regulus grammars and compile them into recognisers. The real power of Regulus comes, however, from the possibility of building recognisers by deriving them from a single general feature grammar. The present chapter presents the details of how do this. The concrete discussion will be exclusively based on the general English grammar supplied as part of the Regulus release. Initial experiments under the MedSLT project suggest that the same methods work well for other languages too (Rayner et al., 2005c, Bouillon et al., 2006).

As explained in Section 1.3.1, the process of deriving a recogniser from the general grammar consists of three main parts. First, it is necessary to write a lexicon containing entries for the domain-specific vocabulary, and also a training corpus. When this has been done, the Regulus grammar specialisation tools can be applied to extract the domain-specific grammar from the general one.

The chapter focusses on the practical issues involved in using the general grammar and the grammar specialisation mechanism. Before reading further, you may find it helpful to look through Chapter 9, which describes the structure of the general English grammar, and Chapter 10, which covers the theoretical aspects of the specialisation process. Chapter 11 also describes quantitative experiments investigating the effect of varying the various parameters which affect the form of the derived recogniser.

Most of the rest of the chapter is organised around a running example, which is introduced in Section 7.2. We describe the config file and the Regulus commands used to compile the general grammar, first into a specialised form that will be used for parsing, and then into a language model. Section 7.3 described issues connected with the training corpus, and Section 7.4 provides a detailed explanation of how to write the extra lexical entries needed to adapt the general grammar to a new domain. There are two different ways to parameterise the specialised grammar. Section 7.5 describes the different types of pre-defined semantics which can be associated with the general and specialised grammars. We postpone discussion of the cutting-up criteria, which determine the way in which the general grammar is "flattened" into the specialised form, until Section 10.2.

The remaining sections handle less central topics. Section 7.6 describes how to define multiple top-level specialised grammars; Section 7.7, how to include lexicon entries directly into the specialised grammar; and Section 7.8, how to handle the problem of potential ambiguity in the general grammar. Section 7.9 provides some pointers towards making the compilation process more efficient, and 7.10 describes how to perform probabilistic tuning of the specialised Nuance grammar.

7.2 Using the general English grammar

This section will describe how to derive a recogniser from the general English feature grammar in the directory `$REGULUS/Grammar`. As our running example, we will use the grammar in the directory `$REGULUS/-Examples/Toy1Specialised`. This has roughly the same coverage as the Toy1 grammar from Chapters 5 and 6, but is produced using the specialisation process described in detail below.

7.2.1 The config file

As with the simple Regulus grammars shown in earlier chapters, the first step is to write a config file. The config file for our running example is shown in Figure 65, and specifies the three linguistic components of the process: the general grammar to be specialised, the corpus of training examples and the "cutting-up" or "operationality" criteria[17] that determine the structure of the specialised grammar. They are defined in the following three entries:

1. As in other config files, `regulus_grammar` defines the files that make up the grammar, which in this case is the general grammar together with the domain-specific lexicon. It consists of four files. Three of them (`general_eng`, `gen_eng_lex` and `linear_sem`)

[17] For historical reasons, the term "operationality criteria" is standard in the Machine Learning literature.

```
file_search_path(
     general_regulus_grammars,
     '$REGULUS/Grammar').
file_search_path(
     toy1_regulus_grammars,
     '$REGULUS/Examples/Toy1Specialised/Regulus').
file_search_path(
     corpora,
     '$REGULUS/Examples/Toy1Specialised/corpora').
file_search_path(
     toy1_runtime,
     '$REGULUS/Examples/Toy1Specialised/Generated').
file_search_path(
     toy1_prolog,
     '$REGULUS/Examples/Toy1Specialised/Prolog').
file_search_path(tmp,'C:/Temp').

% The Regulus grammar consists of these files
regulus_config(
     regulus_grammar,
     [general_regulus_grammars(general_eng),
      general_regulus_grammars(gen_eng_lex),
      general_regulus_grammars(linear_sem),
      toy1_regulus_grammars(toy1_lex)
     ]).

% The top-level category is .MAIN
regulus_config(top_level_cat, '.MAIN').

% EBL training will use this training corpus.
regulus_config(ebl_corpus,
               [corpora('toy1_corpus.pl')]).

% Operationality criteria are defined in this file.
regulus_config(ebl_operationality,
     file(toy1_prolog('operationality.pl'))).

% Specialised Nuance grammar is put in this file.
regulus_config(
     ebl_nuance_grammar,
     toy1_runtime(toy1_specialised_recogniser)).

% Working files go here.
regulus_config(
     working_file_prefix,
     toy1_runtime('toy1')).
```

FIGURE 65 Config file for Toy1Specialised application
($REGULUS/Examples/Toy1Specialised/scripts/toy1_specialised.cfg)

come from the Regulus general grammar directory; the fourth, **toy1_lex**, is specific to the Toy1 application, and defines the lexicon entries needed for this domain. We will discuss the lexicon file in Section 7.4 below.

2. **ebl_corpus** points to the training corpus used to build the grammar. This is discussed in Section 7.3.

3. **ebl_operationality** defines the cutting-up or operationality criteria. The rules in **Prolog/operationality.pl** produce a specialised grammar in which the constituents are full utterances, noun phrases, post-modifier phrases, and lexical items. We will say more about cutting-up criteria in Section 10.2.

7.2.2 Parsing with the general grammar

Once the config file has been written, we can load the general grammar directly, by starting the Regulus top-level and invoking the LOAD command. We can then parse utterances in the usual way. Figure 66 shows an analysis of a typical utterance. The first thing to notice is that the parse-tree is complex, with multiple levels of nesting. (The general grammar's detailed structure is discussed in Chapter 9; it will not, however, be very important in this chapter).

By using the LINE_INFO_ON command (cf. page 67), you will also be able to see which files the rules and lexical entries come from. You should find that all the rules, and also the entry for the function word "the", come from files in the general grammar directory, while the entries for the content words "switch", "on" and "light" come from the domain-specific lexicon file.

The semantic represention is presented as a list of pairs. This reflects the decision to use the "linear" semantics (cf. Section 7.5), defined by the semantics macros in the file **linear_sem**.

7.2.3 Creating the specialised grammar

The specialised version of the grammar is then created using the Regulus command EBL_ANALYSIS. The processing consists of three stages. First, the training corpus is parsed, using the general grammar, to create a "treebank" of training examples. Next, specialised rules are extracted from the parsed examples in the treebank. The granularity of the learned rules is determined by the value of **ebl_operationality**, which should be of the form `file(<File>)`, where `(<File>)` contains the "cutting-up rules"; the format of these rules is described in Section 10.2. Finally, the extracted rules are combined into a specialised

```
>> switch on the light

Return value:

[[utterance_type, imp], [tense, imperative],
 [pronoun, you], [action, switch], [prep, on],
 [spec, the_sing], [device, light]]

Parse tree:

.MAIN
   top
   /  utterance_intro null
   |  utterance
   |     s
   |        s
   |           vp
   |           /  vp
   |           |  /  vbar
   |           |  |     v lex(switch)
   |           |  |  p lex(on)
   |           |  |  np
   |           |  |  /  np
   |           |  |  |  /  d lex(the)
   |           |  |  |  |  nbar
   |           |  |  |  \     n lex(light)
   |           |  \  \  post_mods null
   |           \  post_mods null
   \  utterance_coda null
```

FIGURE 66 Analysis of "switch on the light" using the general grammar

grammar[18].

The specialised grammar is in fact produced in two different forms, which differ with respect to whether or not the rule binarisation transform has been applied[19]. Both versions are stored in "working files", and thus have names which begin with the value of `working_file_prefix`. In the case of our running example, the value of `working_file_prefix` is

$REGULUS/Examples/Toy1Specialised/Generated/toy1

[18]It is also possible to perform each of these operations separately, using the commands `EBL_TREEBANK`, `EBL_TRAIN` and `EBL_POSTPROCESS`.

[19]The binarisation transform is described in Section 8.6.2.

The version of the grammar which includes rule binarisation is in

```
<Prefix>_specialised_default.regulus
```

and the version without rule binarisation is in

```
<Prefix>_specialised_no_binarise_default.regulus
```

In most further processing, the binarised version is used.

Once the specialised grammar has been created, it can be loaded with the command `EBL_LOAD`. This command has exactly the same effect as the `LOAD` command, except that the specialised grammar is loaded instead of the general one. When the grammar has been loaded, it is again possible to parse sentences in the usual way. Figure 67 shows the result of parsing the same sentence as in Figure 66, this time using the specialised grammar. The most important thing to notice here is that, although the logical form produced is identical, the parse tree is much simpler. The category `tmp_cat_1` is an artefect of the binarisation process: as explained in Section 8.6.2, binarisation rewrites the grammar into an equivalent form in which no rule has more than two daughters. This transformation will in general involve introduction of new categories when rules are split up.

7.2.4 Compiling the specialised grammar into Nuance form

The command `EBL_NUANCE` compiles the specialised grammar into Nuance form. Processing is the same as with the `NUANCE` command described in Section 2.5, except that the specialised grammar is used instead of the general grammar. The resulting GSL grammar is placed in the file determined by the `ebl_nuance_grammar` config file entry.

7.3 The training corpus

The training corpus contains a list of utterances, one per record. Records have the format

```
sent('<Utterance>').
```

The corpus used for the running example is shown in Figure 68.

The precise form of the specialised grammar rules extracted from the corpus is determined by the operationality criteria, as discussed in great detail in Chapter 10. In the running example, the operationality criteria cut the examples up into pieces at the levels of single words, NPs, post-modifying phrases, and full utterances. For instance, the first example, "switch on the light", yields four lexical entries of the forms

```
V --> switch
P --> on
```

```
>> switch on the light

Return value:

[[utterance_type, imp], [tense, imperative],
 [pronoun, you], [action, switch], [prep, on],
 [spec, the_sing], [device, light]]

Parse tree:

.MAIN
   utterance
   /  v lex(switch)
   |  tmp_cat_1
   |  /  p lex(on)
   |  |  np
   |  |  /  d lex(the)
   \  \  \  n lex(light)
```

FIGURE 67 Analysis of "switch on the light" using the specialised grammar. Note that the logical form is identical to that in Figure 66, but the parse tree is much simpler.

```
D --> the
N --> light
```

an NP rule of the form

```
NP --> D N
```

generalised from "the light", and a top-level utterance rule of the form

```
UTTERANCE --> V P NP
```

generalised from the whole sentence. The third example, "switch the fan off", yields two new lexical entries,

```
P --> off
N --> fan
```

and a new top-level rule of the form

```
UTTERANCE --> V NP P
```

Combining these rules, the specialised grammar will also be able to cover utterances like "switch off the fan" and "switch the light on".

If it is unclear why the specialised grammar fails to cover some sentence, the best thing to do is usually to start by looking at the generated

```
sent('switch␣on␣the␣light').
sent('switch␣on␣the␣light␣in␣the␣kitchen').
sent('switch␣the␣fan␣off').
sent('dim␣the␣light␣in␣the␣living␣room').
sent('is␣the␣light␣switched␣on').
sent('is␣the␣light␣in␣the␣kitchen␣switched␣off').
sent('dim␣the␣light').
sent('is␣the␣light␣on').
sent('is␣the␣light␣off').
```

FIGURE 68 Training corpus for Toy1Specialised application

files. Both the binarised and the non-binarised forms of the grammar are formatted to be human-readable. They list the rules and lexical entries, ordered by the number of training examples associated with each rule, with the relevant training examples included as comments. This makes it easy to see how each training example has been used in the rule extraction process.

7.4 Adding lexical entries

When building a specialised version of the general grammar, the most difficult task is writing the extra domain-specific lexicon entries. This will be the focus of the present section. Nearly all of the lexicon entries you will write will be for content words. The most important categories are nouns, verbs, adjectives, adverbs and prepositions.

Before beginning your lexicon, you will have to make a basic design decision, and define the sortal types required for your domain. Sortal types are essential in order to constrain the range of contexts in which each word can occur[20]. Once you have decided on the sortal types, you will be able to define the lexicon entries themselves; you are strongly advised to do so using the *lexicon macros* provided with the general grammar. We will start by looking informally at some examples taken from the Toy1Specialised example grammar. In Section 7.4.1, we will present a systematic description of the different types of lexicon entries.

In our lexicon, examples from which are presented in Figure 69, we have two nouns that refer to devices, "light" and "fan". Let's suppose that we want to distinguish between nouns referring to devices that can be turned on and off, to which we'll assign the sortal class `switchable`, and nouns referring to devices that can be dimmed, which we'll assign to the class `dimmable`. These two domain-specific sortal type values are

[20] Experiments supporting this claim are described in Section 11.4.

```
% Extra domain-specific feature values
feature_value_space(n_type,
                    [[switchable, dimmable]]).

% Entry for device noun 'light'
@noun([light, lights],
      [device, light],
      [switchable\/dimmable],
      [takes_det_type=def,
       n_pre_mod_type=loc, takes_loc_pp=y]).

% Entry for transitive verb 'dim'
@v_transitive(
    [dim, dims, dimmed, dimmed, dimming],
    [action, dim],
    [agent, dimmable],
    [takes_loc_pp=y]).

% Entry for locative preposition 'in'
@preposition(in,
             in_loc,
             [loc, loc],
             []).

% Entry for predicative adjective 'on'
@adjective(on,
           [adj, on],
           [switchable\/dimmable],
           [adjpos=pred]).
```

FIGURE 69 Examples of entries from Toy1Specialised lexicon file

declared in the `feature_value_space` declaration for the value space `n_type`.

The first lexicon entry is the one for the noun "light". The entry is defined using the lexicon macro `noun`; all the lexicon macros are defined in the file `$REGULUS/Grammar/gen_eng_lex_macros.regulus`. The four arguments to `noun` convey the following information:

- `[light, lights]` gives the surface form of the word, in the singular (`light`) and plural (`lights`). This argument must always be a list of two atoms.
- `[device, light]` gives the piece of semantic structure associated

with the noun. This argument also needs to be a list of two atoms. Typically, the first one will be some kind of general category (here `device`), and the second one will be a constant specific to the entry (here `light`).

- `[switchable\/dimmable]` specifies the noun's sortal type. This argument must be a list containing one sortal type term. The disjunction `\/` says that the sortal type can be either `switchable` or `dimmable`.
- `[takes_det_type=def, n_pre_mod_type=loc, takes_loc_pp=y]` is a list containing the remaining feature specifications for the noun:

  `takes_det_type=def` constrains the noun only to be associated with determiners that are categorised as definite. Since spoken determiners tend to be easily confusable (think for example about "a" and "the"), it can be useful to constrain them in this way.

  `n_pre_mod_type=loc` says that the noun can be pre-modified by nouns of sortal type `loc`, as in e.g. "kitchen light".

  `takes_loc_pp=y` says that the noun can take locative PP modifiers. There are several related features for other types of PP.

Nouns and their associated features are described in Section 9.5.

The next item defines an entry for the verb "dim", encoded using the lexical macro `v_transitive`. The argument structure for `v_transitive` is similar to that for `noun`:

- `[dim, dims, dimmed, dimmed, dimming]` is a list of five atoms giving the various inflected forms of "dim".
- `[action, dim]` is the piece of semantic representation associated with the verb. Once again, this is a list of two elements, where the first is general type (`action`) and the second is a constant specific to the entry (`dim`).
- `[agent, dimmable]` defines the sortal types for the two arguments to the verb, namely its subject and object. The first element says that a subject NP associated with the verb must have sortal type `agent`. The second says that the object NP must have sortal type `dimmable`.
- `[takes_loc_pp=y]` is again a list of all the remaining feature specifications. Here, this says that the verb may take locative modifiers.

Verbs and verb features are described in Section 9.6.

The last two entries in Figure 69 are respectively for the preposition "in" ("dim the light **in** the kitchen") and the adjective "on" ("is the fan **on**?"). The lexical macros used to define them are similar to those used above for nouns and verbs. "In" is defined using the macro `preposition`, where the arguments have the following meanings:

- `in`. The surface form of the preposition.
- `in_loc`. The piece of semantic representation associated with the preposition.
- `[loc, loc]`. A list of two items, specifying the sortal type (`loc`) of a PP whose preposition is "in", and the sortal type (also `loc`) of the associated NP.
- `[]`. All other feature specifications: here, an empty list.

The adjective "on" is defined using the macro `adjective`, whose arguments are similar to those we have seen in the other lexical macros:

- `on`. The surface form of the adjective.
- `[adj, on]`. The piece of semantic representation associated with the adjective.
- `[switchable\/dimmable]`. The adjective can combine with nouns whose sortal type is `switchable` or `dimmable`.
- `[adjpos=pred]`. All other features. `adjpos=pred` says that the adjective can only be used predicatively; so for example "is the light on?" is allowed, but not "*the on light".

7.4.1 More about lexical entries

Following on from the preceding illustrative examples, this section presents a more formal description of how to write lexical entries. We break it down by categories:

Nouns

Nouns are defined using the macro `noun`, whose general form is as follows:

```
@noun([SingularForm, PluralForm],
      [SemType, SemConst],
      [SortalType],
      OtherFeatures).
```

As we saw in the example for "light", `SingularForm` and `PluralForm` are the singular and plural surface forms, `SemType` and `SemConst` are semantic identifiers, and `SortalType` specifies the sortal type of the noun. The other features are optionally used to restrict the complements and adjuncts that can be combined with the noun, as follows:

`takes_det_type` Constrains the types of determiner that can combine with the noun. Determiners have the following possible types: `numeric` ("one", "two", ...), `def` ("the", "that", ...), `indef` ("a", "an"), `quant` ("some", "all", "several", ...), `ordinal` ("the first", "the last", ...), `null` (no determiner).

`n_pre_mod_type` Constrains the sortal type of a possible nominal pre-modifier. Example (the constrained phrase is in bold): "the **kitchen** light". Default value is `none`.

`n_post_mod_type` Constrains the sortal type of a possible nominal post-modifier. Example: "plan **nine**". Default value is `none`.

`n_appositive_mod_type` Constrains the sortal type of a possible appositive modifier. Example: "table one **row three**". Default value is `none`.

`n_of_mod_type` Constrains the sortal type of a possible "of" PP modifier. Example: "the front **of the head**". The sortal type of the "of" modifier is defined to be the sortal type of its NP. Default value is `none`.

`takes_loc_pp` **etc** There is one such feature for each distinct sortal type of PP, determining whether that type of PP can be used as a nominal modifier[21]. By default, all these features have the value `n`.

Verbs

Verbs come in different types depending on their complement structure (intransitive, transitive, ditransitive etc), and there is a separate lexicon macro for each distinct type. All these macros have the common form

```
@<MacroName>(
    [Base, 3PersonSing, Past, PastPart, PresPart],
    [SemType, SemConst],
    <ListOfSortalTypes>,
    OtherFeatures).
```

As in the example for "dim" in Figure 69, the first argument lists the inflected forms of the verb in the order `Base` ("I **eat**"), `3PersonSing` "he **eats**", `Past` ("I **ate**"), `PastPart` ("I have **eaten**") and `PresPart` ("I am **eating**"). In the second argument, `SemType` and `SemConst` are, as before, semantic identifiers. The third argument lists the sortal types of the arguments to the verb. Its form depends on the specific macro used; the details are presented in Figure 70. The fourth argument specifies other optional features, as follows:

`takes_loc_pp` **etc** (one feature for each separate type of modifier) Specifies whether the verb can take that type of PP modifier.

`takes_adv_type` Specifies which sortal types of adverb can modify the verb. The possible values will be domain-dependent.

[21] PP features are described in more detail in Section 9.7.

subj_nform Can be used to constrain verbs to take a dummy subject. Possible values are there (e.g. "**there** is a light") it (e.g. "**it is raining**") or normal (non-dummy subject). Default value is normal.

can_be_gerund If value is y (default), verb can be used to form gerunds.

elliptical_v If value is y, verb can be used for elliptical correction expressions, e.g. "no i said **read**". Default value is n.

In the rest of this section, we will present examples showing how to write entries for various kinds of verbs; mostly of these are taken from the MedSLT English lexicon (cf. Section 1.4.2). We start with the intransitive verb "occur", which appears in utterances like "how often do the headaches **occur**?" or "does the pain **occur** in the morning?". The entry is as follows:

```
@v_intransitive(
   [occur, occurs, occurred, occurred, occurring],
   [state, occur],
   [symptom\/behavior],
   [takes_time_pp=y, takes_duration_pp=y,
    can_be_gerund=n])).
```

The first two arguments specify the list of inflected forms and the associated semantic information. The third argument specifies the sortal types for the arguments. Since an intransitive verb only has one argument, its subject, this list has one element. symptom\/behavior consequently says that the subject must be a noun phrase with sortal type symptom or behavior. The fourth argument specifies the remaining syntactic features:

- **takes_time_pp=y** says that "occur" can take temporal PP modifiers (e.g. "do the headaches occur **in the morning**?").
- **takes_duration_pp=y** says that "occur" can take duration PP modifiers (e.g. "have the headaches occurred **for more than a week**?").
- **can_be_gerund=n** says that "occurring" may not be used to form a gerund.

The next example is the transitive sense of the verb "eat", e.g. "do you get headaches when you **eat** nuts?". We use the macro v_transitive:

```
@v_transitive(
   [eat, eats, ate, eaten, eating],
   [action, eat],
   [agent, substance],
   [takes_time_pp=y])).
```

As before, the first two lines give the inflected forms and the semantic value. Since a transitive verb has two arguments, subject and object, the third argument is a two-element list. The value `[agent, substance]` specifies that the subject is of sortal type `agent` and the object of sortal type `substance`. Note that these are the "deep" subject and object; if the verb is used in the passive ("were the nuts **eaten** by you?"), then the NP in the by-PP ("you") is constrained to be of type `agent`, while the surface subject ("the nuts") is constrained to be of type `substance`. The last argument says that "eat" can take a temporal PP modifier.

Ditransitive verbs are similar to transitive ones, except that they require an extra argument. The following entry is for the verb "give", e.g. "does red wine **give** you headaches?". This takes both a direct object (here "headaches") and an indirect object (here "you"). The entry is as follows:

```
@v_ditransitive(
    [give, gives, gave, given, giving],
    [action, give],
    [cause\/action, symptom, agent],
    []).
```

The format of the first two arguments is similar to those in earlier examples. Since ditransitive verbs take a subject, an object and an indirect object, the third argument is a list with three elements. The first of these elements says that the subject NP must have sortal type `cause` or `action`. Note here that the general grammar is constructed to give gerundive NPs the sortal type `action`. Thus the feature specification allows a gerund to be the subject of "give", e.g. "does **drinking red wine** give you headaches?".

The second and third elements in the list that makes up the third argument specify the sortal types of the object and indirect object complements: the direct object must be a `symptom`, and the indirect object an `agent`. The general grammar function-word lexicon assigns a sortal type of `agent` to all personal pronouns ("i", "you" etc). There are no additional constraints, so the final argument is an empty list.

Our fourth example is for the sense of the verb "make" taking both a direct object and an adjective, e.g. "what **makes** your headaches worse?", or "are your headaches **made** worse by drinking red wine?":

```
@v_object_adj(
    [make, makes, made, made, making],
    [event, make_adj],
    [cause\/action, agent\/symptom],
    []).
```

`v_intransitive(Words, Sem, [Subj], More)` "John **sleeps**".
`v_transitive(Words, Sem, [Subj, Obj], More)` "John **loves** Mary".
`v_ditransitive(Words, Sem, [Subj, Obj, IndObj], More)` "Mary **gave** John a book".
`v_pp(Words, Sem, [Subj, PP], More)` "John **agreed** with Mary".
`v_adj(Words, Sem, [Subj], More)` "Mary **became** angry".
`v_measure(Words, Sem, [Subj, Obj], More)` "John **ran** 1000 metres".
`v_object_pp(Words, Sem, [Subj, Obj, PP], More)` "John **put** the book on the table".
`v_object_particle(Words, Sem, [Subj, Obj, P], More)` "John **switched** off the light" or "John **switched** it off".
`v_vp_ing(Words, Sem, [Subj], More)` "John **stopped** sleeping".
`v_to_vp(Words, Sem, [Subj], More)` "John **wants** to sleep".
`v_clause(Words, Sem, [Subj], More)` "John **says** he loves Mary".
`v_question(Words, Sem, [Subj], More)` "Mary **wonders** if John loves him".
`v_object_question(Words, Sem, [Subj, Obj], More)` "Mary **asked** John if he loved her".
`v_object_adj(Words, Sem, [Subj, Obj], More)` "John **made** Mary angry".
`v_object_to_vp(Words, Sem, [Subj, Obj], More)` "Mary **allowed** John to sleep".
`be_np(Sem, [Subj, Predicate], More)` "John **is** a man".
`be_adj(Sem, [Subj], More)` "Mary **is** angry".
`be_adj(Sem, [Subj, PP], More)` "John **is** at home".

FIGURE 70 Verb macros. For each type of macro, we give the structure of the macro call and an example of a relevant verb. In the macro call, `Words` is a list of five inflected surface forms, `Sem` is the semantic value, `More` is a list of other feature specifications, `Subj`, `Obj` and `IndObj` are NP sortal types, `PP` is a PP sortal type, and `P` is a particle sortal type.

The first two arguments are as before. The third argument is a list of only two sortal types: the first of these is for the subject, and the second for the object. The verb also has a third argument, namely the adjective: however, the grammar unifies the sortal type of the adjective with that of the subject, so no extra sortal type needs to be specified.

The value `cause\/action` captures the requirement that the subject can be either an NP of sortal type **cause** ("does **exercise** make the pain worse?") or a gerund ("does **avoiding movement** make the pain better?"). The value `agent\/symptom` allows the object to be either a `symptom` ("make **the pain** worse") or an **agent** ("make **you** worse"). As in the previous entry, personal pronouns are of type **agent**.

Our final example is for the sense of "associate" taking a direct object and a "with"-PP, e.g. "are the attacks **associated** with nausea?".

```
@v_object_pp(
   [associate, associates, associated, associated,
    associating]
   [action, associate_with],
   [agent, cause\/symptom, with],
   []).
```

Although we are in practice mostly interested in the passive form "associated", the macro as usual requires us to define all the inflected forms of the verb. The third argument is a list containing three elements, representing the sortal types of the subject, the object and the PP. The first element restricts the subject to being an **agent**, e.g. "do **you** associate the attacks with nausea?". Similarly, the second element, `cause\/symptom`, defines the object to be a **cause** or `symptom`. When "associate" appears as a passive, as it usually does in the MedSLT domain, note that the surface subject is the object, and that the subject is omitted. Finally, the third element, `with`, specifies that the PP complement's **sem_pp_type** feature value must be `with`. Possible values for the **sem_pp_type** feature are listed in Table 71.

Adjectives

Adjective entries are defined using the `adjective` macro, which is similar to those we have already seen for nouns and verbs. Its general form is as follows:

```
@adjective(SurfaceForm
           [SemType, SemConst],
           [SortalType],
           MoreFeatures).
```

The first argument is the surface form of the adjective, and the second one the semantic form. The third argument restricts the sortal type of

NPs to which the adjective may be related. The last argument is a optional list of additional feature specifications. The following possibilities are available:

`adjpos` Specifies the positions in which the adjective may occur. Possible values are `prenom` (before the noun, e.g. "the **red** light"), `postnom` (after the noun, e.g. "flights **available**") and `pred` (predicative complement, e.g. "is the pain **severe**?"). The value will often be a disjunction of two of these types.

`can_be_nbar` If value is `y`, specifies that the adjective can also be used as a noun.

`takes_loc_pp` **etc** If the adjective can be used as a noun, specifies whether that noun can be modified by each sortal type of PP.

Adverbs

Adverb entries follow the same pattern. The relevant macro is `adverb`, whose general form is:

```
@adverb(SurfaceForm
        [SemType, SemConst],
        [SortalType],
        MoreFeatures).
```

The `SortalType` argument specifies the sortal type of the adverb, which must match the modified verb's `takes_adv_type` feature.

The only feature which can occur in the `MoreFeatures` list is `advpos`, which specifies the syntactic positions in which the adverb can occur. Possible values are `prev` (before the verb, e.g. "she **sometimes** walks to town"), `postv` (after the verb, e.g. "she walked **quickly** to town"), `postvp` (after the VP, e.g. "she walks to town **occasionally**") and `fronted` (as part of an adverb question, e.g. "how **often** does she walk to town?").

Particles, prepositions and postpositions

Particles, prepositions and postpositions are defined using the macro `preposition`:

```
@preposition(SurfaceForm
             SemConst,
             [PPType, NPType],
             MoreFeatures).
```

As usual, the first argument is the surface form, and the second is the semantic representation. The third argument is a list of two elements. The first element is the sortal type of the preposition itself, which also becomes the sortal type of any PP formed from it: this must be a `loc` Locative, e.g. "switch on the light **in the kitchen**", "is the pain **above the eye**?", "**where** is the pain?".

`from` Source (usually "from"), e.g. "give me flights **from Denver**", "remove it **from the holder**".

`to` Destination (usually "to"), e.g. "i want flights **to Boston**", "does the pain spread **to the left arm**?".

`time` Time of occurrence, e.g. "do you have headaches **in the morning**", "do they appear **at night**?", "**when** do they appear?", "something **this afternoon**".

`date` Date of occurrence, e.g. "i want flights leaving **on** tuesday", "something **in** june or july", "records **for** march twenty two", "a flight departing **june twelfth**".

`duration` Duration of occurrence, e.g. "does the pain last **for** more than an hour?".

`frequency` Frequency of occurrence, e.g. "do you have the headaches several times **per** week?".

`cost` Cost, e.g. "trips **under** six hundred dollars", "something **for** two hundred fifty".

`about` e.g. "tell me **about the special offers**".

`with` e.g. "is the pain associated **with nausea**?".

`attribution` e.g. "the reading **according to the sensors**".

FIGURE 71 Possible values for `sem_pp_type` feature

possible value for the `sem_pp_type feature`, as listed in Figure 71. The second element restricts the sortal type of NPs combining with the preposition, and will be an NP sortal type. It is important to distinguish between `PPType` and `NPType`.

The other features which may occur in the list composing the fourth argument are as follows:

`postposition` If set to `y`, marks the particle as a postposition (e.g. "ago") rather than a preposition. The default is `n`.

`def` Can be used to constrain the definiteness feature for NPs combining with this preposition.

PPs are described further in Section 9.7.

7.5 General grammar semantics

As suggested earlier on page 152, we can obtain different types of semantic representations from the general grammar, depending on which set of semantic macros we choose to include. The directory

$REGULUS/Grammar currently contains three different semantics macro files, respectively called linear_sem, nested_sem and riacs_sem. In the rest of this section, we briefly describe the representations produced by each set. We illustrate with the running example "is the light in the kitchen switched on?".

7.5.1 linear_sem

The simplest version of the semantics is the one in the file linear_sem. As with the hand-coded Toy0 grammar from Chapter 4, the basic idea is that a representation will in most cases be a list, and the semantics of a constituent will usually be formed by concatenating the lists representing its component parts. In the linear semantics, the representation of the example sentence is:

```
[[utterance_type, ynq],
 [voice, active], [tense, present], [verb, be],
 [spec, the_sing], [device, light], [prep, in_loc],
 [spec, the_sing], [location, kitchen],
 [adj, on]]
```

There are a small number of exceptions to the principle of making all representations into flat lists, most importantly for conjunction and subordinate clauses. For instance, the representation of "the light and the fan" is

```
[[utterance_type,phrase],
 [np_and,[[spec,the_sing],[device,light]],
         [[spec,the_sing],[device,fan]]]]
```

7.5.2 nested_sem

The file nested_sem produces a more standard structured semantics. Representations are again lists, but this time the lists are nested, using tags to identify functional roles. In this version, the example sentence produces the following representation,

```
[[ynq,
   [[tense,present],
    [verb,be],
    [subj,[[spec,the_sing],
           [device,light],
           [in_loc,[[spec,the_sing],
                    [location,kitchen]]]]],
    [adj,[[adj,on]]]]]]
```

In contrast to the linear representation, the piece of logical form representing "the kitchen" is explicitly marked as the object of "in"; similarly, the representation of "the light in the kitchen" is marked as the subject of "is".

In general, the information contained in the linear representation is a strict subset of that contained in the nested one. For many applications, however, the linear version is adequately expressive, and offers significant advantages in terms of easier processing. In particular, the non-trivial speech translation applications built under the MedSLT project all use the linear semantics.

7.5.3 riacs_sem

The file `riacs_sem` implements a slightly more elaborate version of the "nested" semantics, developed at RIACS/NASA Ames, which also involves post-processing of the representation produced by the rules by a Prolog predicate. This makes the "RIACS" version only suitable for Prolog-based applications.

The main structural difference between the "nested" and "RIACS" versions of the semantics is that the RIACS version is more explicit about distinguishing the parts of the representation of each phrase which denote heads and modifiers. Looking at the RIACS version of the example sentence, as follows,

```
[[ynq,
  form(present,
       [[be,
         term(the_sing,
              light,
              [[in_loc,term(the_sing,
                            kitchen,
                            [])]]),
         on]])]]
```

we can see that the representation of "the light in the kitchen" is a structure schematically of the form

```
term(<'the'>, <'light'>, [<'in-the-kitchen'>])
```

where the first argument to `term` is the spec, the second is the head noun, and the third is a list of modifiers. Similarly, the clause-level structure is

```
[[<'yes/no-question'>,
  form(<'present-tense'>,
       [[<'be'>,
         <'the-light-in-the-kitchen'>,
         <'on'>]])]]
```

where the first argument to the `form` construct is a representation of the tense and aspect information, and the second argument is a list of items, the first of which represents the main verb and its obligatory arguments.

7.6 Multiple top-level specialised grammars

The grammar specialisation mechanism can be used to produce multiple top-level specialised grammars. The most common reason for wanting to do this is that dialogue context may make it possible to use a smaller grammar, thus improving recognition quality (Lemon and Gruenstein, 2004). For example, in a home control domain, we might want to have separate grammars for each room, assuming that people will only want to refer to the devices in the room where they currently happen to be located.

If you want to define several top-level specialised grammars, you must first define a set of tags. Each example in the EBL training corpus uses these tags to specify which grammar or grammars it applies to. For the home control domain example, the tags would be the names of the rooms (`bedroom`, `kitchen`, `living_room` and so on), and typical lines in the training file might then be

```
sent('switch␣off␣the␣light',
    [bathroom, bedroom, kitchen, living_room, wc]).
sent('turn␣on␣the␣tap', [bathroom, kitchen, wc]).
```

The specialised Nuance grammar file produced by the `EBL_NUANCE` command will contain one top-level grammar for each tag. The name of the top-level Nuance grammar corresponding to the tag <*Tag*> will be `.MAIN__`<*Tag*> (note the double underscore), so for example the grammar for `kitchen` will be `.MAIN__kitchen`. The tag `default` is treated specially, and produces the top-level grammar `.MAIN`.

7.7 Including lexicon entries directly

The most straightforward way to add lexicon entries to the specialised grammar is simply to add suitable training examples in the corpus. It is also possible to include lexicon entries directly from the general grammar. To do this, you need to write one or more files of `include_lex` entries, and add an `ebl_include_lex` entry to the config file, which points to them. For example, if your `include_lex` entries are in the file `$MY_APP/my_lex_includes.pl`, your config file needs the line

```
regulus_config(
        ebl_include_lex,
        '$MY_APP/my_lex_includes.pl').
```

The most general format of an include_lex entry is

```
include_lex(<Cat>:[words=<Words>, sem=<Sem>],
            <Tags>).
```

This says to include all lexicon entries of category <Cat>, whose surface form is <Words> and whose logical form contains the atom <Sem>, in the specialised grammars whose tags (cf. Section 7.6) are in the list <Tags>. Thus for example the declaration

```
include_lex(v:[words=start, sem=start_happening],
            [gram1, gram2]).
```

says to include in the grammars whose tags are gram1 and gram2 the v entries whose surface form is start, and whose logical forms contain the atom start_happening. Here, <Sem> can and frequently will be partially instantiated: for example

```
include_lex(v:[sem=[event, _]], [gram1]).
```

says to include in gram1 all the v entries whose logical forms contain a term matching [event, _]. You can use this feature to include all entries of a particular semantic class.

<Words>, <Sem> and <Tags> are optional, and in practice it is most common to omit some or all of them. So for example

```
include_lex(v:[words=start, sem=start_happening]).
```

says to include the v entries whose surface form is start, and whose logical forms contain the atom start_happening in the single default specialised grammar;

```
include_lex(v:[sem=start_happening]).
```

says to include all v entries whose logical forms contain the atom start_happening in the single default specialised grammar; and

```
include_lex(v:[]).
```

says to include all v entries in the single default specialised grammar.

7.7.1 Overriding include_lex declarations

A frequent requirement is to include nearly all of the entries matching some pattern, omitting just a few problem cases. It is possible to do this using dont_include_lex declarations. The format of a dont_include_lex is the same as that of an include_lex, i.e.

```
dont_include_lex(<Cat>:[words=<Words>, sem=<Sem>],
                 <Tags>).
```

As one would expect, **dont_include_lex** entries take precedence over **include_lex** entries. Thus for example the following entries say to include all English verb entries except those for the reduced forms of "is", "are" and "am":

```
% Add all entries for verbs
include_lex(v:[]).

% ... except a few auxiliaries that cause problems
dont_include_lex(v:[words='\'s']).
dont_include_lex(v:[words='\'re']).
dont_include_lex(v:[words='\'m']).
```

7.8 Dealing with ambiguity

In general, the corpus utterances used as input to the treebank may be ambiguous. By default, the first analysis produced is chosen; if this is not acceptable, it is possible to annotate the training corpus so as to pick an analysis with specific properties, specifying these in the optional third argument of the **sent** record. This third argument should be a list of constraints on the logical form. Constraints may currently be of the following forms:

- **lf_includes_structure = <*Structure*>**. The logical form must contain a subterm that unifies with <*Structure*>.
- **lf_doesnt_include_structure = <*Structure*>**. The logical form may not contain any subterm that unifies with <*Structure*>.

For example, suppose that the training utterance is "i read the meter", which is ambiguous since "read" can be either present or past tense. If we want to choose the present tense interpretation and reject the past tense interpretation, we can write the training corpus example in either of the following ways:

```
sent('i␣read␣the␣meter', [default],
     [lf_includes_structure=[tense, present]]).
sent('i␣read␣the␣meter', [default],
     [lf_doesnt_include_structure=[tense, past]]).
```

7.9 Making compilation more efficient

For any given specialised grammar, there will probably be several features deriving from the general grammar which have no appreciable positive effect in terms of constraining the language model. Although these features are essentially useless, they can still slow down Regulus to Nuance compilation very substantially, or even cause it to exceed resource limits.

It is possible to force the compiler to ignore features, by using the `ebl_ignore_feats` config file parameter[22]. For example, the declaration

```
regulus_config(ebl_ignore_feats,
               [syn_type, subj_syn_type,
                obj_syn_type, indobj_syn_type]).
```

says that all the features in the "syn_type" group are to be ignored.

If you want to try to optimise performance by ignoring features, we recommend that you start by looking at the following groups:

1. "syn_type" features: `syn_type`, `subj_syn_type`, `obj_syn_type`, `indobj_syn_type`. These features are historical (they may be removed completely from future versions of the grammar), and can safely be ignored. Doing so will typically reduce the size of the GSL grammar by more than a factor of 3.
2. "def" features: `def`, `subj_def`, `obj_def`, `indobj_def`. These features can be used to constrain NPs with respect to definiteness, but we have found them to be of very limited value, and ignoring them typically reduces the size of the GSL grammar by more than a factor of 2.
3. "advp_type" features: `adv_type`, `takes_adv_type`. These features constrain the sortal types of adverbs that can cooccur with a given verb, and typically increase the size of the generated GSL grammar by a factor of between 1.5 and 2. Unless adverbs are extremely important to the applications, these features can also be ignored without great impact on performance.
4. Agreement feature: `agr`. Ignoring agreement will typically result in a small but significant drop in performance (cf. Section 11.4). It will however also reduce the size of the GSL grammar by about a factor of 2, so this may be worth considering if there are problems with compilation to GSL form.

7.10 Using probabilistic tuning

So far in this chapter, we have only used the training corpus to carry out grammar specialisation. In practice, it is usually desirable to use the same corpus a second time, to perform probabilistic tuning of the derived Nuance language model. This kind of tuning can be done using

[22]Features are ignored both when the grammar is loaded in the Regulus top-level using the EBL_LOAD command, and when it is compiled into GSL using the EBL_NUANCE command.

the Nuance compute-grammar-probs utility. Somewhat surprisingly, probabilistic tuning with even very modest amounts of training data can greatly improve recognition performance (cf. Section 11.6).

The reader is referred to the on-line Nuance documentation for details of how to use compute-grammar-probs. In the minimal invocation, the utility is supplied with an initial untuned GSL grammar and a file of training data; it uses the data to produce a tuned version of the grammar in a specified directory. The form of the invocation is

```
compute-grammar-probs
   -base_grammar_file <Grammar> \
   -data <Data> \
   -output_dir <Dir>
```

Regulus provides a top-level command, EBL_GRAMMAR_PROBS, that converts an EBL training file into a training file formatted for use with compute-grammar-probs. The input and output files are defined by the ebl_corpus and ebl_grammar_probs config file entries respectively.

7.11 Summary

- It is possible to build domain-specific recognisers out of the general Regulus grammar for English.
- In order to build a domain-specific recogniser, you first need to add domain-specific lexical entries to the general grammar, and then perform grammar specialisation on the result.
- Grammar specialisation requires two types of input: a training corpus of examples, and a set of "cutting-up criteria".
- The config file for a grammar specialisation application requires definition of at least the following entries: regulus_grammar (the original unspecialised grammar), ebl_corpus (the training corpus) and ebl_operationality (the cutting-up criteria).
- The grammar specialisation process is invoked by the EBL_ANALYSIS command.
- New lexical entries are added to the general grammar using the lexical macros defined in the file $REGULUS/Grammar/gen_eng_lex_-macros.regulus. There are macros for nouns, verbs, adjectives, adverbs and prepositions.
- A lexical macro specifies the following four pieces of information for each entry: the surface forms, the associated semantic representation, the associated sortal information, and any other features that may be required.

- The cutting-up criteria determine how to decompose the analysis trees resulting from parsing the training corpus. One specialised grammar rule is extracted from each piece of the cut-up tree.
- The semantics produced by the general grammar are parameterised by the semantics file used. Three different files are included, permitting linear representations (lists of attribute/value pairs) and two kinds of nested representations.
- It is possible to produce specialised grammars containing multiple top-level GSL categories.
- By default, lexical entries in the specialised grammar are taken from the training corpus, but it is also possible to add declarations to include lexicon entries directly from the general grammar into the specialised one.
- It is possible to annotate the training corpus to specify which reading of a sentence should be used for training, if the sentence in question is ambiguous.
- The process of compiling a specialised grammar into Nuance form can usually be made more efficient by adding declarations to ignore unnecessary features.
- The performance of recognisers derived from specialised grammars can usually be improved by using the training corpus a second time to do probabilistic tuning. The training corpus can be converted into the appropriate format using the `EBL_GRAMMAR_PROBS` command.

Exercises

1. Load the unspecialised Toy1Specialised grammar into the Regulus development environment. Parse some sentences.
2. Use the appropriate commands to build the specialised version of the Toy1Specialised grammar.
3. Load the specialised Toy1Specialised grammar into the Regulus development environment. Parse some sentences. Compare the results with the ones you obtained from the unspecialised version.
4. Use the appropriate commands to build a recognition package from the specialised version of the Toy1Specialised grammar. Compare performance of the recogniser with that of the Toy1 recogniser.
5. Add some more words to the Toy1Specialised lexicon. Rebuild the specialised grammar and recogniser.
6. Change the cutting-up criteria in the Toy1Specialised file. Remake the specialised grammar. What was the effect on coverage? Rebuild the recogniser. What was the effect on performance?

Part II

How Regulus Works

8

Compiling feature grammars into CFG

Manny Rayner and Beth Ann Hockey

8.1 Introduction

In the previous chapters, we have shown how to build applications using Regulus. We have explained that the central idea is to write grammars in a feature grammar formalism and then transform them into GSL, the CFG-based formalism used by the Nuance platform, but we have said very little about the details. This chapter will focus on the Regulus feature grammar to CFG compilation process. The basic idea behind the algorithm is very straightforward: we exhaustively expand out the FG rules, instantiating each feature in each rule to each possible feature value, and then filter out the expanded rules that are not useful. Implemented in its most naive form, first expanding out all the rules and then filtering, this approach is not realistic; for even modest numbers of features, the process runs out of space due to combinatorial explosion in the expansion phase.

It turns out, however, that with some refinements the expand-and-filter algorithm is powerful enough to deal with quite large grammars. We will start by describing the naive version of the algorithm in Sections 8.2 and 8.3, and then successively introduce the various refinements. Section 8.4 describes how to improve the efficiency of the filtering step, so that filtering time is linear in the number of rules; Section 8.5 introduces the idea of interleaving expansion and filtering; Section 8.6 shows how the size of the expanded grammar can be reduced by suitable pre-processing of the initial FG; and Section 8.7 describes how the output CFG grammar can be simplified. Finally, in Section 8.8, we discuss the issues involved in transforming Regulus semantics into

Nuance GSL semantics.

8.2 Exhaustive expansion

In this and the next section, we illustrate the "naive" version of the the Regulus algorithm using the toy grammar shown in Figure 72. This grammar generates noun-phrases (nps) consisting of a determiner (d), which can be either "this" or "these", followed by a noun (n), which can be either "cat" or "cats". There is a single feature num, which has a range of values {sg, pl}, and whose purpose is to ensure that determiners and nouns must agree in number. Thus we permit "this cat" and "these cats", but not "*this cats" or "*these cat".

```
sigma:[] --> np:[num=X].
np:[num=X] --> d:[num=X], n:[num=X].
d:[num=sg] --> this.
d:[num=pl] --> these.
n:[num=sg] --> cat.
n:[num=pl] --> cats.
```

FIGURE 72 Minimal example feature grammar

We start by exhaustively expanding each rule in the grammar, instantiating each feature to each of its possible values. Clearly the FGs that Regulus can compile into CFGs must have only features with defined finite ranges of values, otherwise the expansion phase would not terminate. In this case, we have just one feature, with two possible values; the expanded grammar is shown in Figure 73. Notice that where the original grammar had a single sigma rule and a single np rule, the expanded version has two rules for each category, corresponding to the two possible values for the num feature. The lexical rules (the last four, all of the form <category> → <surface-word>) do not have variables to be instantiated, so are not affected by the expansion process.

Figure 74 shows the same expanded grammar, written in a standard CFG format. Here, we have converted each fully instantiated category into an atomic symbol, forming the name of the symbol by concatenating the category name and the feature values and upper-casing the result: thus for example np:[num=sg] becomes NP_SG, and so on.

One obvious problem is that if the original FG has more features, the expanded CFG can be very large; in the general case, the number of expanded rules is in fact exponential in the number of features, and the expansion process becomes completely intractable. Fortunately, not all

```
sigma:[] --> np:[num=sg].
sigma:[] --> np:[num=pl].
np:[num=sg] --> d:[num=sg], n:[num=sg].
np:[num=pl] --> d:[num=pl], n:[num=pl].
d:[num=sg] --> this.
d:[num=pl] --> these.
n:[num=sg] --> cat.
n:[num=pl] --> cats.
```

FIGURE 73 Example feature grammar after exhaustive expansion

```
SIGMA --> NP_SG
SIGMA --> NP_PL
NP_SG --> D_SG N_SG
NP_PL --> D_PL N_PL
D_SG --> this
D_PL --> these
N_SG --> cat
N_SG --> cats
```

FIGURE 74 Expanded feature grammar in typical CFG format

rules generated by the expansion phase of the algorithm turn out to be useful. The Regulus algorithm includes a filtering phase to eliminate the useless rules generated by the expansion phase. An initial naive version of this filtering operation is introduced in the next section. In Sections 8.4 and 8.5, we then go on to show how it can be made more efficient.

8.3 Filtering

As just noted, filtering the set of expanded rules is a crucial part of the Regulus FG to CFG compilation algorithm. There are two types of filtering, corresponding to two different reasons why rules may be irrelevant. Top-down filtering removes rules that are irrelevant because they do not connect to the top-level rule. Bottom-up filtering removes rules that are irrelevant because they do not connect to the lexicon. In either case, the irrelevant rules will never be part of a derivation that relates the top level category to actual lexical items; removing these rules therefore reduces the size of the resulting grammar without any effect on coverage. In the rest of this section, we describe each type of filtering in more detail.

8.3.1 Top-down filtering

Top-down filtering removes rules created in the expansion phase that cannot be reached from the top level category. To illustrate this more concretely, consider again our running example, the minimal toy FG from Figure 72. Figure 75 shows a version of this grammar which has been altered slightly, so that the `num` feature in the top level `sigma` rule is restricted to take only the value `sg`. When we expand the grammar, as shown in Figure 76, the rules marked by asterisks are irrelevant, because they cannot be reached from the root category. We can filter them out to get an equivalent smaller grammar, as in Figure 77.

```
sigma:[] --> np:[num=sg].
np:[num=X] --> d:[num=X], n:[num=X].
d:[num=sg] --> this.
d:[num=pl] --> these.
n:[num=sg] --> cat.
n:[num=pl] --> cats.
```

FIGURE 75 Version of minimal example FG modified to demonstrate top-down filtering: value of `num` in top-level rule is set to `sg`

```
sigma:[] --> np:[num=sg].
np:[num=sg] --> d:[num=sg], n:[num=sg].
*np:[num=pl] --> d:[num=pl], n:[num=pl].
d:[num=sg] --> this.
*d:[num=pl] --> these.
n:[num=sg] --> cat.
*n:[num=pl] --> cats.
```

FIGURE 76 Expanded version of grammar from Figure 75, with irrelevant rules marked

8.3.2 Bottom-up filtering

Top-down filtering removed rules that failed to connect to the top-level rule. As the name would suggest, bottom-up filtering is the complementary process, and eliminates rules that do not connect to the lexicon. Figure 78 continues the running example, and this time shows a version of the grammar from Figure 72, with the plural lexical items "cats" and

```
sigma:[] --> np:[num=sg].
np:[num=sg] --> d:[num=sg], n:[num=sg].
d:[num=sg] --> this.
n:[num=sg] --> cat.
```

FIGURE 77 Grammar from Figure 76, with irrelevant rules removed

"these" removed. The range of possible values for the feature num remains {sg, pl}. After expansion, the grammar is as in Figure 79, with irrelevant rules marked by asterisks. With the irrelevant rules removed, the filtered grammar is as in Figure 80.

```
sigma:[] --> np:[num=X].
np:[num=X] --> d:[num=X], n:[num=X].
d:[num=sg] --> this.
n:[num=sg] --> cat.
```

FIGURE 78 Version of minimal example FG modified to demonstrate top-down filtering: plural lexical items have been removed.

```
sigma:[] --> np:[num=sg].
*sigma:[] --> np:[num=pl].
np:[num=sg] --> d:[num=sg], n:[num=sg].
*np:[num=pl] --> d:[num=pl], n:[num=pl].
d:[num=sg] --> this.
n:[num=sg] --> cat.
```

FIGURE 79 Expanded version of grammar from Figure 78, with irrelevant rules marked

```
sigma:[] --> np:[num=sg].
np:[num=sg] --> d:[num=sg], n:[num=sg].
d:[num=sg] --> this.
n:[num=sg] --> cat.
```

FIGURE 80 Grammar from Figure 79, with irrelevant rules removed

8.4 Efficient filtering of CFGs

It is very easy to construct algorithms that carry out the top-down and bottom-up filtering processes for context-free grammars, but it is less obvious how to make these algorithms efficient. It turns out that it is in fact possible to make both algorithms run in time linear in the number of rules. Linear-time top-down filtering is not a challenging problem, and the marker-passing algorithm in Figure 81 has the desired properties.

1. Create a table $left\_to\_right$, which associates each non-terminal symbol T with the set of all non-terminal symbols T' such that there is a rule in which T occurs on the left-hand side, and T' on the right-hand side.
2. Create a table *connected*, which associates each non-terminal symbol with one of the symbols y or n. Initialise this table so that $connected(T) = n$ for all non-terminals T.
3. Initialise the set variable *previous_connected*, to the value $\{\Sigma\}$, where Σ is the start symbol of the grammar. Initialise the set variable *next_connected* to the empty set.
4. For each T in *previous_connected*, and each T' such that $T' \in left\_to\_right(T)$ and $connected(T') = n$, add T' to *next_connected* and set $connected(T')$ to y.
5. Set *previous_connected* to *next_connected*.
6. If *previous_connected* is non-empty then go to (4), else terminate.

FIGURE 81 Linear-time algorithm for top-down filtering of CFG grammar

The idea behind the top-down filtering algorithm in Figure 81 is the obvious one. We want to find all the non-terminal symbols[23] which are connected to the start symbol Σ. We begin with Σ, which we know is connected to Σ by definition; we then find rules which have Σ on the left hand side, and mark as connected all the non-terminals occurring on the right-hand sides of these rules. Next, we take all the new connected non-terminals we have just found, and find rules where *they* appear on the left-hand side; we then mark the non-terminals on the right-hand

[23] All the algorithms in this section operate on arbitrary CFGs, irrespective of how these grammars were produced. By "non-terminal symbol", we mean "non-terminal symbol in the CFG", even if the CFG was derived from a feature grammar. Thus for example, in the CFG from Figure 80, `np:[num=sg]` is a non-terminal symbol, and `np` is not a symbol at all.

sides of these new rules as connected. We repeat the process until we run out of new non-terminals.

The algorithm formalises this idea in a straightforward way. We use the table *connected* to mark which non-terminals have already been discovered to be connected. The table $left\_to\_right$, which is computed once at the start of the process, lets us take a non-terminal T, and look up all the non-terminals T' which we will want to mark as connected if we discover that T is connected. The set variable *previous_connected* contains all the non-terminals which we discovered were connected during the last cycle, and the set variable *next_connected* contains the new ones which have been discovered to be connected during the current cycle. We only visit each non-terminal once, and we consequently only visit each rule once. We can thus be confident that the algorithm executes in a time linear in the number of rules.

It is by no means as clear that the same kind of strategy will work for bottom-up filtering, since the obvious algorithms have quadratic complexity. It has however been known for some time that linear algorithms exist for this task. To the best of our knowledge, this was first demonstrated by Dowling and Gallier (1984), who proved that satisfiability of a propositional Horn-clause theory can be determined in time linear in the size of the theory, and then pointed out that the bottom-up filtering result follows as a corollary. There is a good concise explanation of the main Dowling and Gallier result in (Russell and Norvig, 2003) (pp. 218–219). Since the relationship with propositional Horn clause satisfiability is not necessarily self-evident, we will in the rest of this section present a self-contained explanation, showing how the Dowling/Galliers strategy can be applied to the bottom-up filtering problem. The algorithm is shown in Figure 82.

The basic marker-passing idea in the bottom-up filtering algorithm is similar to that in the top-down version, but the details are more complicated. The key notion is that of "support". We are ultimately interested in determining which rules can be connected to the lexicon, so that we are able to prune out the others. If a rule can be connected to the lexicon, we say that it is "supported".

In order to provide this concept with a clear definition, it will be convenient to broaden it a little, and say that both rules and non-terminals can be supported. The base case is given by the lexical rules; if we have a rule R of the form

$$T \rightarrow w_1, w_2, ..., w_n$$

where all the w_i are terminals, then R is supported. The recursive cases mutually define support for rules and support for non-terminals

1. Create a table *right_to_rules*, which associates each non-terminal symbol T with the set of all rules R such that T occurs on the right-hand side.
2. Create a table *supported*, which associates each non-terminal symbol with one of the symbols y or n. Initialise this table so that $supported(T) = n$ for all non-terminals T.
3. Create a table *missing_support*, which associates each rule with an integer greater than or equal to zero. Initialise this table so that $missing\_support(R)$ is the number of *distinct* non-terminals occurring in the right-hand side of R, for all rules R.
4. Initialise the set variable *previous_supported*, to the set of non-terminals T such that T occurs on the left-hand side of a lexical rule, i.e. a rule which has no non-terminals on its right-hand side. Initialise the set variable *next_supported* to the empty set.
5. For each T in *previous_supported*, and each R such that both $R \in right\_to\_rules(T)$ and $missing\_support(R) > 0$, decrement $missing\_support(R)$ by one. If the new value of $missing\_support(R)$ is zero, add the non-terminal on the left-hand side of R to *next_supported*, and set $supported(R)$ to y.
6. Set *previous_supported* to *next_supported*, and set *next_supported* to the empty set. If *previous_supported* is non-empty then go to (5), else terminate.

FIGURE 82 Linear-time algorithm for bottom-up filtering of CFG grammar

in terms of each other. If we have any supported rule of the form

$$T \rightarrow ...$$

then we say that T is supported; conversely, if we have a rule R of the form

$$T \rightarrow T'_1, T'_2, ..., T'_n$$

where all the T'_i are supported, then we say that R is also supported. In the algorithm, the *supported* table represents the set of non-terminals which have so far been found to be supported.

The trick needed to make the algorithm linear is the introduction of the concept of "missing support for a rule". We use the *missing_support* table to associate each rule R with an integer, which originally is set equal to the number of distinct non-terminals on the right-hand side of R (step 3).

In each cycle, we start with the set of non-terminals *previous_-supported* that were discovered to be supported during the previous cycle; initially, this set consists of the set of non-terminals for which at least one lexical rule is available (step 4). In the inner loop (step 5), we take each newly discovered supported non-terminal T, and use the *right_to_rules* table to look up all the rules R where T occurs on the right-hand side. We decrement $missing\_support(R)$ by one, to mark the fact that we have just determined that T, which is on the right-hand side of R, is supported. If $missing\_support(R)$ is now zero, we have found that all the non-terminals on the right-hand side of R are supported. Hence the non-terminal on the left-hand side of R must also be supported, and we can add it to *new_supported*, which keeps track of all the non-terminals which we have discovered to be supported during the present cycle. When we have finished the cycle (step 6), we move the contents of *new_supported* to *previous_supported*, and empty *new_supported*; then if there are any new non-terminals that have been discovered to be supported, we repeat the cycle again.

Intuitively, the algorithm percolates supported non-terminals upwards from the lexicon, until we reach a fixed-point. The reason why it is linear is that, by construction, we visit each non-terminal at most once, and visit each rule at most as many times as there are non-terminals on the right-hand side.

We illustrate the bottom-up filtering algorithm using the example grammar from Figure 78; in the next few figures, we mark the number of unsupported non-terminals for each rule by placing it before the rule in parentheses. Initially, *previous_supported* is the set of non-terminals appearing on the left-hand side of lexical rules, i.e. {`d:[num=sg]`, `n:[num=sg]`}, and the missing-support relation is as follows:

```
(1) sigma:[] --> np:[num=sg].
(1) sigma:[] --> np:[num=pl].
(2) np:[num=sg] --> d:[num=sg], n:[num=sg].
(2) np:[num=pl] --> d:[num=pl], n:[num=pl].
(0) d:[num=sg] --> this.
(0) n:[num=sg] --> cat.
```

The two non-terminals in *previous_supported* only occur on the right-hand side in one rule, the third one. We consequently subtract two (one for each non-terminal) from the missing-support value of the third rule, reducing it to zero and consequently adding `np:[num=sg]`, the non-terminal on the left-hand side, to *next_supported*. At the end of the cycle, *next_supported* has the value {`np:[num=sg]`}, and the missing-support relation is:

```
(1) sigma:[] --> np:[num=sg].
(1) sigma:[] --> np:[num=pl].
(0) np:[num=sg] --> d:[num=sg], n:[num=sg].
(2) np:[num=pl] --> d:[num=pl], n:[num=pl].
(0) d:[num=sg] --> this.
(0) n:[num=sg] --> cat.
```

At the start of the next cycle, *previous_supported* contains the single non-terminal `np:[num=sg]`. This only occurs in the right-hand side of the first rule, so we subtract one from the missing-support value of that rule, reducing it to zero and adding `sigma:[]` to *next_supported*. At the end of the cycle, *next_supported* is {`sigma:[]`} and the missing-support relation is:

```
(0) sigma:[] --> np:[num=sg].
(1) sigma:[] --> np:[num=pl].
(0) np:[num=sg] --> d:[num=sg], n:[num=sg].
(2) np:[num=pl] --> d:[num=pl], n:[num=pl].
(0) d:[num=sg] --> this.
(0) n:[num=sg] --> cat.
```

previous_supported now contains the single non-terminal `sigma:[]`, but this does not occur on the right-hand side of any rule. At the end of the cycle, *next_supported* is consequently empty, and we terminate. The final filtered grammar consists of the rules that have zero missing support:

```
(0) sigma:[] --> np:[num=sg].
(0) np:[num=sg] --> d:[num=sg], n:[num=sg].
(0) d:[num=sg] --> this.
(0) n:[num=sg] --> cat.
```

Experiments with the Regulus implementation of the bottom-up filtering algorithm confirm that performance is indeed linear in the size of the grammar. Table 4 shows the bottom-up filtering time per rule for a set of grammars possessing similar structure but differing numbers of rules.

8.5 Interleaving expansion and filtering

The obvious drawback of the simple "expand and filter" algorithm is that the number of expanded rules is in the worst case exponential in the number of features. The worst case will only occur if a rule actually contains all the available features, which is unlikely in any substantial grammar; however, experience shows that at least some rules will

#Rules	Time/rule (ms)
1132	0.06
2966	0.05
4037	0.06
18880	0.06
117811	0.07

TABLE 4 Bottom-up filtering time per rule for grammars of different sizes

```
sigma:[] --> vp:[takes_pp=PP].
vp:[takes_pp=PP] -->
  v:[type=Type, quant=Quant, takes_pp=PP],
  np:[type=Type, quant=Quant].
vp:[takes_pp=n] -->
  vp:[takes_pp=y], pp:[].
v:[type=openable, quant=def\/all, takes_pp=n] -->
  close.
v:[type=mobile, quant=def, takes_pp=y] --> move.
n:[type=openable, quant=def] --> connection.
n:[type=openable, quant=all] --> all, connections.
n:[type=mobile, quant=def] --> cursor.
pp:[] --> to, top.
```

FIGURE 83 Example feature grammar used to illustrate interleaved expansion and filtering

usually contain enough features that combinatorial explosion becomes an insuperable problem. In this section, we describe a refinement to the simple algorithm, which attacks the problem by interleaving expansion and filtering. The idea is straightforward: we expand using a subset of the features, filter, and iterate until all the features have been expanded.

We illustrate using another example. Figure 83 shows a feature grammar for a toy desktop command and control domain. Commands have the form of a transitive verb ("close", "move"), followed by an NP object ("connection", "cursor") and an optional PP ("to top"). We want to be able to say things like "close connection" and "move cursor to top", but not "move connection" or "close connection to top".

The features `type` and `quant` are used to restrict cooccurrence of verbs and object NPs. `type` specifies the sortal type of the NP; thus the entries for "cursor" and "move" specify `type=mobile` (cursors are things that can be moved, and "move" is a verb that definition acts on mobile objects). Similarly, the feature **quant** specifies whether the NP refers to one specific object (**quant=def**) or all objects of a class (**quant=all**), and verbs are similarly marked as potentially applying to one object or to all objects. We assume for the purposes of the example that "close" is **quant=def\/all** (you can say both "close connection" and "close all connections"), but "move" is **quant=def** (you can only say "move cursor"). Finally, the feature **takes_pp** defines which verbs can take a PP complement. Here, we say that "move" can take a PP ("move cursor to top"), but that "close" cannot take a PP complement. A more fine-grained treatment would probably differentiate between different types of PP.

The grammar in Figure 83 contains three non-lexical rules. The first is the sigma rule; the second combines a V and an NP to form a VP, using the features **type** and **quant** to control cooccurrence and passing up the **takes_pp** feature to the VP; and the third combines a VP and a PP to form a larger VP. We assume that the feature **type** can have the range of possible features {**mobile, openable**}, the feature **quant** the range {**def, all**}, and the feature **takes_pp** the range {**y, n**}.

Figure 84 shows what happens when we fully expand the grammar, by assigning all possible values to all features; note that the second rule, the one forming the VP out of the V and NP, expands to eight different CFG rules. In the figure, we have tagged each rule with a comment, showing an example in which it could potentially be applicable. Thus for example the second expanded rule,

```
vp:[takes_pp=n] -->  % close connection
  v:[type=openable, quant=def, takes_pp=n],
  np:[type=openable, quant=def].
```

combines an object NP referring to a specific openable object ("connection") with a suitable verb ("close"). The feature setting **takes_pp=n** implies that VPs created with this rule will not be modifiable by a PP. Four of the expanded rules, the ones whose examples are preceded by asterisks, cannot be used; for example, the first one,

```
vp:[takes_pp=y] -->  % *close connection to top
  v:[type=openable, quant=def, takes_pp=y],
  np:[type=openable, quant=def].
```

is irrelevant, since there is no V entry in the lexicon that matches the category

```
v:[type=openable, quant=def, takes_pp=y],
```

```
sigma:[] --> vp:[takes_pp=y].
sigma:[] --> vp:[takes_pp=n].
vp:[takes_pp=y] -->  % *close connection to top
  v:[type=openable, quant=def, takes_pp=y],
  np:[type=openable, quant=def].
vp:[takes_pp=n] -->  % close connection
  v:[type=openable, quant=def, takes_pp=n],
  np:[type=openable, quant=def].
vp:[takes_pp=y] -->  % move cursor to top
  v:[type=mobile, quant=def, takes_pp=y],
  np:[type=mobile, quant=def].
vp:[takes_pp=n] -->  % move cursor
  v:[type=mobile, quant=def, takes_pp=n],
  np:[type=mobile, quant=def].
vp:[takes_pp=y] -->  % *close all connections to top
  v:[type=openable, quant=all, takes_pp=y],
  np:[type=openable, quant=all].
vp:[takes_pp=n] -->  % close all connections
  v:[type=openable, quant=all, takes_pp=n],
  np:[type=openable, quant=all].
vp:[takes_pp=y] -->  % *move all cursors to top
  v:[type=mobile, quant=all, takes_pp=y],
  np:[type=mobile, quant=all].
vp:[takes_pp=n] -->  % *move all cursors
  v:[type=mobile, quant=all, takes_pp=n],
  np:[type=mobile, quant=all].
vp:[takes_pp=n] -->
  vp:[takes_pp=y], pp:[].
v:[type=openable, quant=def, takes_pp=n] --> close.
v:[type=openable, quant=all, takes_pp=n] --> close.
v:[type=mobile, quant=def, takes_pp=y] --> move.
n:[type=openable, quant=def] --> connection.
n:[type=openable, quant=all] --> all, connections.
n:[type=mobile, quant=def] --> cursor.
pp:[] --> to, top.
```

FIGURE 84 Fully expanded version of grammar from Figure 83. The expanded versions of the main VP rule have been annotated with examples of phrases they could potentially cover; the ones marked with asterisks are not actually realisable.

```
sigma:[] --> vp:[takes_pp=y].
sigma:[] --> vp:[takes_pp=n].
vp:[takes_pp=n] --> % close connection
  v:[type=openable, quant=def, takes_pp=n],
  np:[type=openable, quant=def].
vp:[takes_pp=y] --> % move cursor to top
  v:[type=mobile, quant=def, takes_pp=y],
  np:[type=mobile, quant=def].
vp:[takes_pp=n] --> % move cursor
  v:[type=mobile, quant=def, takes_pp=n],
  np:[type=mobile, quant=def].
vp:[takes_pp=n] --> % close all connections
  v:[type=openable, quant=all, takes_pp=n],
  np:[type=openable, quant=all].
vp:[takes_pp=n] -->
  vp:[takes_pp=y], pp:[].
v:[type=openable, quant=def, takes_pp=n] --> close.
v:[type=openable, quant=all, takes_pp=n] --> close.
v:[type=mobile, quant=def, takes_pp=y] --> move.
n:[type=openable, quant=def] --> connection.
n:[type=openable, quant=all] --> all, connections.
n:[type=mobile, quant=def] --> cursor.
pp:[] --> to, top.
```

FIGURE 85 Expanded and filtered version of grammar from Figure 83

These four rules will be removed by the bottom-up filtering process, leaving the filtered grammar shown in Figure 85.

We will now show how we can convert the grammar into CFG form more economically by performing alternating phases of expansion and filtering. Figure 86 presents the grammar after just the two features `type` and `quant` have been expanded. We write categories in the form `Cat:Feats1:Feats2`, where `Feats1` are the features that have already been expanded (either `type` and `quant` or nothing, depending on the category), and `Feats2` are the remaining features (either `takes_pp` or nothing).

We can filter the partially expanded grammar, by temporarily ignoring the so far unexpanded features. This is a legitimate operation, since if a rule cannot be connected to the root or the lexicon in the partially expanded grammar, it will still be impossible to connect it after further feature expansion. (The converse is not true; even if a rule passes filtering in the partially expanded version, all of its expansions may later

```
sigma:[] --> vp:[]:[takes_pp=PP].
vp:[]:[takes_pp=PP] --> % close connection (*to top)
  v:[type=openable, quant=def]:[takes_pp=PP],
  np:[type=openable, quant=def]:[].
vp:[]:[takes_pp=PP] --> % move cursor (to top)
  v:[type=mobile, quant=def]:[takes_pp=PP],
  np:[type=mobile, quant=def]:[].
vp:[]:[takes_pp=PP] --> % close all connections
                         % (*to top)
  v:[type=openable, quant=all]:[takes_pp=PP],
  np:[type=openable, quant=all]:[].
vp:[]:[takes_pp=PP] --> % *move all cursors (to top)
  v:[type=mobile, quant=all]:[takes_pp=PP],
  np:[type=mobile, quant=all]:[].
vp:[]:[takes_pp=n] -->
  vp:[]:[takes_pp=y], pp:[]:[].
v:[type=openable, quant=def]:[takes_pp=n] --> close.
v:[type=openable, quant=all]:[takes_pp=n] --> close.
v:[type=mobile, quant=def]:[takes_pp=y] --> move.
n:[type=openable, quant=def]:[] --> connection.
n:[type=openable, quant=all]:[] --> all, connections
 .
n:[type=mobile, quant=def]:[] --> cursor.
pp:[]:[] --> to, top.
```

FIGURE 86 Grammar from Figure 83 after expanding only the features **type** and **quant**. Categories are presented in the form `Cat:Feats1:Feats2`, where `Feats1` are the features that have already been expanded, and `Feats2` are the remaining ones. The expanded versions of the main VP rule have been annotated with examples of phrases they could potentially be used in, with parentheses showing variants; the ones marked with asterisks are not actually realisable.

be ruled out when other features are expanded). In this specific case, we have four expansions for the main VP rule. One of these,

```
vp:[]:[takes_pp=PP] --> % *move all cursors (to top)
  v:[type=mobile, quant=all]:[takes_pp=PP],
  np:[type=mobile, quant=all]:[].
```

can immediately be filtered out, since it cannot connect to the lexicon; even without expanding the `takes_pp` features, we know that there is no V entry of the form

```
v:[type=mobile, quant=all]
```

```
sigma:[] --> vp:[]:[takes_pp=PP].
vp:[]:[takes_pp=PP] --> % close connection (*to top)
  v:[type=openable, quant=def]:[takes_pp=PP],
  np:[type=openable, quant=def]:[].
vp:[]:[takes_pp=PP] --> % move cursor (to top)
  v:[type=mobile, quant=def]:[takes_pp=PP],
  np:[type=mobile, quant=def]:[].
vp:[]:[takes_pp=PP] --> % close all connections
                        % (*to top)
  v:[type=openable, quant=all]:[takes_pp=PP],
  np:[type=openable, quant=all]:[].
vp:[]:[takes_pp=n] -->
  vp:[]:[takes_pp=y], pp:[]:[].
v:[type=openable, quant=def]:[takes_pp=n] --> close.
v:[type=openable, quant=all]:[takes_pp=n] --> close.
v:[type=mobile, quant=def]:[takes_pp=y] --> move.
n:[type=openable, quant=def]:[] --> connection.
n:[type=openable, quant=all]:[] -->
  all, connections.
n:[type=mobile, quant=def]:[] --> cursor.
pp:[]:[] --> to, top.
```

FIGURE 87 Grammar from Figure 83 after expanding only the features **type** and **quant** and then filtering. Categories are presented in the form **Cat:Feats1:Feats2**, where **Feats1** are the features that have already been expanded, and **Feats2** are the remaining ones.

The result of performing this filtering is shown in Figure 87. Next, we expand out the remaining **takes_pp** feature, yielding the fully expanded CFG grammar in Figure 88; finally, we filter this grammar to produce the result shown earlier in Figure 85.

To summarise, the advantage of the interleaved expansion and filtering approach, compared to the simple one, is that we can avoid ever creating some expansions; we filter them out while the grammar is still only partially expanded. In the specific example we have just gone through, the simple approach produces 8 expansions of the main VP rule, which are then filtered down to 4. With the interleaved approach, we never have more than 6 expanded rules at any stage in the process.

The difference is of course small in a grammar with three features, but becomes extremely important in a full-scale grammar with several dozen. Table 5 shows what happens in a version of the Clarissa grammar, contrasting behaviour with and without interleaved expan-

```
sigma:[] --> vp:[takes_pp=y].
sigma:[] --> vp:[takes_pp=n].
vp:[takes_pp=y] --> % *close connection to top
  v:[type=openable, quant=def, takes_pp=y],
  np:[type=openable, quant=def].
vp:[takes_pp=y] --> % move cursor to top
  v:[type=mobile, quant=def, takes_pp=y],
  np:[type=mobile, quant=def].
vp:[takes_pp=y] --> % *close all connections to top
  v:[type=openable, quant=all, takes_pp=y],
  np:[type=openable, quant=all].
vp:[takes_pp=n] --> % close connection
  v:[type=openable, quant=def, takes_pp=n],
  np:[type=openable, quant=def].
vp:[takes_pp=n] --> % move cursor
  v:[type=mobile, quant=def, takes_pp=n],
  np:[type=mobile, quant=def].
vp:[takes_pp=n] --> % close all connections
  v:[type=openable, quant=all, takes_pp=n],
  np:[type=openable, quant=all].
vp:[takes_pp=n] -->
  vp:[takes_pp=y], pp:[].
v:[type=openable, quant=def, takes_pp=n] --> close.
v:[type=openable, quant=all, takes_pp=n] --> close.
v:[type=mobile, quant=def, takes_pp=y] --> move.
n:[type=openable, quant=def] --> connection.
n:[type=openable, quant=all] --> all, connections.
n:[type=mobile, quant=def] --> cursor.
pp:[]:[] --> to, top.
```

FIGURE 88 Grammar from Figure 83 after expanding the features **type** and **quant**, filtering, and expanding the feature **takes_pp**.

sion. We expand increasingly large subsets of the feature set, counting the number of expanded rules produced before and after filtering. As expected, the size of the expanded rule set increases a great deal more quickly than the filtered rule set. If we include no filtering, the size of the expanded rule set grows rapidly; when we reach 39 features, we have over 210K rules, and an attempt to expand it further exceeds resource bounds. If we filter after each expansion, the size of the rule set grows much more slowly, and it is possible to continue the expansion process.

	#Rules	
#Features expanded	After expansion	After filtering
5	378	342
10	412	364
15	735	367
20	771	388
25	1189	457
30	2027	468
35	9245	1052
37	56849	1082
39	210933	1086
40	(error)	1132

TABLE 5 Effect on compilation performance of increasing number of features in the grammar, when all features are expanded simultaneously and then filtered. If no filtering is used, the process exceeds resource bounds at 40 features.

8.5.1 Controlling the expansion and filtering process

In the implemented Regulus system, the default behaviour is to expand all the features at once, and then perform filtering. It is possible to invoke the interleaved expansion and filtering mechanism by supplying a `feature_instantiation_schedule` declaration to the grammar. The argument of a `feature_instantiation_schedule` declaration is a list of lists of features,

```
feature_instantiation_schedule(
   [[Feat11, Feat12, ...],
    [Feat21, Feat22, ...],
    ...
    [FeatN1, FeatN2, ...]
   ]).
```

Every feature used in the grammar must be included exactly once. The effect is to perform compilation by expanding the features listed in each sublist in turn, with filtering after each expansion step. So we start by expanding `Feat11`, `Feat12`, etc and then filtering; next we expand `Feat21`, `Feat22`, etc, and filter again; and we continue in this way until all the features have been expanded.

During each round of expansion and filtering, Regulus prints out trace information. This includes the set of features expanded during the current round, the number of rules after expansion, the number of rules after each filtering stage, the five rules which received most expansions, and the time taken. When all the features have been expanded, Regulus also prints summary information for the whole compilation process.

For toy grammars with small numbers of features, the `feature_instantiation_schedule` declaration is hardly ever required. For substantial grammars, it usually necessary. Our experience is that the safest strategy is to expand features in small groups, starting with the ones that can take the smallest number of possible values, and ending with the ones that can take the largest number. Features with the same ranges of values should be grouped together. An example of a non-trivial `feature_instantiation_schedule` declaration occurs in the general English grammar described in Chapter 9; the declaration can be found near the beginning of the file `$REGULUS/Grammar/general_eng.regulus`.

8.6 Pre-processing of feature grammars

The preceding section showed that we can greatly improve the efficiency of the FG to CFG compilation process by interleaving the expansion and filtering steps. Another, orthogonal, method for improving efficiency is pre-processing of the feature grammar. In this section, we describe two transformations used in Regulus: anonymous variable elimination (Section 8.6.1), and binarisation (Section 8.6.2).

8.6.1 Anonymous variable elimination

Feature values can be unbound variables; often, this possibility is used to ensure that the values of two features are the same, by assigning them the same variable value. It can also frequently happen that a feature value in a rule R is an unbound variable X, but that X does not occur anywhere else in R. We call feature values of this kind *anonymous variables.* For example, looking at the grammar presented earlier in this chapter in Figure 83, the variable `PP` in the first rule is anonymous, since it only occurs once. In contrast, none of the variables in the second rule are anonymous, since each of them occurs exactly twice.

It is possible to transform the grammar so as to eliminate anonymous variables, and this can often reduce the size of the CFG expansion. We illustrate with another toy example. Suppose that want to write a rule which combines a transitive verb and a direct object to form a VP, and moreover that we are working in a language, like French or Spanish, which marks nouns for gender and also requires agreement in number and person between the subject and the main verb. A simple version of this rule might be the following:

```
vp:[number=SubjNum, person=SubjPers] -->
   v:[number=SubjNum, person=SubjPers,
      subcat=trans],
   np:[number=ObjNum, gender=Gen].
```

For French or Spanish, there will be two possible values for number (singular and plural), three for person (1, 2 and 3), and two for gender (masculine and feminine). The original rule will thus expand into a total of $2 * 3 * 2 * 2 = 24$ CFG rules.

In this rule, ObjNum and Gen are anonymous variables[24]. We can eliminate them by splitting the rule into two smaller rules, as follows:

```
vp:[number=SubjNum, person=SubjPers] -->
   v:[number=SubjNum, person=SubjPers,
      subcat=trans],
   np:[number=any, gender=any].

np:[number=any, gender=any] -->
   np:[number=Num, gender=Gen].
```

Here, we have added a new value, any, to the sets of possible values that can be taken by the features number and gender; this value is only used in new rules generated by the anonymous variable elimination transform. The point is to ensure that the daughter category

```
np:[number=any, gender=any]
```

in the first rule can only match the mother category in the second one; this is why the two rules are together equivalent to the original one. In the general case, we replace each anonymous variable in the original rule with the value any; for each modified category, we add a new rule of the form $C' \rightarrow C$, where C is the original version of the category, and C' the modified one.

The point of performing the transformation is that we factor the rule into several parts, separating the anonymous variables from the shared ones. The result is that the CFG expansion becomes considerably smaller; in the example, the first "factored" rule produces $2*3 = 6$ expansions, and the second $2*2 = 4$, giving a total of $6+4 = 10$, compared with 24 for the original rule. Since the factorisation process yields an exponential reduction, savings with complex rules containing many features can be much more dramatic. Experience with large grammars

[24]We could if we wished have omitted ObjNum and Gen when writing the rule, using the convention that an unspecified feature value is an unbound variable (cf. page 35). This is a purely notational change, and does not affect the following argument.

shows that the anonymous variable elimination technique is particularly important for coordination rules of the generic form

```
XP:[] --> XP:[] CONJ:[] XP:[]
```

(cf. also Section 9.8) where the majority of the features in the daughter constitutents tend to be anonymous.

8.6.2 Binarisation transform

The problems in FG to CFG compilation primarily come from rules containing many variables. In general, the number of different variables in a rule increases with the number of daughters, so the size of the expanded rule set is roughly exponential in the number of daughters. Another way to improve efficiency is to transform the grammar into a binarised form, in which no rule has more than two daughters.

We illustrate with another toy example. Suppose we have a rule which forms a yes/no question using a transitive verb ("do cats eat bats") out of an auxiliary verb ("do"), a subject NP ("cats"), a transitive verb ("eat") and an object NP ("bats"). We require the subject and the auxiliary verb to agree in grammatical number, though the main verb, being in the infinitive form, is not marked for number. Also, as in the Toy1 grammar from Chapter 4, we mark NPs for sortal type, and add features to the main verb to constrain the sortal types of the subject and object. The resulting rule will look something like this:

```
s:[] -->
   aux_v:[num=SubjNum],
   np:[num=SubjNum, sem_np_type=SubjType],
   v:[num=MainVNum, vform=infinitive,
       subj_sem_np_type=SubjSem,
       obj_sem_np_type=ObjSem],
   np:[num=ObjNum, sem_np_type=ObjSem].
```

If we suppose that num can take two possible values, and that the sortal type features can take five, this gives us a total of $2 * 2 * 2 * 5 * 5 = 200$ CFG expansions for the rule. Since MainVNum and ObjNum are anonymous variables, we can improve things by applying the transform from Section 8.6.1, and replacing the rule with the following three rules:

```
s:[] -->
   aux_v:[num=SubjNum],
   np:[num=SubjNum, sem_np_type=SubjType],
   v:[num=any, vform=infinitive,
       subj_sem_np_type=SubjSem,
       obj_sem_np_type=ObjSem],
   np:[num=any, sem_np_type=ObjSem].
```

```
v:[num=any, vform=infinitive,
   subj_sem_np_type=SubjSem,
   obj_sem_np_type=ObjSem] -->
  v:[num=MainVNum, vform=infinitive,
     subj_sem_np_type=SubjSem,
     obj_sem_np_type=ObjSem]

np:[num=any, sem_np_type=ObjSem] -->
  np:[num=ObjNum, sem_np_type=ObjSem].
```

We have $2*5*5 = 50$ expansions for the first rule, $2*5*5 = 50$ for the second, and $2*5 = 10$ for the third, to give a total of $50+50+10 = 110$ CFG rules. We can effect a further simplification by applying a binarisation transform, splitting the first of the transformed rules into the three rules

```
s:[] -->
  aux_v:[num=SubjNum],
  tmp1:[num=SubjNum].

tmp1:[num=SubjNum] -->
  np:[num=SubjNum, sem_np_type=SubjType],
  tmp2:[sem_np_type=SubjType].

tmp2:[sem_np_type=SubjType] -->
  v:[num=any, vform=infinitive,
     subj_sem_np_type=SubjSem,
     obj_sem_np_type=ObjSem],
  np:[num=any, sem_np_type=ObjSem].
```

where `tmp1` and `tmp2` are new category symbols that do not occur elsewhere in the grammar; `tmp1` will have only the feature `num`, and `tmp2` only the feature `subj_sem_np_type`. Note that no other features are needed; for example, `tmp1` does not need the feature `subj_sem_np_type`, since the auxiliary verb in the first rule contains no instance of the variable `SubjType`. The first of the new rules produces 2 expansions, the second $2*5 = 10$, and the third $5*5 = 25$, for a grand total of $2+10+25+50+10 = 97$ expansions for all of the five rules produced by the two transformation.

Here, the net reduction due to binarisation is from 110 to 97; as usual, savings are typically more substantial in large-scale grammars with many features. The excessively artificial nature of the example is however not an accident. The reader is quite right if they feel that it would normally make no sense to write a rule like the one used here, and that the grammar should be structured using smaller rules, probably including one that forms a VP constituent. In fact, the binarisation transformation usually has no effect on a well-constructed hand-coded grammar. It is however very powerful when applied to grammars constructed using grammar specialisation methods (cf. Chapter 10), which combine together multiple rules from the original grammar to produce larger rules, like the one shown above. The issues involved in applying binarisation to specialised grammars are explored in more detail in (Rayner et al., 2002).

8.7 Transforming the output CFG

The preceding section showed how we can reduce the size of the expanded CFG rule-set by pre-processing the initial feature grammar. In this section, we show how we can also apply CFG to CFG mappings to simplify the output grammar. We consider two kinds of transformations: compaction (Section 8.7.1) and empty production elimination (Section 8.7.2). Since we will in this section only be interested in context free grammars, as opposed to the feature grammars from which they were derived, it will be convenient to use standard CFG notation; so where we would in the rest of the chapter have written something like

```
np:[num=sg] --> d:[num=sg], n:[num=sg].
```

we will here write

```
NP_SG --> D_SG N_SG
```

8.7.1 Grammar compaction

Experiment shows that CFG-based language models can become much more effective if they are subjected to probabilistic training and converted into PCFG models (cf. in particular Section 11.6). Probabilistic training of CFGs works better on smaller grammar, since fewer rules implies fewer parameters to train.

This section presents a simple method, first described in (Dowding et al., 2001), which can be used to reduce the size of a CFG; for the type of CFGs produced by Regulus, the decrease in the number of rules often exceeds 90%. The method consists of the following three transforms, which are applied repeatedly until a fixpoint is reached:

"Absorbing" If a non-terminal symbol N occurs as the LHS in just one rule R, and the RHS of R contains only terminal symbols, replace N everywhere with the RHS of R.

"Duplicate rules" Remove all duplicated rules.

"Duplicate rule groups" If the sets of rules for the non-terminals N_1 and N_2 are the same, replace N_2 everywhere with N_1. By "the sets of rules are the same", we mean that the sets

$$\{R_1 \mid \text{ there is a rule of the form } N_1 \rightarrow R_1\}$$

and

$$\{R_2 \mid \text{ there is a rule of the form } N_2 \rightarrow R_2\}$$

are equal.

We illustrate the compaction algorithm with a toy example that exploits the fact that, in English, the word "sheep" can be either singular ("a sheep") or plural ("several sheep"). The grammar covers simple noun phrases consisting of a determiner followed by a noun; as usual, we require the determiner and the noun to agree in number. The possible determiners shown here are "the" and "some", both of which can also be either singular ("the/some guy") or plural ("the/some guys"). The original grammar is shown in Figure 89.

```
SIGMA --> NP_SG
SIGMA --> NP_PL
NP_SG --> D_SG N_SG
NP_PL --> D_PL N_PL
D_SG --> the
D_SG --> some
D_PL --> the
D_PL --> some
N_SG --> sheep
N_PL --> sheep
```

FIGURE 89 Toy grammar to illustrate the grammar compaction algorithm.

We can apply the "absorbing" transformation twice on the last two rules, since they are the only rules in which the symbols N_SG and N_PL appear on the left, and their right-hand sides contain only terminals. The result is:

```
SIGMA --> NP_SG
SIGMA --> NP_PL
NP_SG --> D_SG sheep
NP_PL --> D_PL sheep
D_SG --> the
D_SG --> some
D_PL --> the
D_PL --> some
```

The sets of possible right-hand sides for `D_SG` and `D_PL` are both {`the, some`}, so we can apply the "duplicate rule groups" transform; for readability, we call the merge of `D_SG` and `D_PL` simply `D`. We now have

```
SIGMA --> NP_SG
SIGMA --> NP_PL
NP_SG --> D sheep
NP_PL --> D sheep
D --> the
D --> some
```

The sets of possible right-hand sides for `NP_SG` and `NP_PL` are now also both equal to {`(D sheep)`}, so we can apply "duplicate rule groups" again. If we write the merge of `NP_SG` and `NP_PL` as `NP`, we now have

```
SIGMA --> NP
SIGMA --> NP
NP --> D sheep
D --> the
D --> some
```

The first two rules are identical, so we can apply "duplicate rules". This gives the final result, which cannot be reduced further:

```
SIGMA --> NP
NP --> D sheep
D --> the
D --> some
```

8.7.2 Eliminating empty productions

For many well-known reasons, it is useful to allow grammars to contain empty productions; in particular, this greatly simplifies the treatment of movement phenomena (cf. Section 9.6.3). When these grammars are expanded into CFG form, the methods we have described so far in this chapter will retain the empty productions. Since the Nuance compiler does not allow empty productions in GSL grammars, it is necessary to remove them.

The empty production elimination method is a CFG to CFG transformation similar in nature to the compaction method in the preceding section; we successively apply a simple transformation to the grammar until we reach a fixpoint. The algorithm is defined in Figure 90, and functions as follows. The main loop consists of steps 2 to 5. In steps (1) and (2), we find all the non-terminal N which have an empty production, and list them in *empty_symbols*; we tag them with a y if they also have a non-empty production (step 2), and with a n if they don't (step 3). We then delete all the empty productions (step 4).

1. If there are no empty productions in the grammar, then terminate. Otherwise, initialise the set variable *empty_symbols* to the empty set.
2. For each non-terminal T such that there is an empty production of the form $N \rightarrow \epsilon$, and also a non-empty production of the form $N \rightarrow RHS$ ($RHS \neq \epsilon$), add a record of the form (N, y) to *empty_symbols*.
3. For each non-terminal T such that there is an empty production of the form $N \rightarrow \epsilon$, and NO non-empty production of the form $N \rightarrow RHS$ ($RHS \neq \epsilon$), add a record of the form (N, n) to *empty_symbols*.
4. Delete all empty productions from the grammar.
5. Non-deterministically rewrite every non-terminal T in the RHS of every rule R in the grammar, as follows:
   (a) If there is a record of the form (N, n) in *empty_symbols*, then remove T from the RHS of R, else
   (b) If there is a record of the form (N, y) in *empty_symbols*, then non-deterministically EITHER delete T from the RHS of R OR leave T unchanged, else
   (c) Leave T unchanged.
6. Go to step 1.

FIGURE 90 Algorithm for eliminating empty productions from a CFG

In step 5, we use the information in *empty_symbols* to non-deterministically expand every occurrence of any symbol T listed in *empty_symbols*, whenever it occurs in the RHS of a rule. If T is tagged with an n, we remove it, since it can only be used in an empty production. If T is tagged with a y (there is also at least one non-empty production for T), we non-deterministically choose between either removing it, or leaving it unchanged. All symbols not listed in *empty_symbols* are left unchanged.

The cycle may need to be repeated more than once, because step 5 can result in new non-terminals acquiring an empty production. For example, suppose that the original grammar is such that there are rules $A \rightarrow B$ and $B \rightarrow \epsilon$, but no rule of the form $A \rightarrow \epsilon$. In the first cycle, we will eliminate the empty production for B, but we will create one for A; this new empty production will be eliminated in the following cycle.

8.8 Semantics

In this chapter, we have so far said nothing about how to deal with semantics, and we have described the compilation process as one of transforming FG to CFG. There are in fact two possible approaches to dealing with semantics when building a language model out of a feature grammar. The first, which we have assumed up to now, is to discard the semantics when creating the language model, and then use the grammar again in the runtime system to reparse the recognition result. This has the advantage of being straightforward and general. The downside is that it is also inefficient, since the utterance is parsed twice; it also requires a separate Prolog parser, which may not be convenient for some applications.

The second approach, which we have already described in some detail in the first half of the book, is to use the semantic elements of the Nuance Grammar Specification Language (GSL), and compile the unification grammar semantics into GSL semantic constructs. (Cf. in particular Sections 2.3 and 4.3). Abstractly, the result is a CFG with semantic annotations. This approach has advantages and disadvantages complementary to the first one. It is more efficient, and requires no additional Prolog process. It is also, however, less general, since not all unification grammar semantics can be compiled into GSL form.

As we have already seen in Chapters 2 and 4, GSL can build structured representations including ordered lists and attribute-value structures, so it is possible to compile simple versions of compositional semantics into GSL form. The issues involved are discussed further in Section 9.4.

8.9 Summary

- We can convert feature grammars into CFG form by first expanding out the features to all their possible values, and then filtering out useless rules. Naive versions of this method suffer badly from combinatorial explosion; but with suitable refinements, performance is good enough to compile quite large grammars.
- Filtering can be top-down (remove rules that can't be connected to the root) or bottom-up (remove rules that can't be connected to the lexicon).
- It is possible to perform filtering in time proportional to the size of the grammar, by implementing it as a marker-passing algorithm.
- The compilation process can be made a great deal more efficient by interleaving expansion and filtering. We expand some features, filter, and then repeat the process until all features have been expanded.

- Another way to make compilation more efficient is to pre-process the input feature grammar into a more suitable form. The most useful transformation involves removing anonymous variables.
- The output CFG can also be post-processed, both to reduce its size and to eliminate empty productions.
- It is possible to map a restricted version of unification grammar semantics into Nuance GSL semantics, so as to build a self-contained recogniser that produces semantic representations as well as recognition strings.

Exercises

1. Compile the Toy0 grammar, and look at the trace output and the resulting GSL. Which of the following methods do you think were used in the compilation process: interleaved expansion and filtering, anonymous variable elimination, binarisation, compaction, empty production elimination? Why?
2. Repeat the process from exercise (1) with the Toy1 grammar. Are your answers the same?
3. Write a `feature_instantiation_schedule` declaration for the Toy1 grammar, so that each feature is expanded in turn, with filtering in between the steps. Compare the trace output with the one you got using the original grammar. Did the `feature_instantiation_schedule` declaration help in any way?
4. Remove a feature from the Toy1 grammar by adding an `ignore_feature` declaration. (Consult the online Regulus documentation to find out how to do this). What is the effect on the resulting GSL grammar?
5. Compile the Toy1Specialised grammar, and examine the trace output. Which features required most time to expand? What is the effect of ignoring these features?
6. Add some more examples to the training corpus for the Toy1-Specialised grammar. How does this affect the behaviour of the compilation process?

9

A general English feature grammar for speech

Manny Rayner and Pierrette Bouillon

9.1 Introduction

In Chapter 4, we introduced the Regulus unification grammar formalism, and showed how we could use it to build the Toy1 grammar. Later, in Chapter 7, we described how to build recognition grammars by specialising them out of the the general Regulus grammar for English. We did not say much about how the general grammar is structured; that is the topic of the current chapter.

Although Toy1 is very small, it contains several of the key ideas we will need in this chapter. Before reading further, the reader may find it helpful to turn back to Chapter 4 for a moment, and review the Toy1 grammar. It may also be useful to look back at Section 1.3.1, which clarifies the relationships between the material in this chapter, Chapter 8 and Chapter 10. As explained in Section 1.3.1, the intention is not to compile the general grammar directly into CFG form. Instead, we first use the grammar specialisation methods of Chapter 10 to extract a domain-specific feature grammar, and only then apply the techniques from Chapter 8 to convert this specialised grammar into a CFG language model.

The general Regulus grammar for English which we describe here is Open Source, like the rest of Regulus, and can be found on the Regulus website in the directory `$REGULUS/Grammar`. The rule set has been developed over the course of about ten different projects (cf. Section 1.4). The basic strategy has been to attempt to cover as large a proportion as we could of the material that turned up in the individual projects, wherever possible using a clean and linguistically motivated approach. The grammar is still under construction, though changes are being made considerably less frequently than they were during the earlier stages of development.

The rest of the chapter is structured as follows. In Section 9.2, we say a few words about why speech grammars are special. Next, in Section 9.3, we describe informally the types of English constructions we are trying to cover. Section 9.4 discusses semantics. The next four sections constitute the main body of the chapter, and describe the rules and features in detail. Section 9.5 describes noun phrases, Section 9.6 verb phrases and clauses, Section 9.7 adjuncts, and Section 9.8 coordination. Finally, Section 9.9 briefly discusses the use of feature defaults in the lexicon.

9.2 What makes speech grammars special

Our top-level goal is to be able to compile a specialised form of the general grammar into a CFG-based language model. (The specialisation process in described in Chapters 7 and 10). This requirement informs most of the non-standard design decisions in this chapter. Most large-scale grammars these days are written in heavily lexicalised formalisms like HPSG (Pollard and Sag, 1994) or LFG (Bresnan and Kaplan, 1985). Unfortunately, the style of grammar typical for formalisms of this kind is not directly adaptable to Regulus. The key problem is that everything needs to be expressible in terms of finite-valued features, so structure-valued features are not allowed unless they reduce to finite-valued features[25]. This means that the modern strategy of heavily lexicalised grammars is not easy to apply directly. The issues involved have been studied by Kiefer and Krieger (cf. Section 1.5), who have investigated in some depth the problem of compiling HPSG into CFG form.

Since we want to make the rules as constrained as possible, we are willing to make some compromises on full linguistic generality. In particular, we introduce sortal constraints of various kinds in many places, and make them an integral part of the grammar's structure. This will be discussed in detail later in the chapter.

9.3 English grammar: basic intuitions

If we examine the form of English sentences, we see that there are certain regularities in the way that words and phrases can combine together. In English, the basic word-orders for sentences, noun phrases

[25] For example, it would be possible to have a structure-valued feature whose value was a specific list of finite-valued features.

and prepositional phrases are respectively Subject-Verb-Object (SVO), Determiner-Adjective-Noun and Preposition-Noun Phrase. Thus for example we have "John loves Mary" (Subject-Verb-Object), "a red car" (Determiner-Adjective-Noun) and "in America" (Preposition-Noun Phrase). In the rest of this section, we will expand on this initial sketch of English syntactic structure, in order to motivate the more formal treatment later in the chapter. We start with sentences and clauses, and then continue with noun phrases.

9.3.1 Sentences and clauses

There are clearly several different types of sentences; the most important ones are declarative sentences, imperatives, yes-no questions and WH-questions. There are also embedded questions, which are not sentences, but look a great deal like them. These constructions are illustrated in Table 6.

1	Declarative	**You drink water**
2	Imperative	**Drink water!**
3	Y-N question	**Do you drink water?**
4	WH-question	**What do you drink?**
5	Embedded question	I need to know **what you drink**

TABLE 6 Most important sentence structures

Further examples are shown in Table 7. Sentences can be embedded in more complex constructions (example 6 and 7), can be modified by adverbs or PPs (examples 9 and 10) or can be passivised (example 8).

6	Subordinate clause	You feel better when **you drink water**
7	Gerund	**Drinking water** makes you feel better
8	Passive	**Water can be drunk**
9	Adverbial modifier	**You often drink water**
10	PP modifier	**You drink water in the morning**

TABLE 7 Other clauses

Obviously all of these constructions are closely related in some way. The grammar should generalise over the various structures, and capture the relevant constraints. At a very general level, the examples above allow the following observations:

- *Declarative sentences* have a subject phrase followed by a verb phrase. In example 1, the verb "drink" typically requires a subject before the verb (e.g. "you") and an object after (e.g. "water").

- Sometimes, we can apparently omit the subject, as in *imperative clauses*, *gerunds* and *passives* (examples 2, 7 and 8).
- Sometimes, the object is not after the verb, but occurs earlier in the sentence (for example "what" in 4 and 5). This is called *movement*; the object is "moved" from its usual position to a different one.
- If we want to form a question, we add the *auxiliary verb* "do" before the subject. It is also possible to use other auxiliary verbs, like "can" or "will". The fact that the auxiliary verb comes before the subject, rather than after, is often referred to as *subject-verb inversion*, or just *inversion*.
- A *transitive* verb like "drink" typically combines with a subject and an object. Other types of verb may require different sets of complements. For example, an intransitive verb like "sleep" will require just a subject ("you sleep"), and a verb like "put" requires a subject, an object and a prepositional phrase ("you put the glass on the table"). The set of complements required by a verb is often called its *subcategorisation frame*.
- Verbs usually place restrictions (*sortal constraints*) on the types of noun phrase that they can take as subject or object. Here, "drink" usually requires a noun phrase designating a person as subject ("I", "you", "most people", "who") and a noun phrase designating a type of liquid as object ("water", "coffee", "alcoholic beverages", "what"). We have already seen examples of sortal constraints in the Toy1 grammar from Chapter 4.
- Verbs can take optional modifiers ("adjuncts"). The simplest kinds are adverbs (example 9) and PPs (example 10). Most verbs can only take certain kinds of adverbs and PPs.

9.3.2 Noun phrases

We can view the noun phrase as being organised around a "head", the central noun in the noun phrase. In the examples in Table 8, the head is *dog* or *dogs*. As we can see, the head can be followed by post-nominal modifiers or preceded by prenominal modifiers.

Before the head, English syntax generally requires a determiner, for example an article (*a* in example 1), a quantifier (*some* in example 2) or a possessive (*his* in example 3). This determiner may be followed by an adjective (example 5) or a noun (example 6). However, the determiner can generally be omitted with plural nouns (example 4), and sometimes also with singular nouns.

After the head, different types of postmodifiers are possible. The most frequent are PPs (examples 7 and 8), postmodifying numbers (ex-

1	Basic noun phrase	a dog
2	Quantifier	**some** dogs
3	Possessive	**his** dog
4	Null determiner	dogs
5	Adjective	a **small** dog
6	Prenominal modifier	a **guard** dog
7	"of" PP	the dogs **of war**
8	Normal PP	that dog **in the window**
9	Postmodifying number	dog **fifteen**
10	Relative clause	the dog **that chased the cat**
11	Non-finite clause	dogs **chasing cats**

TABLE 8 Examples of noun phrases

1	Conjoined NP	the cats and the dogs
2	Conjoined NBAR	the cats and dogs
3	Pronoun	**it**
4	Bare determiner	**either**

TABLE 9 Coordination and pronominalization in nominal phrases

ample 9), relative clauses (example 10) and non-finite clauses (example 11).

As shown in Table 9, noun phrases and nouns can also be linked by conjunctions such as *and* or *or* (examples 1 and 2). Noun phrases do not always need to contain a common noun; for example, they can also consist of a pronoun (example 3) or a bare determiner (example 4).

9.4 Compositional semantics

The previous sections have introduced some of the syntactic structures that we want to be able to handle. We also want the grammar to assign semantic representations to the constructions it licenses. As explained in earlier chapters, each Regulus rule will build up the semantic representation associated with the mother (left hand side) category out of the semantic representations associated with the daugher (right hand side) categories. We have already seen several examples of this in the Toy1 grammar from Chapter 4.

Comparing the general Regulus grammar with other broad-coverage grammars, there are some non-standard requirements with regard to semantics. The most important of these is a practical one. Since we want to be able to produce recogniser packages that will work in standalone Nuance applications, we want the semantics to be such that we can compile it down into Nuance semantic primitives. This means that we are not allowed to use mechanisms as powerful as lambda-calculus or unification (common in many broad-coverage grammars) to build the semantic forms. The main Nuance primitive we have available is `concat`, which just concatenates two lists.

Another consideration is that the same type of semantic representation is not necessarily equally suitable for all applications. We have found that simple applications are often easiest to construct using a reduced linear version of the semantics. This eliminates most of the dependency information, but the linear form is easier to work with if this dependency information is not required. More elaborate applications may require a nested semantic representation, which preserves dependencies. Examples of the different kinds of semantic representations supported by the grammar are shown in Section 7.5.

In order to maintain flexibility with regard to semantics, the grammar is constructed so that all semantic representations in rules are specified using macros. These macros are then defined in a separate file; different independent semantic representations can be supported in parallel, by maintaining different files of macro definitions. The macros combine the semantic representations of the daughter categories, without making any assumptions about the way in which the combination is to be carried out. For example, the S $\rightarrow$ NP VP rule, which we will discuss later in Section 9.6, has the schematic form

```
s:[sem= @np_vp_sem(Np, Vp)] -->
  np:[sem=Np, agr=Agr],
  vp:[sem=Vp, agr=Agr, vform=finite].
```

Here, the definition of the macro `np_vp_sem` will specify how the contributions of the NP and VP constituents are to be combined. In the "linear" semantics, they are concatenated together; in the "nested" semantics, the NP is placed inside a wrapper which marks it as the subject.

In the next few sections, we will describe the structure of the general English grammar in fair detail. There are four main groups of rules, which respectively cover noun phrases (Section 9.5), verb phrases and clauses (Section 9.6), adjuncts (Section 9.7) and coordination (Section 9.8). We will describe in the individual sections how the various groups of rules fit together. We also explain how most of the features in the grammar are used. Since there are many features, it would be highly confusing to present all of them simultaneously. Our expositional strategy will rather be to introduce them in small groups, showing how they are used to solve specific problems. Particularly during our discussion of clausal structure, this means that we will often show rules several times, in different versions with increasing numbers of features.

9.5 Noun phrases

Since they are simplest, we start with the rules for noun phrases (NPs). The most basic type of NP consists of a determiner followed by a noun ("the light", "some dogs"), so a reasonable first idea might be to write a rule of the generic form

```
np:[] --> d:[], n:[].
```

(We write d for determiner and n for noun). If we look at Table 8, we see however that this straightforward approach will create problems. We want to be able to add adjectives (example 5 in the figure) and prenominal modifiers (example 6), and we also want to be able to omit the determiner (example 4). It would be very clumsy to have to write multiple rules which duplicated the determiner and noun structure, e.g.

```
np:[] --> d:[], adj:[], n:[].    % a small dog
np:[] --> d:[], n:[], n:[].      % a guard dog
np:[] --> adj:[], n:[].          % small dogs
np:[] --> n:[], n:[].            % guard dogs
...
```

We consequently introduce a constituent called an NBAR, which consists of the noun, together with prenominal modifiers like adjectives and other nouns, but not including determiners. Our basic rule will then be of the form

```
np:[] --> d:[], nbar:[].         % a (small/guard) dog
```

and we will have NBAR rules like

```
nbar:[] --> n:[].                % dogs
nbar:[] --> adjp:[], nbar:[].    % small dogs
nbar:[] --> n:[], nbar:[].       % guard dogs
nbar:[] --> name:[], nbar:[].    % Disney dogs
```

We can now get NPs with null determiners by adding the rule

```
np:[] --> nbar:[].               % small dogs (NP)
```

Figure 91 shows an example of a Regulus parse tree for a simple NP, produced using the Toy1Specialised grammar (cf. Chapter 7). We will show several examples of this kind throughout the chapter. We will normally use the same format as in Figure 91. Recall (cf. page 67) that it is also possible to display the line numbers by using the LINE_INFO_-ON command; this option is very useful if you want to run the examples yourself, and examine the relevant grammar rules and lexicon entries.

```
.MAIN
   top
   /  utterance_intro null
   |  utterance
   |     np
   |     /  np
   |     |  /  d lex(the)
   |     |  |  nbar
   |     |  |  /  n lex(kitchen)
   |     |  |  |  nbar
   |     |  \  \     n lex(light)
   |     \  post_mods null
   \  utterance_coda null
```

FIGURE 91 Parse tree for "the kitchen light"

Not all NPs need to include an NBAR. In particular, a very common and important case is that of pronouns, where we have a rule of the form

```
np:[] --> pronoun:[].
```

We can also make some determiners into NPs ("do you have **any/a few**?", but not "*do you have **the/a**?". The relevant rule is of the form

```
np:[] --> d:[can_be_np=y].
```

where the feature `can_be_np` captures the relevant distinction. Gerunds are yet another type of NP construction which lacks an NBAR ("Does **drinking red wine** give you headaches?"). The gerund rule is of the form

```
np:[] --> vp:[vform=ing, can_be_gerund=y].
```

The `vform` feature is discussed later, in Section 9.6; `can_be_gerund` is a feature which is set on the V and passed up to the VP, which makes it possible in a given domain to distinguish between verbs that can and cannot form gerunds. The grammar also contains coverage of several special types of NPs, like names, dates and times ("john"; "december seventh"; "sixteen thirty"). Finally, we have the very important construction which combines an NP with a possibly empty list of postmodifiers ("the light **in the kitchen**"; "the light **that you switched on**"). The form of this rule is

```
np:[] --> np:[], post_mods:[].
```

We will postpone discussion of the **post_mods** constituent until Section 9.7, since it is used for both nominal and verbal modifiers.

9.5.1 NP and NBAR features

The NP rules have so far been presented in a highly schematic form. In the rest of this section, we will describe the relevant features, which are summarised in Table 10. Some of these features are linguistically motivated, and enforce standard grammatical constraints; others are basically sortal in nature, and mediate domain-specific pragmatic constraints encoded in the lexicon.

Feature	Description
Features on N and NBAR only	
`takes_det_type`	Sortal type of determiner
`n_pre_mod_type`	Sortal type of pre-modifying N
`n_post_mod_type`	Sortal type of post-modifying N
Features on N, NBAR and NP	
`agr`	Agreement information (§9.6)
`n_appositive_mod_type`	Sortal type of appositive modifier
`n_of_mod_type`	Sortal type of "of"-PP modifier
`sem_n_type`	Sortal type of N/NBAR/NP
`takes_loc_pp` (etc)	NP can take locative PP, etc (§9.7)
`wh`	NP is WH positive or negative
Features on NP only	
`case`	Case of NP (subject/non-subject)
`gapsin, gapsout`	Features for WH-movement (§9.6.3)
`nform`	NP is impersonal "it" or "there"
`pronoun`	NP is pronoun
`takes_post_mods`	Can combine with POST_MODS (§9.7)

TABLE 10 Features for N, NBAR and NP.

Many of these features, both linguistic and non-linguistic, are "head features"; that is, they are set on the head noun and percolated up through the NBAR rules until they reach the NP. Typical examples of head features are **agr**, which encodes agreement information (cf. Section 9.6), and **sem_n_type**, which encodes the sortal type of the noun. Thus for example a more complete version of the rule which forms an NBAR out of an N would be

```
nbar:[agr=Agr, sem_n_type=Type] -->
  n:[agr=Agr, sem_n_type=Type].
```

and a more complete version of the NP → D NBAR rule would be

```
np:[agr=Agr, sem_n_type=Type] -->
  d:[agr=Agr],
  nbar:[agr=Agr, sem_n_type=Type].
```

Most of the head features belong to the sortal group; other examples are `n_of_mod_type`, which gives the sortal type of a possible "of"-PP modifier, and `takes_loc_pp`, which specifies whether the noun can take a locative PP modifier. Features which control nominal and verbal post-modification are discussed further in Section 9.7. The pair of features `gapsin` and `gapsout`, which are used to handle WH-movement, are discussed in Section 9.6.3. First, however, we switch to talking about the rules for verb phrases and clauses.

9.6 Verb phrases and basic clauses

As we saw in Section 9.3.1, clauses can come in many different forms. We want our rules to capture the commonalities between these different types of clauses. Ideally, we would like to have just one rule for clause formation, parameterised by a suitable set of features. This might be feasible in a highly expressive feature grammar formalism like HPSG (Pollard and Sag, 1994). It is however extremely difficult (most likely impossible) to do this in the relatively simple Regulus formalism. What we can do, however, is achieve a reasonable degree of economy formulating our rules for VPs.

Going back to Table 6, we start by considering the two simplest types: declarative clauses (1) and imperatives (2). The rule for declarative clauses is the traditional one, and has the basic form

```
s:[sem= @np_vp_sem(Np, Vp)] -->
  np:[sem=Np, agr=Agr],
  vp:[sem=Vp, agr=Agr, vform=finite].
```

We will present a more complete version of this rule later, when we have discussed some of the other features. For now, we just show the `agr`, `vform` and `sem` features. `agr` encodes number and person, and enforces agreement between subject and verb. The `vform` feature is used to distinguish between the different inflected forms of each verb, according to their grammatical distributions. It can have several possible values, of which the most important are `finite` ("I **drink**", "he **drinks**", "I **drank**"), `imperative` ("**drink!**"), `ing` ("I am **drinking**") and `en` ("I have **drunk**"). As before, the value of the `sem` feature in the mother is specified using a macro that combines the `sem` values of the daughters.

The rule for imperatives is similar, and is of the form

```
.MAIN
  top
  /  utterance_intro null
  |  utterance
  |     s
  |        s
  |        /  np
  |        |     pronoun lex(i)
  |        |  vp
  |        |  /  vp
  |        |  |  /  vbar
  |        |  |  |     v lex(dimmed)
  |        |  |  |  np
  |        |  |  |  /  np
  |        |  |  |  |  /  d lex(the)
  |        |  |  |  |  |  nbar
  |        |  |  |  |  \     n lex(light)
  |        |  |  \  \  post_mods null
  |        \  \  post_mods null
  \  utterance_coda null
```

FIGURE 92 Parse tree for "I dimmed the light"

```
s:[sem= @np_vp_imperative_sem(Np, Vp)] -->
   vp:[sem=Vp, agr=2, vform=imperative]
```

Basically, an imperative clause is treated as a declarative clause with a missing second person subject (i.e. implicitly "you") and a main verb whose `vform` feature has the value `imperative`.

Figure 92 shows an sample derivation tree for a declarative clause, produced using the Toy1Specialised grammar from Chapter 7. The clause "I dimmed the light" is as usual composed of the NP "I" and the VP "dimmed the light". As with the NP discussed earlier in Section 9.5, the VP's outer structure combines an inner VP and a POST_MODS, (cf. Section 9.7) which is this case is empty. A non-empty POST_MODS constituent could for example be a PP ("at ten p m") or an ADVP ("suddenly").

The inner VP is composed of the VBAR "dimmed" and the NP "the light", whose structure we have already discussed. We will explain later why we need the VBAR constituent; for now, think of VBARs as verbs. In the next section, we will say more about the structure of the VP.

9.6.1 Subcategorisation

The basic structure of the VP combines the verb with its obligatory complements; this is often referred to as *subcategorisation*. Thus an intransitive verb has no complements except the subject ("John **ran**"), a transitive verb combines with an NP ("John **drank water**"), a ditransitive verb combines with two NPs ("John **gave Mary a book**"), and so on.

In most modern grammar formalisms, like GPSG (Gazdar et al., 1985), LFG (Bresnan and Kaplan, 1985) or HPSG (Pollard and Sag, 1994), all of these rules will be combined into one single schema, which in Regulus notation might be roughly of the form

```
vp:[] --> v:[subcat=COMPS] COMPS.
```

In other words, there would be a feature on the verb (usually called `subcat`), whose value would be a list of categories. The VP would consist of the verb followed by constituents matching the contents of the `COMPS` variable. Thus for example a lexical entry for a transitive verb like "drink" would have roughly the form

```
v:[subcat=[np:[case=nonsubj,...]] --> drink.
```

In Regulus, rules and lexical entries like these are not possible, since features, in particular the `subcat` feature, have to take values drawn from a predefined finite space. We consequently revert to a more primitive approach, and write one VP rule for each different complement pattern. So for a transitive verb like "dim" in Figure 92, we have a VP rule of the form

```
vp:[sem= @vp_v_np_sem(Verb, Np),
    agr=Agr, vform=Vform] -->
  vbar:[sem=Vp,
        subcat=nx0vnx1, agr=Agr, vform=Vform],
  np:[sem=Np].
```

The names of possible `subcat` values are based on those used in the XTAG project (Doran et al., 1994, XTAG Research Group, 2001). Here, the name `nx0vnx1` reflects the fact that the syntactic pattern associated with a transitive verb combines a subject NP (`nx0`), a verb (`v`) and a second object NP (`nx1`). Note that the right-hand side of the transitive rule contains a VBAR rather than a V; there is a rule of the form

```
vbar:[sem=V,
      subcat=Subcat, agr=Agr, vform=Vform] -->
  v:[sem=V,
     subcat=Subcat, agr=Agr, vform=Vform].
```

which makes Vs into VBARS, passing up the value of the subcat feature. We will have more to say about VBAR rules in Section 9.6.2. The lexical entry for the verb "dim" will be of the form

```
v:[sem= @verb_sem(action, dim),
   subcat=nx0vnx1, agr=(\(3/\sing)),
   vform=finite] --> dim.
```

Here, the value (\(3/\sing)) uses the feature negation operator \ and the feature conjunction operator /\ to construct a value that means "not third-person singular".

Other subcategorisation patterns are handled in a similar way. For example, the rule for VPs with intransitive verbs is

```
vp:[sem= @vp_v_sem(Verb),
    agr=Agr, vform=Vform] -->
  vbar:[sem=Verb,
        subcat=nx0v, agr=Agr, vform=Vform].
```

and that for VPs with ditransitive verbs is

```
vp:[sem= @vp_v_np_np_sem(Verb, NP1, NP2),
    agr=Agr, vform=Vform] -->
  vbar:[sem=Verb,
        subcat=nx0vnx1x2, agr=Agr, vform=Vform],
  np:[sem=NP1],
  np:[sem=NP2].
```

An important case is that of modal verbs, which includes both obvious modals like "can" ("you **can** see it"), and auxiliary verbs like "have" ("**have** you seen it") and "do" ("**do** you see it"). This time, the VP rule is of the form

```
vp:[sem= @vp_v_vp_modal_sem(Verb, VP),
    agr=Agr, vform=Vform] -->
  vbar:[sem=Verb,
        subcat=nx0vvx1_modal, vp_vform=LowerVForm,
        agr=Agr, vform=Vform],
  vp:[sem=VP, agr=Agr, vform=LowerVform].
```

As with NPs, it is important to be able to use sortal features to constrain the possible complements that can combine with a verb. For example, the transitive verb "dim" in the Toy1Specialised grammar requires its direct object to be of sortal type dimmable and its subject to be of sortal type agent. We specify these and similar constraints using the features subj_sem_n_type, obj_sem_n_type, indobj_sem_n_type, pp_sem_pp_type and sem_p_type. Adding the sortal features to the transitive verb rule we saw a little earlier, a more complete form of the rule can be written as follows:

```
vp:[sem= @vp_v_np_sem(Verb, Np),
    agr=Agr, vform=Vform,
    subj_sem_n_type=SubjSem] -->
  vbar:[sem=Verb, subcat=nx0vnx1,
        agr=Agr, vform=Vform,
        subj_sem_n_type=SubjSem,
        obj_sem_n_type=ObjSem],
  np:[sem=Np, sem_n_type=ObjSem].
```

Similarly, a more complete version of the lexical entry for "dim" will be of the form

```
v:[sem= @verb_sem(action, dim),
   subcat=nx0vnx1, agr=(\(3/\sing)), vform=finite,
   subj_sem_n_type=agent,
   obj_sem_n_type=dimmable] --> dim.
```

In Section 7.4, we show how to use macros to write lexicon entries like these in a compact form.

9.6.2 Inversion

The initial discussion in this section only considered declarative and imperative clauses. We will now show how we can extend the grammar to include yes/no questions as well. In Section 9.6.3, we will also add the rules and features needed for WH-questions and relative clauses.

In English declarative clauses, the subject appears before the main verb ("**John can** swim"). By "inversion", we mean the word-order typical of questions, in which the subject instead appears after the verb ("**Can John** swim?"). Most treatments of subject/verb inversion regard it as a type of movement phenomenon (cf. Section 9.6.3); the idea is that the main verb is moved from its surface position before the subject, to appear in its usual position at the beginning of the VP. Thus for example the Core Language Engine grammar for English (Pulman, 1992) has an inverted clause rule of the form

```
s:[inv=y] -->
  v:[subcat=Sub, agr=Agr, ...],
  np:[],
  vp:[sai=[subcat=Sub, agr=Agr, ...].
```

which forms the clause out of the fronted main verb, the subject, and a VP with a missing verb. The information in the fronted verb is moved to the VP, and then down to the normal verb position, through the category-valued feature sai ("subject-auxiliary inversion"). Extending the description of the "standard" (non-Regulus) main VP rule on page 216, the sai feature appears as follows:

```
vp:[subcat=COMPS, sai=Sai] --> v:[sai=Sai] COMPS.
```

saying that the sai feature is shared between the VP and the V. Finally, there is a "gap" V rule of the form

```
v:[subcat=Sub, agr=Agr, ...
   sai=[subcat=Sub, agr=Agr, ...]] --> [].
```

which in effect allows the fronted verb to appear, as a gap constituent, in its normal position at the beginning of the VP.

Although this type of analysis is favoured by most linguists, it is easy to feel that it is somewhat unintuitive. More importantly in the present context, it also introduces many new VP features which are used to describe the properties of the moved verb; in general, since our main goal is to be able to compile versions of the grammar into CFG form, we prefer to reduce the feature set as much as possible. For these reasons, the Regulus grammar for English instead uses a non-standard treatment of inversion in which the main verb and the subject together form a constituent, which we will consider to be a VBAR. Figure 93 shows a simple example, for the sentence "Could you dim the light". Here, the VBAR "Could you" is created by a rule of the form

```
vbar:[sem= @inverted_subj_sem(Verb, Np),
      inv=y, subcat=Sub, agr=Agr, vform=Vform] -->
  v:[sem=Verb, subcat=Sub, agr=Agr, vform=Vform],
  np:[sem=Np, agr=Agr].
```

The inv feature is passed up to the VP through the VP rules that we saw in Section 9.6.1. In particular, the modal verb VP rule on page 217 will include the inv feature as follows:

```
vp:[sem= @vp_v_vp_modal_sem(Verb, Vp),
    inv=Inv, agr=Agr, vform=Vform] -->
  vbar:[sem=Verb, inv=Inv, agr=Agr,
        vform=Vform,
        subcat=nx0vvx1_modal, vp_vform=LowerVForm],
  vp:[sem=Vp, agr=Agr, vform=LowerVForm].
```

Above this, the inverted clause is created using a rule of the form

```
s:[sem= @s_vp_sem_inverted(Vp), inv=y] -->
  vp:[sem=Vp, inv=y].
```

```
.MAIN
   top
   /  utterance_intro null
   |  utterance
   |     s
   |        s
   |           vp
   |           /  vbar
   |           |  /  v lex(could)
   |           |  |  np
   |           |  \     pronoun lex(you)
   |           |  vp
   |           |  /  vp
   |           |  |  /  vbar
   |           |  |  |     v lex(dim)
   |           |  |  |  np
   |           |  |  |  /  np
   |           |  |  |  |  /  d lex(the)
   |           |  |  |  |  |  nbar
   |           |  |  |  |  \     n lex(light)
   |           |  |  \  \  post_mods null
   |           \  \  post_mods null
   \  utterance_coda null
```

FIGURE 93 Parse tree for "Could you dim the light"

9.6.3 Movement

The phenomenon of *movement* occurs in several type of English constructions, most importantly WH-questions (examples 4 and 5 in Table 6) and relative clauses (example 10 in Table 8). Intuitively, in a WH-question like "What do you drink?", the NP "what" is the object of the verb "drink", and has been "moved" from its natural position after the verb to the fronted position at the beginning of the clause. Similar issues pertain in a relative clause like "The water **that you drink**". The Regulus grammar for English implements a standard account of movement, using the mechanism of *gap-threading* (Pereira, 1981), which is in turn closely related to the idea of *slash categories* (Gazdar et al., 1985). Figure 94 shows an example derivation of a WH-question in the Regulus grammar, where the fronted NP "what" is linked to the null NP appearing as the object of "dim".

The linkage is implemented using the two features **gapsin** and **gapsout**, which appear in all the categories that can include gap cat-

```
.MAIN
   top
   /  utterance_intro null
   |  utterance
   |     s
   |        s
   |        /  np
   |        |     d lex(what)
   |        |  s
   |        |     vp
   |        |     /  vbar
   |        |     |  /  v lex(did)
   |        |     |  |  np
   |        |     |  \     pronoun lex(you)
   |        |     |  vp
   |        |     |  /  vp
   |        |     |  |  /  vbar
   |        |     |  |  |     v lex(dim)
   |        |     |  |  |  np
   |        |     |  |  |  /  np null
   |        |     |  |  \  \  post_mods null
   |        \     \  \  post_mods null
   \  utterance_coda null
```

FIGURE 94 Parse tree for "What did you dim?"

egories involved in WH-movement. The two features together encode whether or not the constituent contains a gap, and if so what kind of gap it is. In the present version of the grammar, we only allow the gap features to encode a single gap; the possible range of values for the two gap features are **null**, **np_gap**, **pp_gap**, **adjp_gap** and **advp_gap**, and the two features together act as a "difference list". Thus for instance if **gapsin** has the value **np_gap** and **gapsout** has the value **null**, then the constituent contains an NP gap. If the two features have the same value, then the constituent contains no gap.

In Figure 94, the fronted NP is introduced using a rule of the form

```
s:[sem= @fronting_sem(Np, S),
   wh=y\/rel, wh=Wh, inv=Inv, whmoved=y,
   gapsin=null, gapsout=null] -->
  np:[sem=Np, wh=Wh, gapsin=null, gapsout=null],
  s:[sem=S, wh=n, inv=Inv,
     gapsin=np_gap, gapsout=null].
```

Here, the mother NP is composed of a fronted NP and an inner S. The settings `gapsin=np_gap, gapsout=null` constrain the inner S to contain an NP gap. The rule is intended to be general enough to cover both WH-questions and relative clauses, so the `inv` and `wh` features are left unconstrained, and just passed up to the mother. For a WH-question like the one in Figure 94, we will have `inv=y` (inverted word-order; cf. Section 9.6.2) and `wh=y` (a WH+ NP like "what" or "which light"). For a relative clause, we will have `inv=n` (uninverted word-order), and `wh=rel` (a relative clause introducing NP like "that" or "which"). Both the WH-question and the relative clause have `whmoved=y`, since both contain movement. The issues concerning the `inv`, `whmoved` and `wh` features are discussed futher in Section 9.6.5. Alongside the NP-fronting rule, we also have rules for PP-fronting ("**when** did you dim the light?"), ADJP-fronting ("**how bright** is the light?") and ADVP-fronting ("**how often** do you dim the light?"). The forms of all these rules are very similar to those of the NP-fronting rule, with suitable adjustments to the fronted constituent and the values of the gap features.

Going back to Figure 94, we have under the NP-fronting rule several other S and VP rules which we have discussed earlier; we now present them again, with the gap features added. First, we have the inverted-clause rule from the end of Section 9.6.2. A more complete version of this rule can be written as:

```
s:[sem= @s_vp_sem_inverted(Vp),
   inv=y, gapsin=GIn, gapsout=GOut] -->
  vp:[sem=Vp, inv=y, gapsin=GIn, gapsout=GOut].
```

where we pass the gap features down from the mother S to the daughter VP. Directly underneath, we have the modal verb VP rule, which with gap features added looks like this:

```
vp:[sem= @vp_v_vp_modal_sem(Verb, VP),
    inv=Inv, agr=Agr, vform=Vform,
    gapsin=GIn, gapsout=GOut] -->
  vbar:[sem=Verb,
        inv=Inv, agr=Agr, vform=Vform,
        subcat=nx0vvx1_modal, vp_vform=LowerVForm],
  vp:[sem=Vp, agr=Agr, vform=LowerVform,
      gapsin=GIn, gapsout=GOut].
```

Note that we have passed the gap features down from the mother VP only to the daughter VP; it is impossible for the moved NP to appear inside the VBAR. Next, the transitive VP rule with added gap features is as follows:

```
vp:[sem= @vp_v_np_sem(Verb, Np),
    inv=Inv, agr=Agr, vform=Vform,
    gapsin=GIn, gapsout=GOut] -->
  vbar:[sem=Verb,
        subcat=nx0vnx1,
        agr=Agr, vform=Vform, inv=Inv],
  np:[sem=Np, gapsin=GIn, gapsout=GOut].
```

Here, we pass the gap features down from the VP to the object NP, since it is again impossible for the VBAR to contain a gap.

Finally, we have the rule which creates the gap NP itself: this has the form

```
np:[sem= @np_gap_sem,
    gapsin=np_gap, gapsout=null] --> [].
```

(recall that `[]` denotes an empty right-hand side). Referring once again to Figure 94, note by the way that a gap NP takes modifiers; here they are empty. The motivation for allowing this is provided by examples like "What do you have in size twelve?", where it seems intuitively clear that the PP "in size twelve" modifies "what", and not "have". This is handled in the grammar by making the POST_MODS constituent containing the PP attach to the gap NP.

9.6.4 Passives

The Regulus grammar implements a simple approach to passives, which uses lexical rules of the form V $\rightarrow$ V to produce passive verb entries from the corresponding active forms. There is one such rule for each subcategorisation pattern (cf. Section 9.6.1) which is capable of undergoing passivisation. The simplest case is that of transitive verbs, where the passivisation rule is of the form:

```
v:[sem=Verb,
   subcat=nx0vnx1_passivised, vform=en_passive,
   passive=y,
   subj_sem_n_type=ObjType,
   takes_passive_by_pp=SubjType] -->
  v:[sem=Verb,
     subcat=nx0vnx1, vform=en,
     subj_sem_n_type=SubjType,
     obj_sem_n_type=ObjType].
```

Here, we have a new value for `subcat`, `nx0vnx1_passivised`, which is specific to passive forms of transitive verbs; we also mark the passivised verb with the feature `passive`. (We will soon see why we need this feature). With regard to the sortal features, the sortal type of the object (`obj_sem_n_type`) in the original transitive verb becomes, as one would expect, the sortal type of the subject (subj_sem_n_type) in the passivised version. The sortal type of the subject in the original verb becomes the sortal type of the possible passive "by" PP.

Passives also require some new rules at the VP and clause level. These extra rules are primarily motivated by semantic considerations. The main issue that arises here concerns the semantic representation of the surface subject NP. If the verb is in the active voice (the default), then the surface subject appears in the semantic form as an agent. If the verb is passive, then the surface subject appears in the semantics as an object. If the mechanism for composing semantic fragments were more powerful (for example, function application or unification), then there would be no problem; the rule that creates the passivised verb entry could include appropriate markings for the surface subject, so that the subject NP just needed to be inserted into the right place, e.g. by being unified with the right unbound variable. This kind of approach is not feasible in the rather less expressive Nuance GSL formalism, so we need new rules that create the passive semantic structures explicitly. Thus we have a passive version of the declarative clause rule:

```
s:[sem= @np_vp_sem_passive(Np, Vp),
   vform=finite, inv=n, wh=Wh,
   gapsin=GIn, gapsout=GOut] -->
  np:[wh=Wh, agr=Agr, sem_n_type=ObjType],
  vp:[agr=Agr, inv=n, vform=finite, passive=y,
      subj_sem_n_type=ObjType,
      gapsin=GIn, gapsout=GOut].
```

This rule differs from the standard one in only two respects: the VP is marked passive=y, and the sem value in the mother is constructed using the macro np_vp_sem_passive instead of np_vp_sem. There is also a variant of the inverted VBAR rule,

```
vbar:[sem= @inverted_subj_sem_passive(V, Np),
      inv=y, subcat=Sub, agr=Agr, vform=Vform,
      passive=y] -->
  v:[sem=Vp, subcat=Sub, agr=Agr, vform=Vform,
     passive=y],
  np:[sem=Np, agr=Agr].
```

which is related similarly to the standard version: the V and VBAR constituents are both marked passive=y, and a different macro is used to construct the sem value in the mother.

Lexical rules create passive versions of verbs from their active versions; as we saw in the last two rules, the passive feature also needs to be propagated up to the VP, and then down to a possible inverted

VBAR constituent. The following rule, which is similar to those shown in Section 9.6.1, combines a passive auxiliary with a VP, and sets the `passive` feature on the mother VP.

```
vp:[sem= @vp_v_vp_passive_sem(Verb, VP),
    inv=Inv, agr=Agr, vform=Vform,
    passive=y,
    gapsin=GIn, gapsout=GOut] -->
  vbar:[sem=Verb, inv=Inv, agr=Agr, vform=Vform,
        subcat=nx0vvx1_passive,
        vp_vform=LowerVForm],
  vp:[sem=Vp,
      vform=LowerVForm, vform=(en_passive\/ing),
      agr=Agr, passive=y,
      gapsin=GIn, gapsout=GOut].
```

Note that the value of the daughter VP's `vform` feature can be either `en_passive` (passive participle, e.g. "the light was **dimmed**"), or alternately `ing` (present participle, e.g. "the light was **being dimmed**"). Finally, the modal/auxiliary verb rule from Section 9.6.1 needs to be modified slightly, as follows, to pass the `passive` feature:

```
vp:[sem= @vp_v_vp_modal_sem(Verb, Vp),
    inv=Inv, agr=Agr, vform=Vform,
    passive=Passive,
    gapsin=GIn, gapsout=GOut] -->
  vbar:[sem=Verb, inv=Inv, agr=Agr, vform=Vform,
        passive=Passive,
        subcat=nx0vvx1_modal, vp_vform=LowerVForm],
  vp:[sem=Vp, vform=VForm, agr=Agr,
      vform=LowerVform, passive=Passive,
      gapsin=GIn, gapsout=GOut].
```

Here, the `passive` feature is not just passed up, from the daughter VP to the mother, but also sideways, from the daughter VP to the VBAR. This is how the inverted VBAR constituent in a passive question receives the feature setting `passive=y`.

Figure 95 shows an example of a derivation using a passive verb.

9.6.5 Adding clause-level semantic information

Looking at derivations like those in Figures 92, 93, 94 and 95, the reader may already have noticed that there is an extra level of clause-level structure about which we have so far said nothing. For instance, in Figure 95 there is an S node directly under the UTTERANCE node, and above the S node which dominates the subject NP and VP nodes.

```
.MAIN
   top
   /   utterance_intro null
   |   utterance
   |       s
   |           s
   |           /   np
   |           |   /   np
   |           |   |   /   d lex(the)
   |           |   |   |   nbar
   |           |   |   \       n lex(light)
   |           |   \   post_mods null
   |           |   vp
   |           |   /   vbar
   |           |   |       v lex(was)
   |           |   |   vp
   |           |   |   /   vp
   |           |   |   |       vbar
   |           |   |   |           v
   |           |   |   |               v lex(dimmed)
   |           \   \   \   post_mods null
   \   utterance_coda null
```

FIGURE 95 Parse tree for "The light was dimmed"

Similar S nodes exist in the other derivations. These nodes correspond to a group of rules, all of the generic form

```
s:[] --> s:[]
```

Rules in this group are used to add clause-level semantic information, categorising the clause as a declarative, a YN-question or a WH-question on the basis of the features `inv`, `whmoved` and `wh`. An example is the rule for WH-questions with movement, which has the form

```
s:[sem= @whq_sem(Sem),
   stype=whq, operator_wrapped=y,
   wh=y, vform=finite, whmoved=y] -->
  s:[sem=Sem, operator_wrapped=n,
     wh=y, vform=finite, whmoved=y].
```

Here, the feature `operator_wrapped` ensures that at most one rule from this group is applied in the derivation of each clause, and the feature `stype` classifies the utterance syntactically as being a WH-question for the benefit of utterance-level rules. In parallel, the macro `whq_sem` adds

Feature	Description
Features on V and VBAR only	
subcat	Complement type of verb (§9.6.1)
obj_sem_n_type	Sortal type of direct object (§9.6.1)
indobj_sem_n_type	Sortal type of indirect object (§9.6.1)
pp_sem_pp_type	Sortal type of PP complement (§9.6.1)
sem_p_type	Sortal type of particle (§9.6.1)
vp_vform	vform value for VP complement (§9.6.1)
takes_advp	VBAR can be modified by adverb (§9.7)
Features on V, VBAR and VP only	
agr	Subject/verb agreement information (§9.6)
passive	(Main) verb is in passive voice (§9.6.4)
subj_nform	Subject is impersonal "it" or "there"
subj_sem_n_type	Sortal type of subject (§9.6.1)
takes_post_mods	VP can be modified by POST_MODS (§9.7)
takes_loc_pp (etc)	VP can take locative PP, etc (§9.7)
takes_adv_type	Sortal type of postmodifying adverb (§9.7)
can_be_gerund	Verb can be used in gerund (§9.5)
can_be_postmod	Verb can be used in postmod (§9.7)
Features on V, VBAR, VP and S	
vform	Inflectional form of (head) verb (§9.6)
inv	Subject/verb inversion (§9.6.2)
gapsin, gapsout	Difference list for WH-movement (§9.6.3)
Features on VP only	
takes_post_mods	Can combine with POST_MODS (§9.7)
Features on S only	
whmoved	Contains WH-movement (§9.6.3)
wh	Fronted constituent is WH+ (§9.6.3)
operator_wrapped	Limit use of clause-level rules (§9.6.5)
stype	Syntactic type of clause (§9.6.5)

TABLE 11 Features for S, VP, VBAR and V.

information to the semantic representation, also marking it as a WH-question.

9.6.6 Summary of V, VBAR, VP and S features

As with NPs, we summarise in Table 11 the different features used for V and its projections VBAR, VP and S, divided up according to the categories in which they can occur. For each feature, we provide a short description and a pointer to the section in which it is introduced.

9.7 Adjuncts

The Regulus English grammar implements a somewhat nonstandard treatment of adjuncts, which is largely based on the POST_MODS category. The basic idea is to consider any sequence of post-nominal or post-verbal modifiers as a constituent, which we call a POST_MODS. Thus in Table 12, all the text in bold is considered as examples of POST_MODS.

"Of"-PP	is the pain in the front **of the head**
Locative PP	the light **in the kitchen**
Temporal PP	do you get headaches **in the morning**
Multiple PP	flights **to geneva on friday**
Passive "by"-PP	are the attacks preceded **by nausea**
Subordinate clause	does the pain appear **when you exercise**
Relative clause	the light **that you switched on**
-ing VP modifier	something **leaving tomorrow**
Reduced relative	a man **named smith**
Appositive	my brother **john**

TABLE 12 Examples of POST_MODS

There are two rules which combine an NP or VP with a POST_MODS. These have, respectively, the schematic forms

```
np:[takes_post_mods=n] -->
  np:[takes_post_mods=y],
  post_mods:[post_mod_type=nominal].

vp:[takes_post_mods=n] -->
  vp:[takes_post_mods=y],
  post_mods:[post_mod_type=verbal].
```

The feature takes_post_mods is used to prevent an NP or VP from being modified by more than one POST_MODS. (We will discuss other features relevant to POST_MODS shortly). Figure 96 shows an example analysis tree for a post-modified NP.

The analysis in terms of POST_MODS is linguistically somewhat dubious (most linguistic theories do not make sequences of post-modifying expressions into constituents), but in the context of the Regulus programme it offers some concrete advantages. The most important of these is that the POST_MODS constituent permits more efficient generalisation when deriving specialised grammars; it is very convenient to

```
.MAIN
   top
   /   utterance_intro null
   |   utterance
   |      np
   |      /   np
   |      |   /   d lex(the)
   |      |   |   nbar
   |      |   \       n lex(light)
   |      |   post_mods
   |      |   /   pp
   |      |   |   /   p lex(in)
   |      |   |   |   np
   |      |   |   |   /   np
   |      |   |   |   |   /   d lex(the)
   |      |   |   |   |   |   nbar
   |      |   |   |   |   \       n lex(kitchen)
   |      |   |   \   \   post_mods null
   |      \   \   post_mods null
   \   utterance_coda null
```

FIGURE 96 Parse tree for "the light in the kitchen"

be able to divide up NPs and VPs into a "core" part and a set of modifiers, and learn rules for each part separately. The details are presented in Section 10.3.3.

In line with the grammar's general emphasis on the use of sortal restrictions, we differentiate between several different kinds of PPs: locative, temporal, from, to and so on. Each type of PP is associated with a head feature set on both nouns and verbs, which defines whether the noun or verb can be modified by the specified type of PP. Thus for example an entry for a noun that can be modified by both a locative and a temporal PP will have the form

```
n:[..., takes_loc_pp=y, takes_time_pp=y] --> ...
```

(cf. also Section 7.4). These features are passed to the POST_MODS constituent.

9.8 Coordination

The final major group of rules is for constituent coordination. The grammar supports coordination of NPs, Ns, PPs, ADJPs, NUMBERs and Ss. The basic pattern is illustrated for the case of NPs. We introduce an auxiliary category called NPCONJ and a feature called `conj`, which are used in rules of the following forms:

```
np:[conj=y] --> npconj:[].

npconj:[] --> np:[conj=n], conj:[], np:[conj=n].

npconj:[] --> np:[conj=n], conj:[], npconj:[].
```

The intent is to permit left-branching construction of coordinated NPs with any number of conjuncts. The treatment of N and PP coordination is similar; ADJP, NUMBER and S coordination are handled in a less elaborate way, since, at least in the kinds of domains that the Regulus grammar has been designed for, they rarely form conjunctions with more than two conjuncts. For example, NUMBER conjunction is handled by a single rule of the form

```
number:[] --> number:[], conj:[], number:[].
```

Conjunction rules pose a problem for the sortal features. As already noted, sortal features are very important for the grammar (in Section 11.4, we will investigate this claim quantitatively). Unfortunately, there is no obvious way to assign a sortal value to a conjunction in which the conjuncts are of different sortal types. At the moment, the rules are implemented so as only to allow conjunction of constituents with the same sortal type: thus for example the first of the two NPCONJ rules referred to above sets the sortal features as follows:

```
npconj:[sem_n_type=Type] -->
  np:[sem_n_type=Type],
  conj:[],
  np:[sem_n_type=Type].
```

If the sortal type system is sensibly designed, however, it seems that there are in practice very few cases where conjunction of differently typed NPs can occur.

9.9 Feature defaults

As we have seen in Tables 10 and 11, both noun and verb projections in the general grammar have a great many features. In any specific context, most of these features are irrelevant. For example, the verb projection feature `pp_sem_pp_type` defines the sortal type of a verb's PP complement, if it has one. Most verbs, however, do not subcategorise for a PP complement.

For rules and lexical entries where the PP complement is not referred to, the question arises of what value to give to the feature `pp_sem_pp_-`

type. For example, looking at the transitive verb rule on page 218, we have written it without mentioning the feature pp_sem_pp_type at all, which implies that its value is an unbound variable. In terms of encoding the desired linguistic constraints, there is nothing wrong with this. However, the feature grammar to CFG compilation algorithm described in the preceding chapter works by non-deterministically assigning to each variable all its possible values. Unbound variables consequently increase the size of the space of expanded rules, and with many unbound variables we can easily fall victim to a combinatorial explosion.

The general solution we have chosen to alleviate this problem is to arrange things so that many features have a neutral value, typically none, which is conventionally assigned in cases where the feature's value is irrelevant. The neutral feature values are set explicitly in rules. For compactness, the Regulus formalism also provides declarations which allow the grammar-writer to specify a default feature value for lexical entries. A declaration of the form

```
% comment
  lexical_feature_default(<Feature>, <Value>).
```

specifies that the default value of <Feature> in a lexical entry is <Value>. Rather more than half of the features in the general grammar (45 out of 79) are currently provided with a default value.

9.10 Summary

- The Regulus grammar for English is Open Source, and is available from the Regulus website. It is a broad-coverage grammar for spoken dialogue applications, which has been developed over about ten projects.
- The main problem with writing a broad-coverage grammar in the Regulus formalism is that features must be finite-valued. This makes it impossible to write heavily lexicalised grammars.
- The semantic formalism used in Regulus is also more restrictive that that used in most large-scale grammars, and does not allow semantic forms to be built up using full unification.
- The grammar makes heavy use of sortal features, since they are important for recognition performance. In particular, NPs have a sortal type feature called sem_n_type, and verbs subcategorise for NPs of specified sortal types.
- The four main rule groups in the grammar respectively cover NPs, VPs and clauses, adjuncts, and constituent coordination.

- NP structure is organised in terms of three main levels: nouns (N), NBARs, and NPs. Most of the features are "head features", which are set in the lexicon, and percolate up to the NP level.
- Verb subcategorisation is handled using the `subcat` feature. There is one VP rule for each possible value.
- Subject-verb inversion is handled by treating the combination of verb and inverted subject as a constituent, which we call a VBAR. This enables us to use fewer features, which is good when compiling grammars into CFG form. The `inv` feature marks whether a VBAR is inverted or not.
- WH-movement is implemented using a gap-threading treatment. The relevant features are called `gapsin` and `gapsout`.
- Passivisation is implemented by lexical rules of the form V → V.
- The `POST_MODS` category represents sequences of post-nominal or post-verbal modifiers, in particular PPs. Nouns and verbs have features which specify which PPs they can combine with. The `POST_MODS` rules only allow at most one PP of a given type to modify a given head.
- There are rules to allow constituent coordination of NPs, Ns, PPs, ADJPs, NUMBERs and Ss. Only constituents of similar sortal types can be conjoined.

Exercises

1. Load the Toy1Specialised grammar into the Regulus development environment, and try parsing the examples shown in this chapter.
2. Use the `LINE_INFO_ON` command to find the rules used. Look at some of these rules, and try to work out what the features are being used for.
3. In the utterance "switch on the light", identify a) the NBAR, b) the VBAR.
4. In the utterance "are the light and fan switched on", identify a) the NBAR, b) the VBAR.
5. In the utterance "has the light been switched on", explain why the analysis tree contains three different VP nodes.
6. In the utterance "what did you switch on", identify a) the fronted NP, b) the gap NP, c) all the constituents which participated in linking the fronted NP to the gap.

10

Grammar specialisation using Explanation Based Learning

Manny Rayner

10.1 Explanation Based Learning

In Chapter 7, we described how to use the grammar specialisation mechanism, without ever really explaining how it worked. Later, at the beginning of Chapter 9, we said that grammar specialisation was the essential link between the general grammar on the one hand, and the feature-grammar-to-CFG compilation methods of Chapter 8 on the other, but did not elaborate on the details. The present chapter will make good these two omissions. The presentation will be reasonably informal, and will focus on the role played by the "cutting-up criteria" (cf. Section 10.2), which define the way in which a general grammar is converted into specialised form. Our main goal is to describe the theoretical background well enough that readers will be in a position to understand what is involved in defining a new set of cutting-up criteria, or choosing between already existing sets. In Chapter 11, we will describe experiments where we investigate the effect on performance of varying the cutting-up criteria.

Grammar specialisation is performed using the mechanism of Explanation Based Learning (EBL; van Harmelen and Bundy (1988)). The basic idea of EBL is simple, and dates back to the "macro-operator" learning of Fikes and Nilson (1971). We assume that our problem can be specified by a set of backward-chaining rules. If we now have an example of a successfully solved instance of the problem, G, the fact that we are working in a backward-chaining system implies the existence of a derivation tree. (See diagram 97). At the root of the tree, we have G. Below it it, we have the conditions $A_1, A_2, ..., A_i$ that immediately

Backward-chaining rules

$$G \leftarrow A_1, A_2, ..., A_i$$
$$A_1 \leftarrow B_1, B_2, ...$$
$$B_1 \leftarrow C_1, C_2, ...$$
$$... \leftarrow L_1, L_2, ...$$
$$... \leftarrow L_j, L_{j+1}, ...$$
$$... \leftarrow L_{k-2}, L_{k-1}, L_k$$

Training example

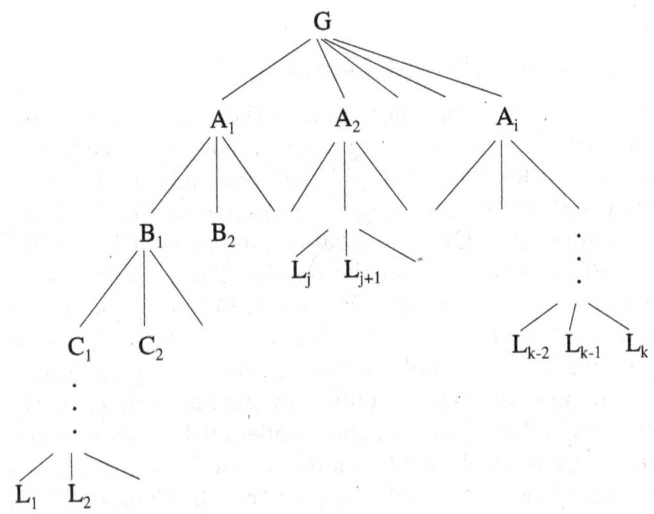

Derived rule

$$G \leftarrow L_1, L_2, ...L_k$$

FIGURE 97 Schematic picture of the EBL process. The leaves in the derivation tree become the conditions in the learned rule.

justify G. Each condition is justified by the entries below it, until we reach the leaf nodes $L_1, ...L_k$. The EBL idea is that we can collapse this tree to form a new rule

$$G \leftarrow L_1, L_2, ...L_k$$

whose left-hand side is G and whose right-hand side is the $L_1, ...L_k$. The term "Explanation Based Learning" comes from the fact that we have extracted the new rule from the derivation tree, which can be viewed as an "explanation" of G.

In the rest of the chapter, we will show how we can apply the general schema to the concrete case of unification grammars. For pedagogical reasons, we will present the idea in several versions, starting in Section 10.1.1 with CFGs and working up to the general case in Section 10.1.5. After this, Section 10.2 discusses cutting-up criteria.

10.1.1 Version 1: CFGs

We start our description of the EBL algorithm with the simplest case, that of a CFG. Figure 98 presents a toy CFG containing five rules and five lexicon entries, together with the training example

```
john has a red car
```

We wish to extract a single rule that summarises the grammatical structure of the example.

We do this by combining the grammar rules in order, starting from the root of the tree. We have the two rules

```
S --> NP VP
VP --> V NP
```

The first rule says that we can rewrite `S` to the sequence `NP` followed by `VP`, and the second says that we can rewrite `VP` to the sequence `V` followed by `NP`. It follows that we can rewrite `S` to the sequence

```
NP V NP
```

Continuing down the tree in Figure 98, we next use the rule

```
NP --> NAME
```

to rewrite the first occurrence of `NP` to `NAME`, showing that `S` can be rewritten to

```
NAME V NP
```

By using the remaining rules in a similar way, we can demonstrate that it is possible to rewrite `S` to the sequence

```
NAME V DET ADJ NBAR
```

Grammar fragment

```
S --> NP VP
VP --> V NP
NP --> DET NBAR
NP --> NAME
NBAR --> ADJ NBAR

NAME --> john
V --> has
DET --> a
ADJ --> red
NBAR --> car
```

Training example

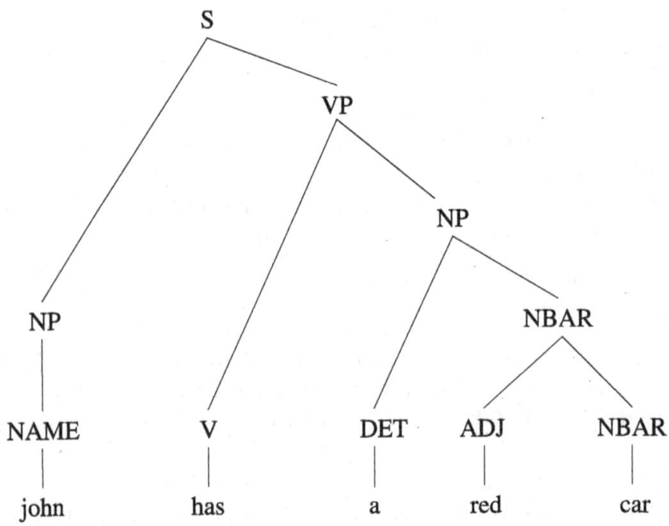

Derived rule

```
S --> NAME V DET ADJ NBAR
```

FIGURE 98 EBL on Context Free Grammar

But this is equivalent to saying that the *derived rule*

```
S --> NAME V DET ADJ NBAR
```

follows from the rules already given in the grammar. The construction we have employed is very general; we could have used any non-terminal N in the tree as the left-hand side of the derived rule, and let the right-hand side be the set of leaves of any subtree T rooted in N.

In the example, we chose the root node N to be the root of the whole tree, and the subtree T to be the subtree formed by deleting all the terminal nodes; this means that the set of leaves of T, and hence the right-hand side of the derived rule, consists of the *pre-terminal* nodes of the whole tree. We could equally well have made other choices for N and T. For example, if we let N be the VP node and again let T be the subtree under N which omits the pre-terminal nodes, we derive the rule

```
VP --> V DET ADJ NBAR
```

If, on the other hand, we let N be the NP node dominating the phrase "a red car", and T be the subtree which includes all the nodes below N except the one for the terminal red, we derive the rule

```
NP --> a ADJ car
```

A little later, we will see how choices like these can be used to construct interesting derived grammars.

10.1.2 Version 2: DCGs

In Version 1, presented in Section 10.1.1, we used a CFG grammar, conceptualised as a set of rewriting rules. Version 2 will now generalise this to the case of a Definite Clause Grammar (DCG; (Pereira and Warren, 1980)), so that we can include semantic values and agreement constraints.

Figure 99 shows the same example, but this time in a simple DCG form. Recall that a DCG rule is a syntactic notation for a Prolog clause, formed by adding two extra arguments to each terminal and non-terminal; these form a "difference list" representing the surface string associated with the phrase in question. For example, the grammar rule

```
np([DET, NBAR], Agr) -->
  det(DET, Agr),
  nbar(NBAR, Agr).
```

is equivalent to the Prolog clause

Grammar fragment

```
s([NP, VP]) --> np(NP, Agr), vp(VP, Agr).
vp([V, NP], Agr) --> v(V, Agr), np(NP, _).
np([DET, NBAR], Agr) -->
  det(DET, Agr), nbar(NBAR, Agr).
np(NAME, sing) --> name(NAME).
nbar([ADJ, NBAR], Agr) -->
  adj(ADJ), nbar(NBAR, Agr).

name(john) --> [john].
v(have, sing) --> [has].
det(a, sing) --> [a].
adj(red) --> [red].
nbar(car, sing) --> [car].
```

Training example

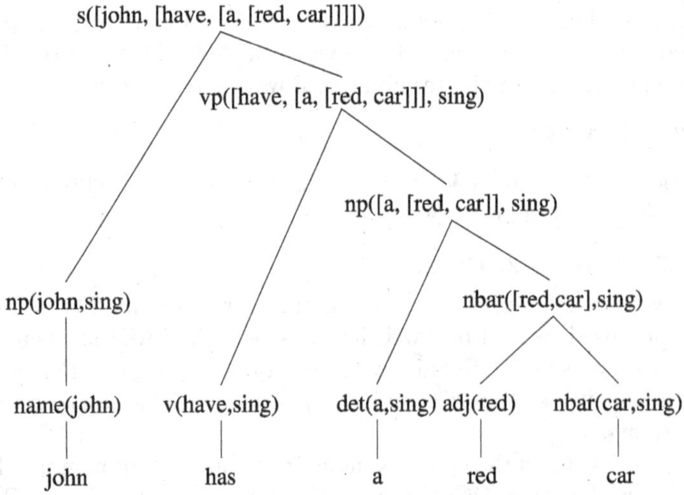

Derived rule

```
s([NAME, [V, [DET, [ADJ, NBAR]]]]) -->
   name(NAME),
   v(V, sing),
   det(DET, Agr),
   adj(ADJ),
   nbar(NBAR, Agr).
```

FIGURE 99 EBL on Definite Clause Grammar

```
np([DET, NBAR], Agr, In, Out) :-
    det(DET, Agr, In, Next),
    nbar(NBAR, Agr, Next, Out).
```

Here, the first argument in `np`, `det` and `nbar` represents the semantics of the constituent, and the second represents the grammatical number (`sing` or `plur`), which must have the same value in both daughters. The last two argument are together a difference list, representing the associated surface string. The `det` daughter's difference list is `(In, Next)`, the `nbar` daughter's is `(Next, Out)`, and the mother's is `(In, Out)`; taken together, this encodes the fact that the mother spans a string consisting of the concatenation of the strings spanned by the two daughters. Similarly, the lexical item

```
adj(red) --> [red].
```

is equivalent to the Prolog clause

```
adj(red, [red | Out], Out).
```

Once again, the first argument in the Prolog version is the semantics, and the last two form a difference list, which here says that the surface form is the single word "red".

We will now show how we can again extract a single derived grammar rule by combining together the rules used to parse the training example. The method is schematically similar to the one used in Version 1, but the mechanism used to compose rules is more a little complex. We start as before with the root node. The top rule is

```
s([NP, VP]) --> np(NP, Agr), vp(VP, Agr).
```

which is equivalent to the Prolog clause

```
s([NP, VP], In, Out) :-
   np(NP, Agr, In, Next),
   vp(VP, Agr, Next, Out).
```

Under this, we have the rule

```
vp([V, NP], Agr) --> v(V, Agr), np(NP, _).
```

equivalent to

```
vp([V1, NP1], Agr1, In1, Out1) :-
   v(V1, Agr1, In1, Next1),
   np(NP1, _, Next1, Out1).
```

We now want to combine the two rules; we renamed the variables in the second rule as a preparatory step. Following the *resolution inference schema* (Section 9.5 of (Russell and Norvig, 2003)), we want to expand the vp goal in the first rule, using the definition of vp in the second one. The resolution schema says that can do this if we can find a *unification substitution* for the two goals

```
vp(VP, Agr, Next, Out)
```

and

```
vp([V1, NP1], Agr1, In1, Out1)
```

In this case, there is a unification substitution, namely

```
VP = [V1, NP1]
Agr = Agr1
Next = In1
Out = Out1
```

(Intuitively, these are the identities that have to hold if the two goals are to match). We apply the substitution to both rules and then substitute the right-hand side of the second rule for the vp goal in the first rule, giving the result

```
s([NP, [V1, NP1]], In, Out) :-
   np(NP, Agr, In, Next),
   v(V1, Agr, Next, Next1),
   np(NP1, _, Next1, Out).
```

which we can also write in DCG form as

```
s([NP, [V1, NP1]]) -->
   np(NP, Agr),
   v(V1, Agr),
   np(NP1, _).
```

This rule is a composition of the S → NP VP rule and the VP → V NP rule; note that it preserves the agreement constraints in both rules, and also composes the semantic values.

We can continue in the same way, just as with Version 1, to combine the new rule we have just created with other rules further down the parse tree; when we have combined all the rules, we will have the result shown at the bottom of Figure 99. It is possible to prove (Rayner, 1988) that we produce the same result irrespective of the order in which the rules are combined.

10.1.3 Version 3: feature grammars

We are not really interested in working with DCGs, but rather with feature grammars. It is, however, well known that feature grammars of the type we consider in this book are just a notational variant of DCGs.

Grammar fragment

```
s:[sem=[NP, VP]] -->
   np:[sem=NP, agr=Agr], vp:[sem=VP, agr=Agr].
vp:[sem=[V, NP], agr=Agr] -->
   v:[v=V, agr=Agr], np:[sem=NP].
np:[sem=[DET, NBAR], agr=Agr] -->
   det:[sem=DET, agr=Agr], nbar:[sem=NBAR, agr=Agr].
np:[sem=NAME, agr=sing] --> name:[sem=NAME].
nbar:[sem=[ADJ, NBAR], agr=Agr] -->
   adj:[sem=ADJ], nbar:[sem=NBAR, agr=Agr].

name:[sem=john] --> john.
v:[sem=have, agr=sing] --> has.
det:[sem=a, agr=sing] --> a.
adj:[sem=red] --> red.
nbar:[sem=car, agr=sing] --> car.
```

Training example

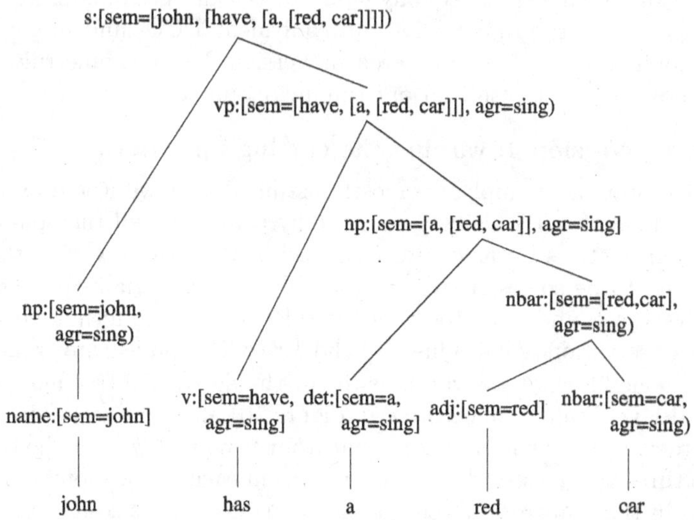

Derived rule

```
s:[sem=[NAME, [V, [DET, [ADJ, NBAR]]]]] -->
   name:[sem=NAME],
   v:[sem=V, agr=sing],
   det:[sem=DET, agr=Agr],
   adj:[sem=ADJ],
   nbar:[sem=NBAR, agr=Agr].
```

FIGURE 100 EBL on feature grammar

Figure 100 shows the grammar and example from Figure 99 rewritten in Regulus feature-grammar notation. It should be clear that the two grammars contain exactly the same information; for example, the S → NP VP rule, which we previously wrote as

```
s([NP, VP]) -->
  np(NP, Agr),
  vp(VP, Agr).
```

is now written as

```
s:[sem=[NP, VP]] -->
 np:[sem=NP, agr=Agr],
 vp:[sem=VP, agr=Agr].
```

All we have done is to give names to the argument positions in each goal: the first argument is always called **sem**, and the second argument in np and vp is called agr.

It follows that grammar specialisation of the kind we have already seen can be carried out equally easily on feature grammars; we transform the feature grammar into an equivalent DCG, and perform the manipuluation we have just seen in Version 2 to combine rules. Figure 100 shows the result for our running example.

10.1.4 Version 4: varying the cutting up criteria

In our running example, we mostly assumed that we would extract a derived rule from a training example by combining all the non-lexical rules. In fact, as we have already noted in the case of CFGs, there is no need to be so restrictive; we can take any contiguous piece of the analysis tree, and unify together the rules inside it to form a new rule. This observation remains just as valid for DCGs and feature grammars.

In general, what we will do is to cut the derivation tree into pieces, and derive a rule from each piece. Figure 101 shows an example of this strategy, using the feature grammar from Version 3: we cut the tree up into three subtrees, and extract a rule from each one by combining the rules in that subtree. We cut at the NP nodes, and also make explicit the fact that we are excluding the lexical rules at the bottom of the tree.

Thus, subtree 1 gives a rule with an s on the left-hand side and nps on the right, while subtrees 2 and 3 produce rules for np. Since the tree is so small, one of the subtrees (subtree 2) actually only contains one rule, and it follows that the rule derived from this subtree is one of the rules in the original grammar.

Grammar fragment

(Same as in Figure 100)

Training example

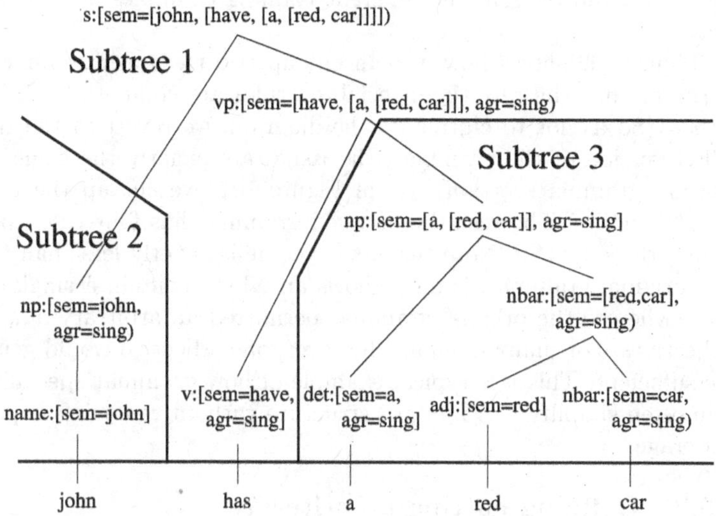

Derived rules

Rule derived from Subtree 1:

```
s:[sem=[NP1, [V, NP2]]] -->
   np:[sem=NP1, agr=Agr],
   v:[sem=V, agr=Agr],
   np:[sem=NP2]
```

Rule derived from Subtree 2:

```
np:[sem=NAME, agr=sing] -->
   name:[sem=NAME].
```

Rule derived from Subtree 3:

```
np:[sem=[DET, [ADJ, NBAR]], agr=Agr] -->
   det:[sem=DET, agr=Agr],
   adj:[sem=ADJ],
   nbar:[sem=NBAR, agr=Agr].
```

FIGURE 101 EBL on feature grammar, cutting up tree to derive several different rules. Note that the rule derived from Subtree 2 is one of the rules in the original unspecialised grammar.

10.1.5 Version 5: multiple training examples

We have so far only considered how to extract rules from a single training example. In general, of course, we will have a whole corpus of training examples. If we want to extract a useful derived grammar, we need to cut up the trees in the different training examples in a consistent way.

Figure 102 shows how we can cut up two trees using uniform criteria, so that the resulting specialised rules are compatible with each other. (So as not to clutter up the diagram, we revert to the simpler CFG version of the grammar; the issues are exactly the same in the feature grammar version). As in Figure 101, we cut up the trees at the NP nodes. The resulting derived grammar has four rules, one for S and three for NP. Note that its coverage is strictly less than that of the original grammar; it only allows an NP to contain a single adjective, whereas the original grammar permitted an arbitrary number of adjectives. For many domains, however, one adjective would generally be sufficient. This is a typical example of how grammar specialisation can often simplify a grammar's structure without removing important coverage.

10.2 Defining cutting-up criteria

As we saw in Section 10.1, the way in which we cut up the analysis trees determines the form of the specialised grammar. In this section, we will describe the formalism used in Regulus to specify cutting-up criteria. In Section 10.3, we will consider different ways to cut up analysis trees produced by the general grammar for English described in Chapter 9.

The `ebl_operationality` file (cf. page 152) contains declarations which specify how example trees from the "treebank" file are to be cut up into smaller trees, which are then flattened into specialised rules. The basic idea is to traverse the tree in a downward direction, starting with the root node: throughout the traversal process, the system maintains a value called the "context", which by default remains the same when moving downwards over a node. Each node is labelled with the associated category. Operationality declarations can do one of two things. Usually they will cut the tree, starting a new rule and simultaneously changing the value of the context. Occasionally, they will just change the value of the context without cutting the tree.

Operationality rules of both types syntactically have the form of Prolog rules. They are respectively of the forms

```
change_rule_and_context(<InContext>, <OutContext>) :-
        <Conditions>
```

Grammar fragment

(Same as in Figure 98)

Training example

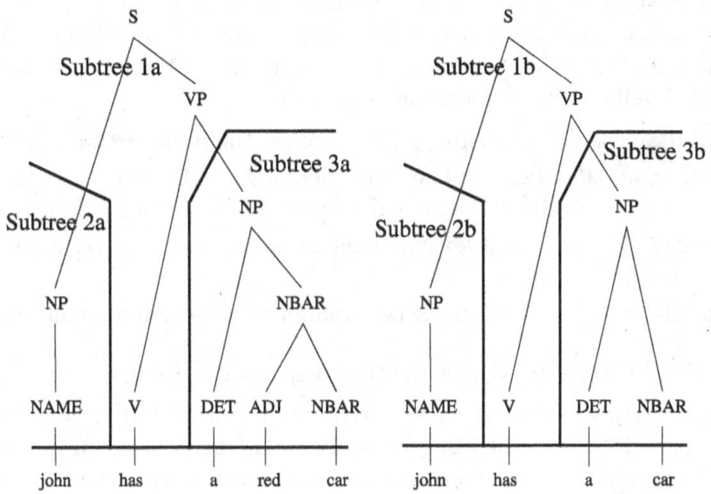

Derived rules

Rule derived from Subtrees 1a and 1b:

```
S --> NP V NP
```

Rule derived from Subtrees 2a and 2b:

```
NP --> NAME
```

Rule derived from Subtree 3a:

```
NP --> DET ADJ NBAR
```

Rule derived from Subtree 3b:

```
NP --> DET NBAR
```

FIGURE 102 EBL on CFG grammar, cutting up two trees in compatible ways. Subtrees 1a and 1b produce the same rule, as do 2a and 2b.

```
change_context(<InContext>, <OutContext>) :-
      <Conditions>
```

where <InContext>, <OutContext> are respectively the old and new values of the context, and <Conditions> is a set of conditions on the node.

The <Conditions> have the form of the body of a Prolog rule, and can include the usual Prolog logical connectors: conjunction (","), disjunction (";") and negation ("\+"). Four different primitives are currently available for constraining the node:

cat(<CatName>) The category symbol for the node is <CatName>.

dominates(<CatName>) The node dominates (directly or indirectly) another node whose category symbol is <CatName>.

lexical The node is a lexical node, i.e. dominates only terminal symbols.

gap The node has null yield, i.e. dominates no terminal symbols.

10.3 Different kinds of cutting-up criteria

This section will describe how to write sets of cutting-up criteria, using the formalism described in Section 10.2. The basic tradeoff is between coverage and efficiency: cutting the analysis trees into smaller pieces makes the grammar more general and flexible, but less efficient and more challenging to compile into CFG form. We will look at several different versions, based on different cutting-up criteria.

10.3.1 Version 1: flat specialised grammar

The simplest way to structure the specialised grammar is the one we have already seen several times in Section 10.1, for example in Figure 100; we combine all the non-lexical rules in each tree, producing a completely "flat" grammar with only one non-pre-terminal category. The cutting-up criteria are correspondingly simple, and consist of the two rules in Figure 103. We cut the tree at the utterance node at the

```
change_rule_and_context(_Context, utterance) :-
    cat(utterance).

change_rule_and_context(_Context, lexical) :-
    lexical.
```

FIGURE 103 Operationality definitions file for flat grammar

```
% Start new rule at UTTERANCE
change_rule_and_context(_Context , utterance) :-
    cat(utterance),
    \+ gap.

% Start new rule at NP if under UTTERANCE
change_rule_and_context(utterance , np) :-
    cat(np),
    \+ gap.

% Start new rule at lexical node
change_rule_and_context(_Context , lexical) :-
    lexical.
```

FIGURE 104 Operationality definitions file for two-level grammar

top (the first rule), and at all lexical nodes at the bottom (the second rule). We have no need for the "context" variable, so we leave it uninstantiated in both rules.

10.3.2 Version 2: two level grammar

Next, we show how to produce a two-level grammar of the kind shown in Figure 101; we have `utterance` and `np` constituents, with the `np` nodes coming between the `utterance` node at the top and the lexical nodes at the bottom. An operationality definitions file for a two-level grammar of this type is shown in Figure 104.

Note that, in this set of operationality definitions, we need to use the grammar specialisation context. Since NPs can potentially contain NPs (cf. Section 9.5), without the context we would create recursive NP rules, which is not our intention here. As it is, we only cut at an NP node if the context is `utterance`, after which we change the context to `np`. This blocks cutting at lower `np` nodes.

10.3.3 Version 3: generalising over modifiers

Versions 1 and 2 produced very simple specialised grammars. We now show how to produce a complex specialised grammar, which generalises over the modifiers defined in the general English grammar from Chapter 9. Figure 105 illustrates schematically how we will cut up a typical tree; the cutting-up rules themselves are shown in Figure 106.

Looking from left to right in Figure 105, we first see at the bottom left-hand corner that we cut at the `vbar` constituent (cf. Section 9.6.2) to enable us to generalise over adverbial modification of verbs. More importantly, we add structure to the np constituents in the specialised grammar. As shown in the figure, an np can now dominate both a post_mods constituent and an inner np.

We consequently learn two sets of np rules, distinguished by whether or not they dominate a post_mods constituent; we differentiate them by using the grammar specialisation context, setting the context to np for an np that dominates a post_mods constituent, and to simple_np for one which doesn't. This is why rules for cutting at np nodes come in pairs. For example, the two rules

```
change_rule_and_context(utterance, np) :-
        cat(np), \+ gap, dominates(post_mods).
change_rule_and_context(utterance, simple_np) :-
        cat(np), \+ gap, \+ dominates(post_mods).
```

say that if the context is utterance (we are under an utterance node in the specialised grammar), and we have now reached an np node, we will cut to form a new constituent, changing the context to np if the current node dominates a post_mods constituent (first rule), and simple_np if it doesn't (second rule).

Most of the cutting-up rules require that the constituent where the cut is to be made has to be non-empty[26]; this is the import of the condition \+ gap which appears in the majority of the rules. It is convenient, however, to allow null post_mods constituents in the specialised grammar. (The null post_mods constituents have been omitted from Figure 105 to save space). Cutting at null post_mods constituents allows us to generalise over clauses containing empty and non-empty post_mods.

We still need to explain the change_context rules that appear at the bottom of Figure 106. These arise from a subtle technical problem. In a training example which involves WH-movement of an NP (cf. Section 9.6.3), we can descend through a null np node, and find a null post_mods daughter; we don't, however want to extract a rule at this point. We consequently need to distinguish the empty NP context from the normal NP context, to block application of the rule

```
change_rule_and_context(np, post_mods) :-
        cat(post_mods).
```

This is precisely the function of the change_context rules.

[26]Note that there is no such restriction on the dominates construction; a constituent is regarded as "dominated" irrespective of whether or not it is empty.

Grammar

General English grammar

Training example in schematic form

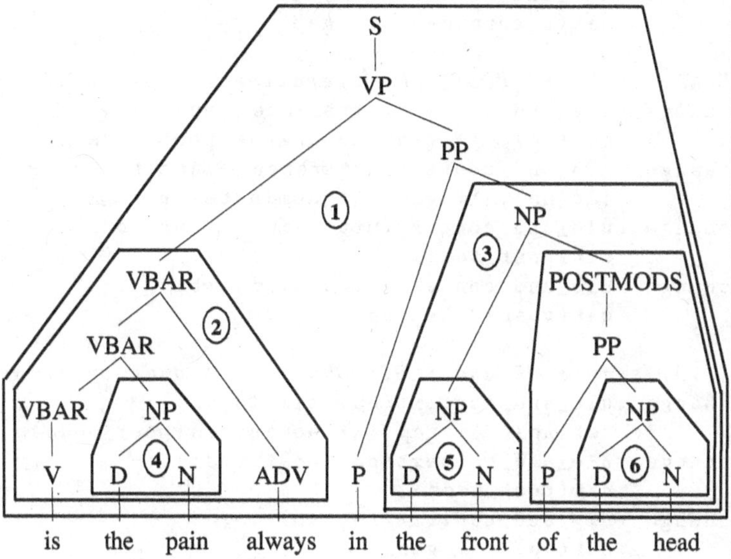

Derived rules

Rule derived from Subtree 1:

```
S --> VBAR P NP
```

Rule derived from Subtree 2:

```
VBAR --> V NP ADV
```

Rule derived from Subtree 3:

```
NP --> NP POSTMODS
```

Rule derived from Subtrees 4, 5 and 6:

```
NP --> D N
```

FIGURE 105 EBL on general English grammar, using cutting-up criteria in which subtrees from VBAR and POSTMODS constituents are turned into rules. The empty POSTMODS constituents in the tree have been omitted to simplify the diagram.

```
% TOP rule highest, UTTERANCE operational under it
change_rule_and_context(_Context, top) :-
        cat(top), \+ gap.
change_rule_and_context(top, utterance) :-
        cat(utterance), \+ gap.

% NP, VBAR and POST_MODS operational under UTTERANCE
change_rule_and_context(utterance, np) :-
        cat(np), \+ gap, dominates(post_mods).
change_rule_and_context(utterance, simple_np) :-
        cat(np), \+ gap, \+ dominates(post_mods).
change_rule_and_context(utterance, post_mods) :-
        cat(post_mods).
change_rule_and_context(utterance, vbar) :-
        cat(vbar), \+ gap.

% VP, simple NP and POST_MODS operational under NP
change_rule_and_context(np, simple_np) :-
        cat(np), \+ gap, \+ dominates(post_mods).
change_rule_and_context(np, post_mods) :-
        cat(post_mods).
change_rule_and_context(np, vp) :-
        cat(vp), \+ gap.

% NP operational under POST_MODS, VBAR and VP
change_rule_and_context(post_mods, np) :-
        cat(np), \+ gap, dominates(post_mods).
change_rule_and_context(post_mods, simple_np) :-
        cat(np), \+ gap, \+ dominates(post_mods).

change_rule_and_context(vbar, np) :-
        cat(np), \+ gap, dominates(post_mods).
change_rule_and_context(vbar, simple_np) :-
        cat(np), \+ gap, \+ dominates(post_mods).

change_rule_and_context(vp, np) :-
        cat(np), \+ gap, dominates(post_mods).
change_rule_and_context(vp, simple_np) :-
        cat(np), \+ gap, \+ dominates(post_mods).

% Lexical goals operational anywhere
change_rule_and_context(_Anything, lexical) :-
        lexical.

% Treat gap NPs specially
change_context(utterance, gap_np) :- cat(np), gap.
change_context(vp, gap_np) :- cat(np), gap.
```

FIGURE 106 Operationality definitions file for complex specialised grammar

10.3.4 Version 4: specialised grammars with larger lexical items

In Version 3 of the specialised grammar, the structure of a typical NP is as shown in Figure 105. Looking at the right hand side of the parse tree, we see the `np` "the front of the head" consists of two constituents: an inner `np`, "the front", and a `post_mods`, "of the head". The inner `np` consists of a `d`, "the", and an `n`, "front".

Usually, this is the structure we want. Depending on the nature of the domain, however, it may also be advantageous to extract a slightly different version of the grammar, where the inner `nps` are lexical items. Figure 107 shows a revised version of the tree from Figure 105, which has been cut up in this way. This time, the specialised grammar contains no rule of the form

```
NP --> D N
```

Instead, it contains three lexical rules of the form

```
NP --> the pain
NP --> the front
NP --> the head
```

A grammar of this kind will be appropriate if there is very little variation in the forms of inner NPs, and in particular in the choice of article that accompanies a given noun. If the grammar is used for recognition, the additional constraints may increase accuracy. We have also found that grammars of this kind are often suitable for generation; the issues involved are discussed in more detail in Section 6.2.2.

10.4 Summary

- Grammar specialisation in Regulus is performed using the Explanation Based Learning (EBL) method. EBL is a macro-rule learning method, which uses examples to combine old rules into new ones.
- The coverage of a specialised grammar is always a strict subset of the coverage of the original general grammar. The advantage is that since the specialised grammar is more constrained, processing is usually more efficient.
- Training examples for EBL, as used in Regulus, are parse trees.
- To perform EBL rule extraction on a training example, we first decompose the parse tree into a number of contiguous pieces. We extract a specialised rule from each piece by sticking together the original grammar rules in that piece.
- The rules which determine how the parse-trees are to be decomposed are called "cutting-up criteria" (alternately, "operationality

Grammar

General English grammar

Training example in schematic form

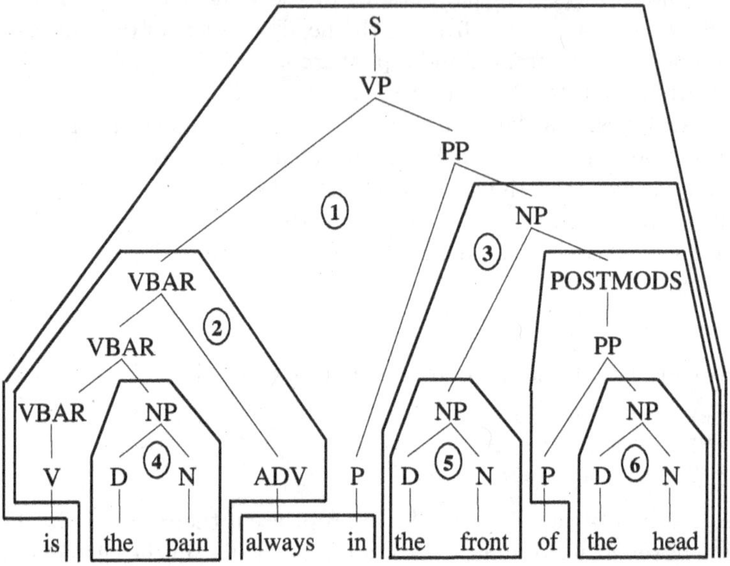

Derived rules

Rule derived from Subtree 1:

```
S --> VBAR P NP
```

Rule derived from Subtree 2:

```
VBAR --> V NP ADV
```

Rule derived from Subtree 3:

```
NP --> NP POSTMODS
```

Rule derived from Subtree 4:

```
NP --> the pain
```

Rule derived from Subtree 5:

```
NP --> the front
```

Rule derived from Subtree 6:

```
NP --> the head
```

FIGURE 107 EBL on general English grammar, using cutting-up criteria in which simple NPs become lexical rules.

criteria"). Regulus provides a simple language for defining cutting-up criteria.

- The process of cutting up the parse tree operates by descending through the tree, maintaining a context variable and deciding at each node whether or not to cut. The cutting-up criteria language make the decision to cut conditional on properties of the subtree rooted in the current node.
- Complex cutting-up criteria make it possible to define specialised grammars that generalise over modifiers, and which can contain null productions.

Exercises

1. Extract a flat specialised grammar from the Toy1Specialised grammar in Chapter 7.
2. Extract a two-level specialised grammar from the Toy1Specialised grammar.
3. Extract a complex specialised grammar from the Toy1Specialised grammar, using the cutting-up criteria defined in Figure 106.
4. Experiment with the three specialised grammars you have produced. Compare their coverage.
5. Compile the three specialised grammars you have produced into speech recognisers. Compare their performance.
6. Define and test a new set of cutting-up criteria.

11

Performance of grammar-based recognisers

Manny Rayner, Beth Ann Hockey and Pierrette Bouillon

11.1 Introduction

In the previous chapter, we saw that one of the main advantages of Regulus is the ability to derive several different types of specialised recogniser from a single general grammar. We will now quantitatively investigate how the performance of a family of specialised recognisers varies, as we vary different parameters that affect the form of the specialised grammar. We will carry out several different versions of this experiment. Section 11.2 uses different sizes of vocabulary; Section 11.3, different amounts of coverage; Section 11.4 manipulates the grammar by systematically suppressing sets of features inherited from the general grammar; and Section 11.5 contrasts different cutting-up criteria. In the last two sections, we investigate a couple of related issues that arise naturally in the course of the chapter. Section 11.6 describes experiments which measure the impact of performing probabilistic training on the language model, in other words transforming it from a CFG into a PCFG. Section 11.7 looks at recognisers derived directly from the general grammar, that is without performing grammar specialisation.

All the experiments were carried out using the headache subdomain grammar for the MedSLT application (cf. Section 1.4.2). The baseline grammar was created using the cutting-up criteria defined in Section 10.3.3, with a training set of 650 utterances. The training set was then used a second time to perform PCFG training. Finally, the resulting recogniser was tested on the set of 801 American-dialect MedSLT utterances recorded during the two data collections described in (Rayner et al., 2004) and (Rayner et al., 2005a). Each of the variant recognisers was trained and tested in a similar manner. Since performance is very different on in-coverage and out-of-coverage utterances, we present seperate figures for each subset. Viterbi beam width (the Nuance feature `rec.Pruning`) is set uniformly to 1200, which for most of the recognisers is close to the point at which performance tops out with increasing beam-width.

In each case, we measure the coverage of the different derived grammars on a uniform test set, and the performance of the associated recognisers. Performance is evaluated using three parameters: Word Error Rate (WER), Sentence Error Rate (SER) and Semantic Error Rate (SemER). To make SemER relevant to the MedSLT speech translation task, we say that recognition has assigned a correct semantic representation R to an English utterance U if and only if the result of translating R into an interlingual representation and then back into English ("back-translation") results in a paraphrase of U acceptable in the context of the task. This implies that several types of recognition errors, in particular confusions between singular and plural, will usually be considered semantically acceptable; in the context of the task, there is for example no difference between "does **the headache** usually last for more than an hour" and "do **the headaches** usually last for more than an hour", since both versions produce the same interlingual representation and are thus translated uniformly.

We evaluate the significance of differences between two different versions of the recogniser for both the SER and SemER metrics, using the McNemar test. We will report significance as being one out of "not significant", "$p < 0.05$", "$p < 0.01$" or "$p < 0.001$".

11.2 Varying vocabulary size

In our first set of experiments, we create the variant recognisers by increasing the size of the lexicon, keeping the grammar rules, features and cutting-up criteria constant. We derive the new lexicon entries from the Medical Subject Headings thesaurus,[27] a controlled vocabulary produced by the National Library of Medicine which is used for indexing, cataloging, and searching for biomedical and health-related information and documents. We used 3868 thesaurus entries, belonging to four different semantic classes potentially relevant to the MedSLT task:

- 829 body part nouns ("myenteric plexus", "optic nerve", "shoulder joint");

[27] `http://www.nlm.nih.gov/mesh/introduction2005.html`

Version	Lex	Vocab
0	0	429
1	374	946
2	755	1392
3	1079	1742
4	1469	2096
5	1817	2394
6	2204	2698
7	2569	2969
8	2956	3266
9	3351	3538
10	3701	3788

TABLE 13 Different versions of the MedSLT recogniser, built by adding extra vocabulary to the baseline recogniser. For each version, we list the number of extra lexical entries added (Lex), and the total number of surface words in the vocabulary (Vocab).

- 1899 symptom nouns ("adenomatous polyps", "fungal meningitis", "laryngeal granuloma");
- 323 names of drugs ("copaxone", "pravachol", "rocephin");
- 817 therapy nouns ("ambulatory electrocardiography", "pancreatic function tests", "reticulocyte count")

We built 10 different versions of the lexicon by successively adding larger subsets of the lexical entries from the thesaurus, in randomly chosen increments of about 10% at a time. On average, this amounted to about 370 new entries for each version. Since thesaurus entries are often multi-word phrases, the surface vocabulary initially increases between versions by more than the number of new lexical entries added. Table 13 summarises the new information added for each version of the grammar, Table 14 the performance of the resulting recognisers, and Table 15 the significance results.

None of the extra vocabulary added to the variant versions appeared in the test material, so we expected that performance would gradually degrade as the vocabulary size increased; the search space becomes larger, but the only possibilities added are irrelevant ones. This is indeed what happened, though the rate of decline was fairly slow. For Version 1, vocabulary has increased from 429 to 946, a factor of 2.2; SemER increases from 7.6% to 8.3% (9% relative to the baseline). At Version 4, vocabulary has increased to 2096, a factor of 2.2 relative to Version 1; this time, SemER increases to 9.3% (12% relative to Version 1).

Version	In coverage			Out of coverage		
	WER	SER	SemER	WER	SER	SemER
(Baseline)	4.9%	15.9%	7.6%	50.4%	96.6%	77.8%
Version 1	5.3%	16.2%	8.3%	53.1%	95.5%	80.1%
Version 2	5.2%	16.2%	8.5%	52.6%	95.5%	80.5%
Version 3	5.6%	16.9%	9.0%	52.9%	95.5%	80.5%
Version 4	5.8%	17.1%	9.3%	53.7%	95.5%	80.5%
Version 5	5.9%	17.2%	9.5%	54.2%	95.9%	80.5%
Version 6	6.0%	17.2%	9.4%	53.5%	95.9%	80.5%
Version 7	6.2%	17.6%	10.0%	53.7%	95.9%	81.0%
Version 8	6.0%	17.6%	9.8%	54.0%	95.9%	81.4%
Version 9	6.6%	18.5%	10.9%	54.6%	95.5%	81.9%
Version 10	6.5%	18.3%	11.0%	54.2%	95.5%	81.9%

TABLE 14 Word, Sentence and Semantic error rates for versions of the MedSLT recogniser built adding different numbers of extra lexical entries, on in-coverage and out-of-coverage data.

First	Second	SER		SemER	
		Score	Significance	Score	Significance
Baseline	Version 1	4–2	Not signif.	6–0	$P < 0.05$
Baseline	Version 2	6–4	Not signif.	9–2	$P < 0.05$
Baseline	Version 3	8–2	Not signif.	9–0	$P < 0.01$
Baseline	Version 4	10–3	Not signif.	13–1	$P < 0.01$
Baseline	Version 5	11–3	$P < 0.05$	13–0	$P < 0.001$
Baseline	Version 6	11–3	$P < 0.05$	13–0	$P < 0.001$
Baseline	Version 7	13–3	$P < 0.05$	15–0	$P < 0.001$
Baseline	Version 8	13–3	$P < 0.05$	15–0	$P < 0.001$
Baseline	Version 9	19–4	$P < 0.01$	22–0	$P < 0.001$
Baseline	Version 10	18–4	$P < 0.01$	22–0	$P < 0.001$

TABLE 15 Significance of differences in SER and SemER on in-coverage data between the baseline MedSLT recogniser and variant versions produced by adding extra vocabulary.

By the time we reached Version 10, vocabulary is 3788, a factor of 1.8 compared to Version 4, while SemER increases to 11.0% (18% relative).

In general, we can say that a doubling of vocabulary results in a degradation in task performance by about 1–2% absolute, or 10–20% relative. All versions were significantly worse than the baseline on the SemER metric. The smaller number of significant differences on the strict SER metric is due to recognition errors involving articles; these are essentially a source of noise, which is filtered out by the SemER metric.

11.3 Varying linguistic coverage

The second set of experiments investigated the effect of changing the coverage; starting with the baseline grammar, we created different versions which successively removed coverage of various constructions. As we made the grammar smaller, we measured the change in recognition performance on in-coverage material. We expected to find that, as the grammar's coverage shrank, performance *on the material still in coverage* improved[28]. We used six versions of the grammar, as follows:

Version 0 Baseline specialised grammar

Version 1 We remove the rules for subordinate clauses, ("is the pain better **when you lie down**?") and gerunds ("does **lying down** make the pain better?").

Version 2 As (1), but also remove rules for phrasal utterances, in particular lone NPs ("chocolate?") and lone PPs ("in the morning?").

Version 3 As (2), but also remove rules for passives ("is the pain **accompanied by nausea**?").

Version 4 As (3), but also remove rules for WH-questions, ("**where** is the pain?", "**how long** do the headaches last?")

Version 5 As (4), but also remove rules for adverbs, ("does bright light **usually** give you headaches?")

Version	Removed from previous version	In-C	Loss
	(Baseline)	(580)	(0)
1	Subordinate clauses and gerunds	537	7.4%
2	Phrasal utterances	510	12.1%
3	Passives	356	38.6%
4	WH-questions	345	40.5%
5	Adverbs	306	47.2%

TABLE 16 Coverage of versions of the baseline grammar, reduced by removing sets of rules. "In-C" measures the number of in-coverage sentence out of a total of 801; "Loss" measures the proportion of utterances for each grammar that are out of coverage for that grammar, but in coverage for the original baseline grammar.

[28]Performance over the whole dataset will however get worse, since a smaller portion of it will be within coverage.

We present the results in three tables; Table 16 tracks coverage, Table 17 recognition performance and Table 18 significance. In order to be able to make clear comparisons, all the performance figures are evaluated on the material that is within the coverage of Version 5, the most restricted grammar, and hence within the coverage of all the other grammars too[29].

	WER	SER	SemER
Baseline	6.0%	18.3%	10.5%
Version 1	6.1%	18.6%	10.5%
Version 2	5.4%	17.7%	9.2%
Version 3	5.3%	17.7%	8.5%
Version 4	5.0%	17.3%	8.2%
Version 5	5.0%	17.3%	8.2%

TABLE 17 Word, Sentence and Semantic error rates for versions of the MedSLT recogniser, derived from the different grammars in Table 16, on the set of 306 utterances that are in-coverage for Version 5.

First	Second	SER		SemER	
		Score	Significance	Score	Significance
Baseline	Version 1	2–1	Not signif.	1–1	Not signif.
Baseline	Version 2	4–6	Not signif.	2–6	Not signif.
Baseline	Version 3	3–5	Not signif.	2–8	Not signif.
Baseline	Version 4	3–6	Not signif.	1–8	$P < 0.05$
Baseline	Version 5	6–9	Not signif.	1–8	$P < 0.05$
Version 5	Baseline	9–6	Not signif.	8–1	$P < 0.05$
Version 5	Version 1	9–5	Not signif.	8–1	$P < 0.05$
Version 5	Version 2	6–5	Not signif.	4–1	Not signif.
Version 5	Version 3	6–5	Not signif.	2–1	Not signif.
Version 5	Version 4	5–5	Not signif.	4–1	Not signif.

TABLE 18 Significance of differences between versions of the MedSLT recogniser, derived from the different grammars in Table 16, on the set of 306 utterances that are in-coverage for Version 5.

[29]Note that recognition performance of the baseline version on the subset of the data that is within coverage of Version 5 is somewhat worse than its performance on the whole set. This is due to the fact that utterances within the coverage of the smaller grammar are more challenging than average.

Table 16 shows that all the groups of deleted rules are relevant to the domain; as each group is removed, coverage drops substantially. The largest drop occurs between Versions 2 and 3: removing passive constructions reduces relative coverage by 26.5%, reflecting the importance in the medical query domain of words like "caused", "relieved", "aggravated" and "preceded". The smallest drop (1.9%) is between Versions 3 and 4, where WH-questions are removed.

Table 17 is most naturally read from bottom to top. In this direction, we conceptualise it as starting with the most restricted grammar, and then successively adding coverage; the table measures how recognition performance degrades on the original coverage as the new rules are added. The largest drop occurs between Versions 2 and 1 (addition of rules for phrasal utterances), where WER increases from 5.4% to 6.1% (13% relative), and SemER from 9.2% to 10.5% (14% relative). Over the whole set, WER increases from 5.0% to 6.0% (16% relative), and SemER from 8.2% to 10.5% (28% relative). Scalability with respect to coverage extensions was quite good; on the SemER metric, the McNemar test showed that the addition of no individual construction resulted in a significant degradation in recognition performance, though the composition of several additions was significant. None of the versions displayed significant differences against the baseline on the SER metric.

Our overall conclusion is that specialised grammars are fairly robust to small increases in grammar coverage. Adding any particular piece of new coverage has little effect on recognition performance; it is only the cumulative effect of multiple coverage extensions that will in general result in significant degradation. This contrasts sharply with the behaviour of recognisers derived from general linguistically motivated grammars, where small tweaks to the rule-set can result in dramatic changes to recognition performance (Rayner et al., 2000c).

11.4 Varying the feature set

The next set of experiments investigated the effect on recognition performance of global constraints encoded in the general grammar's feature set, and inherited by the specialised grammars. This time, we created the variant grammars by suppressing groups of related features; as we remove features and their associated constraints, the language models become looser, and we expect recognition to become less accurate. We created four variant grammars, as follows:

No sortal features Suppress the sortal features (cf. Section 9.3.1) on nouns, verbs and adjective. With these features removed, the grammar would for example permit "does the pain spread to the **coffee**" or "do you get headaches when you drink **neck**".

No agreement features Suppress the agreement features (cf. Section 9.6) on nouns, verbs and DETs. Without these features, the grammar permits examples like "**are** the pain frontal" or "**does** you get headaches in the morning".

No PP features Suppress the features on nouns, verbs and prepositions that control PP modifications (cf. Section 9.7). Without them, we get examples like "does the pain last **in the head**" or "does the pain occur **for more than ten minutes**".

No DET features Suppress the features that restrict cooccurrence of nouns and DETs (cf. Section 9.5.1). Without these features, we can for example get "**a head**" or "**the minutes**".

Table 19 shows performance results. It is interesting to see that the WER, SER and SemER metrics once again paint very different pictures. In terms of WER on the in-coverage data, removing the sortal features produces the largest degradation in performance (4.9% to 6.7%; 37% relative), fairly closely followed by removing the agreement features (4.9% to 6.2%; 27% relative). In terms of SER, the largest difference in performance results from removing the agreement features (15.9% to 23.3%; 47% relative), ahead of the sortal features (15.9% to 19.8%; 25% relative). With the SemER metric, removing the sortal features results in a huge difference (7.6% versus 14.2%; 87% relative), but removing the agreement features makes no difference at all; the second largest difference arises from removing the PP features (7.6% versus 8.8%; 16% relative).

	In coverage			Out of coverage		
	WER	SER	SemER	WER	SER	SemER
No sortal	6.7%	19.8%	14.2%	48.6%	96.3%	84.7%
No agreement	6.2%	23.3%	7.6%	50.9%	96.8%	77.8%
No DET	5.7%	20.8%	8.1%	50.4%	96.4%	78.1%
No PP	5.3%	17.0%	8.8%	50.4%	96.6%	83.6%
(Baseline)	4.9%	15.9%	7.6%	49.7%	96.4%	77.8%

TABLE 19 Word, Sentence and Semantic error rates for versions of the MedSLT recogniser formed by removing features from the grammar, on in-coverage and out-of-coverage data.

Table 20 shows the results of using the McNemar test to compare the baseline recogniser with the four variants on in-coverage data. In terms

First	Second	SER		SemER	
		Score	Significance	Score	Significance
Baseline	No agr	52–9	$P < 0.001$	6–6	Not signif.
Baseline	No DET	29–2	$P < 0.001$	5–3	Not signif.
Baseline	No PP	12–6	Not signif.	9–3	Not signif.
Baseline	No sortal	32–10	$P < 0.001$	38–3	$P < 0.001$

TABLE 20 Significance of differences between the baseline MedSLT recogniser and four versions produced by removing features from the grammar, measured on in-coverage data. "Score" shows the number of items in each direction for which one version was right, and the other wrong.

of the strict SER metric, the differences for "no agreement", "no DET" and "no sortal" are all significant at $P < 0.001$. This is consistent with the findings of Rayner et al. (2001b), which reported small but statistically significant differences in recognition performance when agreement constraints were removed from three different grammar-based recognisers. In contrast, only the "no sortal" version displays a significant difference in performance when we evaluate using the task-based SemER metric.

The fact that we get widely differing results from the various metrics should not be surprising; WER often correlates badly with task error rate (Wang et al., 2003). In this case, the nature of the task means that singular/plural distinctions are usually irrelevant to the semantic representation. Although including agreement constraints makes a substantial difference to the surface measures, this does not translate into corresponding semantic differences. It is not clear to us that either metric can be regarded as a "true" performance measure. Singular/plural distinctions happen to be irrelevant to the MedSLT task, but there are certainly other tasks where they would be important.

11.5 Varying the cutting-up criteria

In the fourth set of experiments, we compare the effect of using different cutting-up criteria (cf. Chapter 10) to build the specialised grammar. The basic parameter we will vary is the "flatness" of the specialised grammar; we start with a completely flat grammar, and introduce successive levels of complexity. As the grammars become more complex, they become looser. As in Section 11.3, we expected that this would result in the derived recognisers offering less accurate performance on the material that they covered. The compensation is that coverage increases, since the more complex grammars are also more flexible.

Specifically, we used the following cutting-up criteria, all taken from Section 10.3:

Flat The specialised grammar is completely flat. The cutting-up criteria are defined in Section 10.3.1.

Two-level The specialised grammar contains two levels, for `utterance` and `np` constituents. The cutting-up criteria are defined in Section 10.3.2.

Recursive 1 A simplified version of the specialised grammar produced by the cutting-up criteria defined in Section 10.3.3. The grammar contains the three possible non-pre-terminals `utterance`, `np` and `post_mods`. The grammar is potentially recursive, since `post_mods` can be a constituent under `np`, and `np` can be a constituent under `post_mods`.

Baseline The specialised grammar produced by the cutting-up criteria defined in Section 10.3.3. This grammar is used for the baseline recogniser used for all the experiments in this chapter.

Version	In-C	Loss
Flat	412	31.7%
Two-level	553	8.4%
Recursive 1	577	4.5%
Baseline	580	3.9%
(General)	604	(0)

TABLE 21 Coverage of grammars built using different cutting-up criteria. "In-C" measures the number of in-coverage sentence out of a total of 801; "Loss" measures the proportion of utterances for each grammar that are out of coverage for that grammar, but in coverage for the general grammar.

	In coverage			Out of coverage		
	WER	SER	SemER	WER	SER	SemER
Flat	4.0%	13.8%	5.8%	49.9%	98.5%	72.2%
Two-level	4.1%	15.2%	6.0%	52.4%	97.2%	78.6%
Recursive 1	4.4%	15.3%	6.6%	50.6%	96.4%	77.7%
Baseline	4.9%	15.9%	7.6%	50.4%	96.6%	77.8%

TABLE 22 Word, Sentence and Semantic error rates for versions of the MedSLT recogniser built using different cutting-up criteria, on in-coverage and out-of-coverage data.

First	Second	SER		SemER	
		Score	Significance	Score	Significance
Two-level	Flat	17–15	Not signif.	6–3	Not signif.
Rec. 1	Two-level	3–3	Not signif.	0–2	Not signif.
Baseline	Rec. 1	4–8	Not signif.	2–7	Not signif.

TABLE 23 Significance of differences between different versions of the MedSLT recogniser produced by varying the cutting-up criteria, measured on in-coverage data only.

First	Second	SER		SemER	
		Score	Significance	Score	Significance
Two-level	Flat	130–15	$P < 0.001$	87–10	$P < 0.001$
Rec. 1	Two-level	24–3	$P < 0.001$	22–6	$P < 0.01$
Baseline	Rec. 1	7–8	Not signif.	5–9	Not signif.

TABLE 24 Significance of differences between different versions of the MedSLT recogniser produced by varying the cutting-up criteria, measured on all data.

Table 21 shows the coverage of the four different specialised grammars on the 801 utterance test set, and Table 22 shows recognition performance. Tables 23 and 24 give the significance results. Table 23 compares performance on in-coverage data only, and thus ignores effects due to gain or loss of coverage; Table 24 compares performance on all the data.

The general grammar covers 604 utterances. As we would expect, the Flat grammar loses a great deal of coverage (31.7%) since it has no ability to generalise; it has however the best recognition performance on the material it does cover, with WER at 4.0% and Sem at 5.8%.

Moving to the Two-level grammar reduces the relative coverage loss from 31.7% to only 8.4%, at the cost of an insignificant degradation in WER (4.0% to 4.1%) and SemER (5.8% to 6.0%). This is clearly a large win, as we can see from the first line of Table 24.

As we move to the more complex sets of cutting-up criteria, the two effects come more closely into balance. Moving from Two-level to Recursive 1 reduces the relative coverage loss from 8.4% to 4.5%, while WER increases from 4.1% to 4.4%, and SemER from 6.0% to 6.6%. This is still a significant improvement on both evaluation criteria (second line of Table 24), but the gain is much smaller than the one we saw when moving from Flat to Two-level.

The final transition, from Recursive 1 to Baseline roughly marks the point where the process of enriching the specialised grammar tops out. The relative coverage loss still decreases, but only from 4.5% to 3.9%. This is counterbalanced by an increase in WER from 4.4% to 4.9%, and in SemER from 6.6% to 7.6%. All the test data was produced by naive users, and for these subjects moving from Recursive 1 to Baseline is in fact a backwards step; the loss in recognition performance is slightly worse than the gain in coverage. The third line of Table 24 shows no significant difference on either the "strict" or the "task" metric. For expert users, anecdotal evidence suggests that the Baseline version is somewhat better, with the increased flexibility of the recogniser appearing more important than the slight degradation in performance.

11.6 Comparing CFG and PCFG language models

All the recognisers that we have discussed so far in this chapter use PCFG language models. The training corpus is used twice; first for grammar specialisation, to produce a CFG language model, and then for PCFG training, using the Nuance `compute_grammar_probs` utility. Our final set of experiments evaluate the contribution made by PCFG tuning. We used the 11 grammars from Section 11.2, and built versions of the recognisers which omitted the PCFG tuning step, and instead compiled the recogniser directly from the CFG grammar produced by Regulus. We then evaluated the resulting recognisers in the same way as we did for the original PCFG versions in Table 14. The new results are shown in Table 25.

Although we have only a few hundred sentences of training data, it turns out that probabilistic tuning makes a huge difference to the recognition quality. Comparing Tables 14 and 25, we find that PCFG tuning on the baseline version reduces in-coverage WER from 8.9% to 4.9% (45% relative), and in-coverage Sem from 12.1% to 7.6% (37% relative). As we add more vocabulary, the difference becomes successively greater. By the time we reach Version 10 (vocabulary 3788 words), PCFG tuning reduces in-coverage WER from 14.5% to 6.5% (55% relative), and in-coverage Sem from 22.8% to 11.0% (52% relative).

These differences are so large that we felt we needed to make some effort to check that they were not in some way artefacts of the experimental setup. In particular, one possible explanation which occurred to us was that the fairly modest degradation in performance we observe in Table 14 might be due to probabilistic tuning in practice removing all the new lexical items added from the thesaurus, giving them such low probabilities that they are effectively eliminated from the language

Version	In coverage			Out of coverage		
	WER	SER	SemER	WER	SER	SemER
(Baseline)	8.9%	29.8%	12.1%	56.3%	96.4%	80.1%
Version 1	10.5%	31.0%	15.0%	59.5%	95.9%	83.3%
Version 2	11.3%	32.4%	16.2%	60.8%	95.9%	85.1%
Version 3	11.6%	32.4%	16.7%	61.0%	95.9%	84.6%
Version 4	12.4%	33.3%	17.8%	60.6%	95.9%	85.1%
Version 5	13.3%	33.8%	19.5%	61.4%	95.9%	85.5%
Version 6	13.9%	34.5%	20.0%	60.5%	95.9%	85.5%
Version 7	13.6%	35.0%	20.9%	61.0%	95.9%	85.5%
Version 8	14.2%	35.3%	21.7%	61.8%	95.9%	85.5%
Version 9	14.4%	36.0%	22.6%	62.3%	95.9%	86.0%
Version 10	14.5%	36.2%	22.8%	63.2%	95.9%	86.9%

TABLE 25 Results for versions of the recognisers in Table 14, built without inclusion of the PCFG tuning step.

model. Since we are testing on data exclusively from the coverage of the baseline grammar, this effect would not show up in the evaluation.

It is challenging to construct a good experimental protocol to test performance on the new vocabulary under normal conditions of system use, but an informal test was enough to satisfy us that the new vocabulary is genuinely available. We randomly selected 50 items from the thesaurus, and for each one constructed a test sentence using a suitable pattern: for example, a symptom word would get the pattern "do you have ⟨symptom⟩?", or a body part word would get "is the pain in the ⟨body_part⟩?". A subject then read out each example sentence to Version 10 of the recogniser; 44 of the utterances (88%) were correctly recognized. Although it is inappropriate to compare these results directly with the ones in Table 14 they certainly make it clear that the new vocabulary is not spurious. The overall conclusion is that, even with small amounts of training data, PCFG tuning produces a very substantial improvement in performance for this kind of recognition grammar.

11.7 Deriving recognisers from general grammars

All the experiments described so far in the chapter have also been performed on recognisers derived from specialised versions of the grammar. It is natural to wonder what performance we would get from a recogniser that was derived from the original *general* grammar. Unfortunately, we have so far not been able to compile the general grammar directly into recogniser form, since the compilation process exceeds resource bounds during the expansion phase (cf. Chapter 8).

It is however possible to compile the general grammar into CFG form if we ignore enough features; in particular, we can do it if we ignore both the "sortal" and the "PP" groups of features (cf. Section 11.4). The resulting Nuance grammar can then be compiled into a recogniser, but tests show that it is in practice completely useless. With a beam-width of 400, recognition speed is 15×RT, but the recogniser is still so inaccurate that it fails to recognise any of the utterances in the test set.

It is *a priori* conceivable that the main problem is the missing features, and that if we were able to enhance the compilation process in order to compile the full general grammar, including the sortal and PP features, we would produce interesting performance. The results presented earlier in this chapter, in particular in Section 11.4, however argue against this hypothesis. The PP features appear to make very little difference to performance of the specialised grammar, and although the contribution of the sortal features is significant, it does not appear to be remotely large enough to make the kind of difference that would be required here; it would be surprising if things were radically different for the general grammar. Other experiments we have carried out involving attempts to compile general grammars directly into recognisers (cf. in particular (Rayner et al., 2000c)) also suggest that the process is extremely fragile, and has poor scalability properties. Our overall conclusion is that grammar specialisation is an essential step, if we wish to derive useful recognisers from general linguistically motivated grammars.

11.8 Summary

- We have argued that meaningful comparisons can be carried out between grammar-based language models, if all the language models to be compared are derived in a well-defined manner from a single general grammar.
- We have described a case study where we applied the methodology to investigate variation in performance as we modified the baseline grammar along several different dimensions: vocabulary size (Section 11.2), coverage (Section 11.3), presence or absence of grammatical features (Section 11.4), structure of the specialised grammar (Section 11.5), and whether or not probabilistic training was used (Section 11.6).
- We evaluated with respect to word error, sentence error and semantic

error. We used the McNemar test to determine significance for both sentence error and semantic error.

- In agreement with the results of Wang et al. (2003), we found that task error often correlated very poorly with word error and sentence error; this was particularly striking in the experiments where we varied the grammar's feature set.
- As expected, all the language models performed enormously better on in-coverage than on out-of-coverage data. Somewhat more surprisingly, given the small amount of training data, probabilistic training of the CFG language models improved performance very substantially on all metrics.
- The structural factor which most affected performance was generality; flat grammars incurred a large coverage loss due to their lack of ability to generalise, but did not offer significantly better recognition performance on in-coverage material compared to the more complex versions.
- Sortal features, most of which distinguish semantically distinct types of nouns, also had a large impact on performance.
- Degradation in performance resulting from the addition of new grammatical constructions varied greatly depending on the nature of the construction, with elliptical phrases making the largest difference. Although the addition of no single new construction was significant on its own, the combined effect of adding several new constructions was significant.
- Other factors had a smaller effect. The grammars were fairly robust to addition of new vocabulary; the vocabulary size needed to be approximately doubled to produce a significant drop in task performance. On the semantic criterion, all groups of features except the sortal ones could be omitted without a significant effect, though the difference was significant in terms of strict sentence error.

Exercises

1. Create a version of the Toy1Specialised grammar and recogniser which ignores some features. Compare it with the baseline version.
2. Create a version of the Toy1Specialised grammar and recogniser which uses a different set of cutting-up criteria. Compare it with the baseline version.
3. Create a version of the Toy1Specialised grammar and recogniser which adds some more grammatical constructions. Compare it with the baseline version.

4. Create a version of the Toy1Specialised grammar and recogniser which adds some more vocabulary. Compare it with the baseline version.

12

Comparison of rule-based and robust approaches

Manny Rayner, Beth Ann Hockey, Pierrette Bouillon, Nikos Chatzichrisafis and Marianne Starlander

12.1 Introduction

The claim made in Chapter 1, that grammar-based language models produce superior speech recognition performance in controlled-language, user-initiative applications, is a critical motivation for the Regulus approach that is the topic of this book. Regulus reduces the effort required to produce grammar-based language models, but this is only interesting if grammar-based language modelling methods are competitive with standard data-driven approaches. In the current chapter, we present evidence that this is indeed the case for the type of application domains Regulus is designed for, in which the users are experienced, complete understanding of utterances is required, and there are only small amounts of training data available.

Currently, most spoken dialogue systems use some version of an architecture where speech recognition is carried out using a statistical language model (SLM), usually a class bigram or trigram model, and word-strings produced by the recogniser are converted into a semantic representation using some kind of phrase-spotting or robust parsing method. We will describe experiments, performed on the Regulus-based Clarissa and MedSLT systems (cf. Section 1.4), where we carried out a direct comparison of Regulus with a mainstream speech understanding architecture. In both cases, we constructed a plausible alternate version of the existing system using a class N-gram/robust approach, taking care to do this in a way that made the correspondence between the two versions as direct as possible; N-gram language models were built using the Nuance SayAnything© tool. We then compared performance with respect to WER, SER and semantic error rate.

In the rest of the chapter, we describe the methodological issues that arise when trying to set up a fair comparison of the two types of architecture (Section 12.2), the experiments carried out on each system (Sections 12.3 and 12.4), and the conclusions we can draw from this data (Section 12.5).

12.2 Methodological issues

It is easy to argue that grammar-based and data-driven approaches to speech recognition are too different for a comparison to be meaningful. Data-driven methods are trained from a well-defined corpus, while grammar-based ones rely on hard-to-specify linguistic intuitions. Recognisers built using N-gram language models usually only produce a recognition string, while grammar-based recognisers often give a direct semantic representation as well. If the comparison is to be at the level of semantic representations, this implies that the N-gram based recogniser also needs a robust parser, further complicating the picture. Finally, we may be asking the wrong question: perhaps the correct thing to do is not to compare performance of the two types of architecture, but rather to combine them in some suitable way.

We do not deny the validity of any of these objections, but at the end of the day it is often necessary to make a practical decision. If we have a limited amount of training data, and wish to construct a recogniser for a functioning system, we can base it on a standard class N-gram language model; alternately we consider using a different architecture, like Regulus. It is almost certainly impossible to produce a watertight experiment that will prove, beyond all reasonable doubt, that one method gives better results than the other. None the less, we will argue in the rest of this section that the methodological problems can be addressed convincingly enough for the outcome to shift the burden of proof to the other side. For the types of applications and evaluation metrics that are of practical interest to us, we obtain considerably better performance using Regulus than we do with data-driven methods. It is always conceivable that better data-driven methods could reverse this result, but the question is what evidence we have for believing this.

We will begin our detailed discussion of the methodological issues by summarising an earlier study (Knight et al., 2001), in which some of us were involved. Two speech understanding systems were constructed for the same domain, a medium-vocabulary command and control task, with both systems running on the Nuance 7 platform. The first had a hand-coded GLM, compiled using the standard Nuance Toolkit into a recognition package. The second system instead used a trigram language model, trained using the SRILM package (Stolcke, 2002) on a corpus of about 4000 domain utterances. A robust parser post-processed the word-strings produced by the trigram-based recogniser; it built semantic representations in the format used by the grammar-based system, so that an exact comparison was possible. The trigram/robust system had a slightly lower WER, but a considerably higher semantic error rate when evaluated on data provided by experienced users who knew the system's coverage. When evaluated on naive users who were encouraged to experiment with different constructions, the trigram/robust version comfortably outperformed the GLM one. Both systems, however, performed very poorly on the naive subjects.

The difficulties involved in carrying out a fair comparison of grammar-based and statistical/robust methods are well illustrated by this study. In the rest of this section, we will use it to illustrate the key problems, and go on to describe how we have addressed them in the experiments on MedSLT and Clairissa described later.

12.2.1 Making the recognisers comparable

The first and most obvious problem is how to ensure that the comparison between a grammar-based recogniser and a class N-gram recogniser is meaningful at all. A class N-gram recogniser is built from a training corpus; most grammar-based recognisers are constructed by hand, based on linguistic intuitions that are generally hard to quantify. This objection clearly applied to (Knight et al., 2001). However, since Regulus also constructs its language model using a corpus of training examples, a comparison does become meaningful, since both versions of the recogniser can be trained from the same data. We have done this in both the MedSLT and Clarissa experiments.

The importance of the training corpus is obvious. A related, and somewhat somewhat more subtle issue, is that the class definitions used in the class N-gram model typically also reflect unquantifiable linguistic intuitions (cf. Section 1.2.1) . Regulus provides a mechanism for addressing this problem too, by making it possible to derive class definitions directly from the Regulus lexicon: the implementor specifies two or three examples of the class, and the tool adds the surface forms of all the other lexicon entries which match the least common generalisation of the examples. We derived the N-gram classes in this way for the MedSLT experiments. There were 32 class definitions, which mostly consisted of groups of semantically similar words and phrases. For example, the verbs "radiate", "spread" and "extend" form a class, and the body-part nouns "head", "eye", "face", "neck" and "jaw" form a second class.

The N-gram classes for the Clarissa experiments were constructed by hand. There were only three classes, for numbers, times, and objects that could appear as arguments to the "show" command. Although these classes were not automatically derived from the lexicon, they corresponded exactly with sets of phrases defined by relevant subgrammars of the Regulus grammar.

12.2.2 Choosing appropriate metrics

As always, it is important to find suitable evaluation metrics. The simplest and in practice most widely used metric is WER; however, as demonstrated in (Wang et al., 2003), WER often correlates very poorly with semantic measures of speech understanding performance. "Semantic error rate" is unfortunately not straightforward to define either. In many systems, the data structure built up at the level of semantic representation contains information irrelevant to the task: it is often possible to get the same processing result from different semantic representations. (Knight et al., 2001), which was carried out in a home automation domain, suffered badly from this problem. Since determiners and articles were sometimes significant ("Switch off the light" versus "Switch off all the lights"), they were part of the semantic representation, and an interpretation which got the article wrong was scored as semantically incorrect. In most cases, though, the article actually made no difference: "Switch off kitchen light" and "Switch off the kitchen light" would produce the same system response.

In the MedSLT and Clarissa experiments, the primary evaluation metrics are at the task level. For MedSLT, we consider that an utterance has been correctly recognised if the result of translating back from the interlingua into the source language ("back-translation") results in an acceptable paraphrase of the transcribed source-language utterance. For Clarissa, recognition results are interpreted into task-oriented representations ("dialogue moves"), and evaluated at this level.

12.2.3 Making semantic understanding comparable

We have just argued that we wish to compare performance at the level of semantic interpretation, but this introduces another problem. N-gram-based recognisers will only return a string of words. Regulus grammars can directly produce logical forms, but these will not necessarily be useful as task-level semantic representations, and will in general require some kind of post-processing (cf. Section 5.3). To make the comparison between the two architectures more neutral, we would prefer a uniform semantic interpretation framework, which can take either surface strings or logical forms as input, and produce task-level semantic representations as output.

Alterf, supplied as part of the Regulus release, is a simple package designed to address these requirements, which characterises semantic analysis as a task slightly extending the "decision-list" classification algorithm (Yarowsky, 1994, Carter, 2000). We start with a set of *semantic atoms*, each representing a primitive domain concept, and define a semantic representation to be a non-empty set of semantic atoms. For example, in Clarissa we represent the utterances "please speak up", "set an alarm for five minutes from now" and "no i said go to the next step" respectively as

```
{increase_volume}
{set_alarm, 5, minutes}
{correction, next_step}
```

where `increase_volume`, `set_alarm`, 5, `minutes`, `correction` and `next_step` are semantic atoms. As well as specifying the permitted semantic atoms themselves, we also define a *target model* which for each atom lists the other atoms with which it may legitimately combine. Thus here, for example, `correction` may legitimately combine with any atom, but `minutes` may only combine with `correction`, `set_alarm` or a number.

Training data consists of a set of utterances, in text form, each tagged with its intended semantic representation. We define a set of *feature extraction rules*, each of which associates an utterance with zero or more features. Feature extraction rules can potentially carry out any type of processing, though we will in practice only be interested in three specific types of rules:

N-grams: The features are the set of all n-grams extracted from the surface string, for some specified n.

String: The features are defined by a set of hand-coded regular expressions, each of which is tagged by the name of the feature in question. For example, a typical String feature extraction rule for the Clarissa domain might be

```
surface_pattern([decrease/reduce,'...',volume],
                decrease_volume).
```

which produces the feature `decrease_volume` if the string contains an occurrence of `decrease` or `reduce`, followed at some point by `volume`.

LF: The features are defined by a set of hand-coded logical form patterns, again tagged by the name of the feature in question. For example, the two Clarissa LF feature extraction rules below correspond to the previous String rule[30]

```
lf_pattern([decrease,_,term(_,volume,_)],
           decrease_volume).
lf_pattern([reduce,_,term(_,volume,_)],
           decrease_volume).
```

The feature extraction rules are applied to all of the examples in the training corpus, and statistics are then compiled to estimate the probability $p(a \mid f)$ of each semantic atom a given each separate feature f, using the formula

$$p(a \mid f) = (N_f^a + 1)/(N_f + 2)$$

where N_f is the number of occurrences in the training data of utterances with feature f, and N_f^a is the number of occurrences of utterances with both feature f and semantic atom a.

The decoding process follows (Yarowsky, 1994) in assuming complete dependence between the features. Note that this is in sharp contrast with the Naive Bayes classifier (Duda et al., 2000), which assumes complete *independence*. Of course, neither assumption can be true in practice; however, as argued in (Carter, 2000), there are good reasons for preferring the dependence alternative as the better option in a situation where there are many features extracted in ways that are likely to overlap.

We are given an utterance u, to which we wish to assign a representation $R(u)$ consisting of a set of semantic atoms, together with a target model comprising a set of rules defining which sets of semantic atoms are consistent. Decoding proceeds as follows:

1. Initialise $R(u)$ to the empty set.
2. Use the feature extraction rules and the statistics compiled during training to find the set of all triples $\langle f, a, p \rangle$ where f is a feature associated with u, a is a semantic atom, and p is the probability $p(a \mid f)$ estimated by the training process.
3. Order the set of triples by the value of p, with the largest probabilities first. Call the ordered set T.
4. Remove the highest-ranked triple $\langle f, a, p \rangle$ from T. Add a to $R(u)$ iff the following conditions are fulfilled:

[30]The Clarissa logical forms are defined using the RIACS semantic macros: cf. Section 7.5.

- $p \geq p_t$ for some pre-specified threshold value p_t.
- Addition of a to $R(u)$ results in a set which is consistent with the target model.

5. Repeat step (4) until T is empty.

Intuitively, the process is very simple. We just walk down the list of possible semantic atoms, starting with the most probable ones, and add them to the semantic representation we are building up when this does not conflict with the consistency rules in the target model. We stop when the atoms suggested are too improbable, that is, have probabilities below a specified threshold.

We used Alterf to perform all semantic analysis in the Clarissa experiments. (We will say more about the details in Section 12.4). For MedSLT, we used the output from the Regulus grammar as the semantic representation in the grammar-based version of the system, and for the statistical/robust version performed semantic analysis on the recognition string using a version of Alterf modified in three repects. First, the large number of semantic atoms and the very limited quantity of training data made it infeasible to attempt to train a statistical association between the two, and we assumed uniform associational weights. Second, it was necessary to take account of the fact that MedSLT representation are not simple linear lists, but permit a single layer of nesting, so as to be able to represent subordinate clauses (Rayner et al., 2005b). In order to do this, processing first segmented the input string using a set of phrase-matching rules that attempted to detect start- and end-boundaries for subordinate clauses. Finally, a set of post-processing rules was applied, which filled in default values for unset features in the representation of each clause. For example, `tense` was by default set to `present`, and `voice` to `active`.

For both sets of experiments (Clarissa and MedSLT), performance of the robust and rule-based versions of the system agreed to over 99% on the development corpus.

12.2.4 Collecting appropriate test data

In general, we expect grammar-based recognisers to do much better on in-coverage data than out-of-coverage data, while the difference for N-gram based recognisers will be less pronounced. (Knight et al., 2001) confirmed this prediction: when evaluated on data from experienced users who knew the system, the grammar-based version scored best, but naive users who had been encouraged to experiment got better results with the N-gram based system. This underlines the fact that the choice of appropriate test data to use when evaluating the recognisers also poses a problem. As subjects use the system, we expect them to adapt to it, and move towards its intended coverage. The controlled-language systems that constitute our primary focus of interest in this book are designed for expert users, so it is reasonable to argue that we should focus on this group. It is however preferable, if possible, to quantify the level of expertise in some way.

For the Clarissa experiments, we would ideally have liked to test on astronaut subjects who had completed the NASA-approved Clarissa training course, but the virtual impossibility of getting significant quantities of astronaut time forced us to adopt a compromise. Comparison of the small amount of astronaut data we were able to obtain against the results of a pilot study using naive subjects with no previous exposure to the system revealed a serious mismatch. The astronauts were very familiar both with the procedure-following task and with use of controlled language, and moreover had a strong motivation to learn to use the system; the naive subjects had neither the relevant background, nor any particular reason to want to acquire the relevant skills. The performance figures reflected this imbalance, with the astronauts scoring enormously better than nearly all of the naive subjects.

We obtained a much closer fit against the data recorded by system developers during the course of the project. Although the developers know the system a little better than the astronaut users, our intuitive observation was that the difference was not large, and that the astronauts would probably catch up after only a relatively short period of use. The experiment were thus based on a sample of 8158 in-domain utterances (23369 words) collected from system developers and transcribed during the course of the project. By "in-domain", we mean here that the utterances expressed commands meaningful in the context of the Clarissa task, and that the system should ideally have responded to them. The data had not previously been used for development purposes, and can be considered as unseen.

For the MedSLT experiments, we wanted to take advantage of the system's intelligent help module (cf. Section 1.4.2), and investigate the extent to which this assisted potential users as they learned to use the system. We collected data from 12 native speakers of English, half of whom used the grammar-based version, and half the N-gram based version. The subjects were encouraged to play the part of a doctor, and conduct an examination interview, through the system, on a team member who simulated a patient suffering from a specific type of headache. The task was to identify the type of headache correctly out of a list of eight possibilities. Before the start of their experimental session, each subject was first given a short acclimatisation session, where they used a prepared list of ten sentences that were in-coverage for the GLM, to learn how to use the microphone and the push-to-talk interface. Half of the subjects were given a version of the system in which the help system was switched on; the remaining subjects had it switched off. No other assistance was given. We collected a total of 870 recorded utterances.

12.2.5 Combining the two methods

A final methodological question is whether the idea of comparing grammar-based and statistical methods is appropriate in the first place. Rather than having the two methods compete, it is reasonable to ask whether they can be productively combined instead. In the full (trainable) version of the Alterf framework used for the Clarissa experiments, it was possible to combine information straightforwardly from the two recognisers. Each recogniser contributed its own set of features. Alterf's discrimination algorithm was able to pick out the most strongly associated semantic atoms in the usual way, since the origin of the features made no difference. This option was not available for the MedSLT experiments, since the version of Alterf used did not include associational training.

In the final section, we will summarise the methodological issues in the two sets of experiments, and discuss how they affect the significance of the results. First, however, we present the experiments themselves in more detail.

12.3 Experiments on MedSLT

Our experiments with the MedSLT system were based on those described in (Knight et al., 2001) but were designed to address several of the problems that arose in the earlier study. We created GLM and N-gram versions of the recogniser; the training corpus issue was resolved by constructing the GLM grammar using Regulus, allowing both recognisers to be derived from the same corpus. We used the Nuance SayAnything© tool to build a standard class trigram model. Evaluation was in terms of performance on the end-to-end speech translation task, giving a more appropriate measure of semantic accuracy. Both versions of the recogniser (GLM and N-gram) were trained from the same corpus of 575 text utterances, and testing was performed using the 870 utterance corpus described in Section 12.2.4[31].

The recorded data was first transcribed, and then processed through offline versions of both the GLM and N-gram/robust processing paths.

[31] These experiments were carried out in December 2004; they used an older version of the MedSLT system than the one used for the experiments in Chapter 11, which were performed about 8 months later.

This was done as follows. We first set the system to translate from English into English (via the interlingua), and then had an English-speaking judge evaluate the "back-translation" of each utterance to determine whether or not it was an acceptable paraphrase of what had been said. Utterances for which the back-translation was judged acceptable were regarded as correctly recognised, and were then translated further into the two target languages French and Japanese.

Table 26 presents overall Word Error Rate (WER), Sentence Error Rate (SER) and Semantic Error Rate (SemER) for both versions of the system, where SemER is measured as the proportion of utterances not receiving an acceptable back-translation. As in the previous chapter, we present separate figures for in-coverage data (417 utterances) and out-of-coverage data (453 utterances).

	In coverage		Out of coverage	
	GLM	N-gram	GLM	N-gram
WER	5.7%	12.7%	57.5%	47.8%
SER	19.4%	36.7%	99.8%	91.4%
SemER	18.5%	28.1%	87.9%	89.0%

TABLE 26 WER, SER and SemER for GLM and N-gram versions of the MedSLT recogniser, on in-coverage and out-of-coverage data. SemER is measured as the proportion of utterances not receiving an acceptable back-translation.

Translations to French and Japanese were judged for acceptability by native speaker judges for each language: there were six judges for French, and three for Japanese. Judges were asked to categorise translations as "good", "acceptable" or "bad". For each target language, and each processing method (GLM or N-gram), we consolidated the results using a majority voting scheme. If two-thirds of the judges (i.e. four for French, or two for Japanese) agreed that the translation was clearly "good" or "bad", we counted the translation as belonging to the appropriate category. Otherwise, we counted it as "acceptable". The results of this judging are shown in Table 27.

For each target language, we extracted the sets of utterances where one type of processing yielded a clearly better result than the other. By "clearly better", we mean that either one result was judged "good" and the other not, or that one was "acceptable" and the other was some kind of error. The balance in favour of GLM processing was 83 clearly better versus 46 clearly worse for French, and 77 versus 41 for Japanese. According to the McNemar sign test, both these results are

	French		Japanese	
	GLM	N-gram	GLM	N-gram
Bad recognition	54.6%	59.8%	54.6%	59.8%
Good translation	34.4%	30.8%	36.4%	32.8%
Acceptable translation	8.7%	7.7%	3.6%	3.3%
Bad translation	0.3%	0.2%	0.5%	0.5%
No translation	2.0%	1.5%	4.9%	3.7%

TABLE 27 Breakdown of English → French and English → Japanese translation using GLM and N-gram versions. Translation judgements have been consolidated using majority voting.

significant at well under the 1% level.

12.4 Experiments on Clarissa

We now describe the experiments carried out on Clarissa, which, in addition to comparing GLM- and SLM-based systems, compare the effect on performance of different types of Alterf features (cf. Section 12.2.3). In particular, this study investigates whether logical-form-based patterns produce more accurate semantic analysis than string-based or N-gram patterns, and whether it is useful to combine several types of pattern.

The Clarissa Regulus grammar was constructed using a training corpus containing 3297 examples; of these, 1349 were hand-constructed to represent specific words and constructions required for the application, while the remaining 1953 were transcribed examples of utterances recorded during system development. The parameters guiding the grammar specialisation process were chosen as described in Section 10.3.4, to produce a fairly "flat" grammar in which many noun-phrases became lexical items. This reflects the generally stereotypical nature of language in the Clarissa domain. We again used the Nuance SayAnything© tool and the same 3297 utterance training set to build a class trigram model.

We experimented with three different kinds of Alterf feature extraction rules: surface N-grams, hand-coded surface patterns and hand-coded logical form patterns. The patterns were developed and debugged using the 3297 utterance training corpus: on this corpus, each set of patterns has a classification error rate of about 0.5%. We used six different sets of Alterf features:

N-grams: N-gram features only.

LF: Logical-form-based patterns only.

String: String-based patterns only.

String + LF: Both string-based and logical-form based patterns.

String + N-grams: Both string-based and N-gram features.

String + LF + N-grams: All types of features.

Recogniser	WER	SER
GLM	6.27%	9.79%
N-gram	7.42%	12.41%

TABLE 28 WER and SER for the Regulus-based Clarissa recogniser (GLM) and a conventional class N-gram recogniser trained on the same data.

Raw recognition performance figures for the two recognisers, measured in terms of WER and SER, are shown in Table 28. The main results are in Table 29, which contrasts speech understanding performance for the Regulus-based recogniser and the class N-gram recogniser, using several different sets of Alterf features. For completeness, we also present results for simulated perfect recognition, i.e. using the reference transcriptions.

12.5 Discussion

Having presented the results, we will now attempt to draw some general conclusions about the relative performance of GLM and N-gram/robust processing in these experiments. Looking first at the MedSLT figures in Table 26, the striking difference is on the in-coverage data; the GLM version scores much better than the N-gram/robust one, especially on WER (5.7% versus 12.7%) and SER (19.4% versus 36.7%). Robust processing lets the N-gram/robust version recover somewhat on SemER (18.5% versus 28.1%), but the GLM still comes out a clear winner. Interestingly enough, although the N-gram/robust version scores better than the GLM on the out-of-coverage data in terms of WER (47.8% versus 57.5%) and SER (91.4% versus 99.8%), the two systems score about equally even here in terms of semantic error rate (87.9% versus 89.0%).

Over the whole dataset, GLM processing is slightly worse on WER (34.3% versus 31.6%), but slightly better on SER (62.0% versus 66.3%), and SemER (54.6% versus 59.8%). This reflects the balance between in-coverage and out-of-coverage utterances in the data. SemER is about 10% better for the GLM on in-coverage data, and the two versions are about equal on out-of-coverage data; since we have about half in-

Version	Rec	Features	Errors		
			Rej	Bad	All
T-1	Text	N-grams	7.3%	5.9%	13.2%
T-2	Text	LF	3.1%	0.5%	3.6%
T-3	Text	String	2.2%	0.8%	3.0%
T-4	Text	String+LF	0.8%	0.8%	1.6%
T-5	Text	String+LF+N-grams	0.4%	0.8%	1.2%
G-1	GLM	N-grams	7.4%	9.7%	17.1%
G-2	GLM	LF	1.4%	4.9%	6.3%
G-3	GLM	String	2.9%	4.8%	7.7%
G-4	**GLM**	**String+LF**	**1.0%**	**5.0%**	**6.0%**
G-5	GLM	String+LF+N-grams	0.7%	5.4%	6.1%
N-1	N-gram	N-grams	9.6%	11.9%	21.5%
N-2	N-gram	String	2.8%	7.4%	10.2%
N-3	N-gram	String+N-grams	1.6%	8.0%	9.6%

TABLE 29 Speech understanding performance for 8158 Clarissa test sentences recorded during development, on 13 different configurations of the system. The "Rec" column indicates either simulated perfect recognition ("Text"), recognition using the Regulus-derived grammar-based language model ("GLM") or recognition using a class N-gram language model ("N-gram"). The "Features" column indicates the Alterf features used. Errors are subdivided into rejections ("Rej") and incorrect interpretations ("Bad").

coverage and half out-of-coverage, the GLM does about 5% better overall.

The ratio of in-coverage to out-of-coverage in the dataset is mainly a function of how familiar the subjects are with the system's coverage. An experienced user will produce mostly in-coverage data; a novice user will produce mostly out-of-coverage data. Performance improves with increased familiarity, and this favours the GLM system: as people become more expert, they gravitate towards the intended coverage. One way to quantify this effect is to contrast performance for the two architectures, averaged over the first and last quarters of each session.

Table 30 presents the results, divided up according to whether the help system was enabled or not. Even without the help system, performance improved on average by about 7% over the course of the session. With GLM processing and the help system turned on, the improvement was much larger, averaging over 17%.

The Clarissa data is mostly in-coverage; again, the GLM version

Part session	Help OFF		Help ON	
	GLM	N-gram	GLM	N-gram
First quarter	58.6%	65.8%	63.1%	64.1%
Last quarter	52.1%	58.1%	45.9%	56.0%
Improvement	6.5%	7.7%	17.2%	8.1%

TABLE 30 Performance of MedSLT GLM and N-gram/robust processing, measured by proportion of unacceptably recognised utterances, for versions with and without access to help system.

performed very considerably better than the N-gram/robust. Looking at Table 29, we see that the best N-gram/robust version, N-3, had a semantic error rate of 9.6%, while the best GLM version, G-4, had an error rate of 6.0%, a relative improvement of 37%. Part of this is clearly due to the fact that the GLM recogniser has better WER and SER than the N-gram one. However, Table 28 shows that the relative improvement in WER is only 15% (7.42% versus 6.27%), and that in SER is 21% (12.41% versus 9.79%). The larger improvement by the GLM version at the level of semantic understanding is most likely accounted for by the fact that it is able to use logical-form-based features, which are not accessible to the N-gram/robust version. Although logical-form-based features do not appear to be intrinsically more accurate than string-based features (contrast rows T-2 and T-3), the fact that they allow tighter integration between semantic understanding and language modelling is intuitively advantageous.

It is interesting to note that the combination of logical-form-based features and string-based features outperforms logical-form-based features alone (rows G-4 and G-5). Although the difference is small (6.0% versus 6.3%), a pairwise comparison shows that it is significant at the 1% level according to the McNemar sign test. There is no clear evidence that N-gram features are very useful. This supports the standard folk-lore result that semantic understanding components for command and control applications are more appropriately implemented using hand-coded phrase-spotting patterns than general associational learning techniques.

12.5.1 Summary of methodological issues in experiments

We have presented the results of the MedSLT and Clarissa experiments, but there is still the question of methodological soundness. In Section 12.2, we identified six potential problems when attempting to compare grammar-based and N-gram language models. Table 31 summarises how well the two sets of experiments answer to our criteria.

On the positive side, both sets conform to the first three requirements (uniform training corpus, N-gram classes linked to lexicon and task-level evaluation metric). The last requirement (possibility to combine both architectures) seems to us less important, though it is pleasant that we were able to address this in the Clarissa experiments. If there is doubt about the validity of the comparisons, it will be because of the "no" answers in row 4 for MedSLT, and 5 for Clarissa.

Methodological Feature	**MedSLT**	**Clarissa**
Trained both recognisers from same corpus	yes	yes
N-gram classes from Regulus lexicon	yes	yes
Task-level evaluation metric	yes	yes
Uniform semantic interpretation framework	no	yes
Users trained through online help module	yes	no
Combined both recognition architectures	no	yes

TABLE 31 Methodological features for the two experimental domains

Looking first at the MedSLT experiments, the key question is thus whether the Alterf-based robust interpretation method yields sufficiently good performance in the N-gram based version of the system. Evidently, the comparison fails to be interesting if the N-gram architecture's results are poor simply because of a substandard robust parser. In fact, the evidence at our disposal strongly suggests that this is not the case, and that the disparity in performance on in-coverage data is primarily due to worse recognition performance. The most obvious reason for believing this is the N-gram recogniser's very much poorer WER and SER on in-coverage material (cf. first two columns of Table 26). Hand-examination of the data confirmed our initial impression: incorrect semantic analyses produced by the N-gram system are typically due to misrecognition of a critical content word, and it is in most cases not obvious how better robust parsing would help.

Turning to the Clarissa experiments, the main methodological problem is that the test data came from system developers. The comparison could be biased against the N-gram recognizer if the developer data had very many more more in-coverage utterances than fully trained astronauts (the intended user population) would produce. However, from the small amount of astronaut data that we have seen, there is no reason to believe that the difference would be large. Anecdotally, new system developers who joined the Clarissa project were using the system as effectively as everyone else after about a week of exposure, and astronauts clearly learned more quickly than average. Even with only the statutary one hour of official NASA training, the astronauts we collected data from were rapidly approaching the error rates seen in the developers' data.

To sum up, our basic conclusion for both application domains is substantially the same. In terms of WER, the grammar-based version performs better on in-coverage data, and the N-gram/robust version performs better on out-of-coverage data; which version wins overall depends on the proportion of data that is within grammar coverage. In terms of semantic error rate, the grammar-based system constructed using Regulus offers substantially better performance on the in-coverage data, and neither system does at all well on the out-of-coverage data. For systems like Clarissa and MedSLT, where only complete understanding is useful and users typically will have had enough exposure to the system to have become familiar with its coverage, it seems reasonable to claim that the grammar-based version is clearly preferable.

12.6 Summary

- The most common architecture for spoken dialogue systems combines speech recognition using a class N-gram language model with a robust parser. We would like to compare Regulus-based systems against mainstream alternatives. We carried out experiments of this kind on both the MedSLT and Clarissa systems.
- There are several methodological problems involved in comparing grammar-based recognisers with class N-gram recognisers. Class N-gram language models are derived directly from a corpus, but it is often hard to specify what information was used to construct a grammar-based language model. It is important to evaluate in terms of a task-level metric, but introducing a robust parser for the class N-gram recogniser complicates the picture. It is also not obvious how to collect suitable test data.
- Using Regulus solves the most urgent methodological problem, since the language model is also produced using a data-driven method, and can be built from the same training corpus.
- We can address the problem of choosing appropriate training data in two ways. If we can assume that users will receive formal training in use of the system, it is reasonable to focus only on in-coverage data. If we are interested in performance of new users who do not know system coverage, we can make the comparison objective by providing an intelligent help system, and arranging the experiments so that subjects only receive instruction though the help system.
- For both MedSLT and Clarissa, we found that the Regulus-based

version strongly outperformed the class N-gram based version on in-coverage data. Both versions performed very badly on out-of-coverage data. This behaviour is at least partly explained by the fact that the task in both domains is "all or nothing", with partial results not being useful.

- For the Clarissa experiments, we used the Alterf robust parser to compare the effectiveness of semantic interpretation from different levels of representation. Semantic interpretation from the level of logical form strongly outperforms semantic interpretation from surface level, and semantic interpretation using a combination of logical form and surface level information marginally outperforms semantic interpretation using only logical form information.
- For the MedSLT experiments, we were able to contrast subject performance depending both on the type of architecture (Regulus or class N-gram/robust), and on whether or not an intelligent help system was available. Subjects improved their performance most quickly for the combination of Regulus-based recognition and availability of a help system.

Exercises

1. Read the Nuance documentation for the SayAnything© tool. Use the tool to build a class N-gram recogniser for the Toy1 application. How do you define suitable classes and a suitable training corpus?
2. Compare the performance of the class N-gram recogniser and the Regulus recogniser in terms of surface strings (WER and SER). How does performance vary as you increase the size of the training corpus?
3. Using Alterf, or some other method, write a phrase-spotting parser which derives semantic interpretations from the strings produced by the class N-gram recogniser. Consult the online Regulus documentation if you need to find out how to write Alterf rules.
4. Compare the performance of the class N-gram recogniser and the Regulus recogniser in terms of semantic accuracy. Use your phrase-spotting parser to produce semantic interpretations for the class N-gram version.
5. Adapt the Toy1 application from Chapter 3 to use the class N-gram recogniser and your phrase-spotting parser. (The Regserver will return an empty list for the semantic interpretation).

13

Summary and future directions

Manny Rayner, Pierrette Bouillon and Beth Ann Hockey

13.1 Summary

In this book, we have tried to achieve two main goals: describing how to use the Regulus system to build real spoken dialogue system, and explaining how it works. In the first half of the book, we showed how to download, install and run the Open Source Regulus platform (Chapter 2), how to use the interactive development environment to write grammars and compile them into recognisers (Chapter 4), and how to use those recognisers to build different types of applications (Chapters 3, 5 and 6). We finished by describing in Chapter 7 how to extract efficient domain-specific grammars from a general linguistically motivated grammar. If you had trouble following Chapter 7, but haven't yet looked at the second half of the book, you might want to try reading Chapters 9 and 10, and then revisit it; hopefully it will make more sense.

The second half of the book is the theoretical part. There are three main topics: the central idea, factors affecting performance, and comparison with other architectures.

13.1.1 The central idea

The basic aim of the whole Regulus project is to be able to build reusable grammar-based speech recognisers capable of delivering performance useful in real applications. We have argued that we can attack these goals by creating the right kinds of general, linguistically motivated grammars, together with compilation tools that can turn these grammars into recognisers. These issues were discussed in Chapters 8, 9 and 10.

We started in Chapter 8 by explaining how we can efficiently compile a feature grammar into the context free grammar (CFG) form required by a recogniser platform. We showed that a suitably enhanced version of the simple "expand-and-filter" algorithm is capable of compiling quite large feature grammars into the CFG form required by the Nuance recogniser platform. The key ideas are an efficient (linear-time) filtering algorithm, interleaving of expansion and filtering, pre-processing of the feature grammar, and post-processing of the CFG.

Next, in Chapter 9, we explained more exactly what we meant by a "linguistically motivated general grammar". We presented a detailed description of the general feature grammar we have built for English. We focussed on the non-standard aspects, which primarily result from two requirements: firstly, that all features be finite-valued, and secondly, that semantics should be capable of compilation to Nuance semantic primitives. These restrictions are fairly serious, and for example rule out use of many of the techniques associated with HPSG. None the less, we showed that, by backing off to a more enumerative and lexicalist approach, it is still possible to build a substantial grammar which covers a large proportion of the core linguistic phenomena of English.

It turns out that if we try to compile the general grammar directly into a recogniser, the resultant language model is not capable of supporting efficient recognition (Section 11.7). However, it is possible to use the Explanation Based Learning technique to extract simpler domain-specific grammars from the general one (Chapter 10). These specialised grammars can be compiled into useful recognisers.

13.1.2 Factors affecting performance

Recogniser performance can vary a great deal, ranging from extremely good to completely useless. We want to know what factors affect the performance of recognisers built using the Regulus platform and methodology: some of the obvious candidates are coverage, vocabulary size, and grammar structure. We examined these questions in Chapter 11, by deriving multiple versions of the same recogniser and comparing recognition performance on speech data.

The results suggested that the structural factor which most affected performance was generality; flat grammars incurred a large coverage loss due to their lack of ability to generalise, but did not offer significantly better recognition performance on in-coverage material compared to the more complex versions. Sortal features, most of which distinguish semantically distinct types of nouns, also had a large impact. Although other features could affect Word Error Rate considerably, their effect on task performance was much smaller; this may however have been partly due to the nature of the MedSLT task, since the distinction between singular and plural was usually not relevant at the task level. Degradation in performance resulting from the addition of new grammatical constructions varied greatly depending on the nature of the construction. The grammars were fairly robust to addition of new vocabulary; the vocabulary size needed to be approximately doubled to produce a significant drop in task performance.

13.1.3 Comparison against other architectures

Regulus is very different from the current mainstream paradigm for spoken language understanding, which is based on statistical language modelling and robust parsing. We want to compare Regulus with the mainstream methods, and see how it performs; we would also like to understand the types of applications where we can reasonably expect it to be able to offer us anything. We investigated these issues in Chapter 12, where we took two Regulus-based systems, and compared them with plausible alternatives built using mainstream methods. For both systems, the pattern was similar: the Regulus-based version gave much better performance on the in-coverage data, and comparable, very bad, performance on out-of-coverage data.

These two applications, and others we have experimented with, suggest that the following characteristics are typical of systems suitable for the Regulus approach. We are primarily interested in applications with medium-size vocabularies (hundreds of words, as opposed to tens or thousands). There should be a moderate level of syntactic complexity (not fixed phrases, and not unrestricted speech), and insufficient data available to train a good statistical recogniser. Precision should be more important than robustness, and it should be feasible for users to learn a controlled language with a well-defined syntax. Although these requirements may seem restrictive, they apply in practice to quite a broad range of mixed-initiative command-and-control or limited-domain speech translation systems.

13.2 Future directions

Regulus is an ongoing Open Source project. This final section lists some of the activities in which we are currently engaged.

Improvements to the English grammar The general English grammar described in Chapter 9 was not developed in a planned manner, and still contains several major holes. The most important of these is a systematic treatment of comparative and superlative adjectives and adverbs. The authors of this book are actively working to improve the coverage of the grammar.

Improvements to grammar specialisation methods With the operationality criteria and other settings that we currently use, we can sometimes produce specialised grammars that fail to compile to CFG form. The specific problem is usually caused by a small number of specialised rules (often as few as one or two rules), which result in combinatorial explosion during expansion. We are investigating different solutions to this problem. Ideally, we would like to be able to stop bad specialised rules from being generated. The second best solution would be to automatically identify bad rules, and remove them.

Grammars for other languages It appears quite possible to apply the Regulus methodology to languages other than English. Under the MedSLT project, we are in the process of writing general grammars for several other languages, and using them to derive recognisers. Grammars for French, Japanese, Spanish, Finnish, and Catalan are currently under active development. We have also done some initial work on Greek. The grammars are available from the MedSLT website (MedSLT, 2006).

Multi-lingual grammars For pairs of closely related languages, it appears completely feasible to write a single, parameterised shared grammar which encodes the information for both languages; our grammar for Catalan (Bouillon et al., 2006) is already implemented in this way, and is in fact a shared grammar for Catalan and French. (Catalan and French are very closely related). We are in the initial stages of developing a more ambitious shared grammar, which will cover at least five different languages.

Lexicon entry tool The lexicon macros described in Section 7.4 simplify the task of writing domain-specific lexicon entries, but it is still quite demanding. We have recently begun work on a GUI-based lexicon wizard, similar in spirit to the one described in (Lewin, 2000), which will simplify this task.

Enhancements to Regserver and client libraries As explained in Chapter 3, we so far only have Regserver client libraries for Java and Prolog. We plan to develop libraries for other languages, most importantly C++. We also intend to further enhance the the Regserver itself, and in particular make it possible to support open microphone speech recognition.

Appendix: Online Documentation

This book is not intended to serve as an exhaustive reference for Regulus, but rather as a source of tutorial and background material. The details are available in the online documentation, which can be obtained from the Regulus website, in the file `$REGULUS/doc/RegulusDoc.htm`. In particular, the following sections are often useful:

- "Using the Regulus development environment" lists all the top-level commands available in the development environment, and provides brief explanations of how they are used.
- "The config file" lists all the possible config file declarations, again with brief explanations.
- "Formal description of Regulus grammar notation" provides an exact definition of the grammar notation and its associated semantics.

References

Allen, J., D. Byron, M. Dzikovska, G. Ferguson, L. Galescu, and A. Stent. 2000. An architecture for a generic dialogue shell. *Natural Language Engineering, Special Issue on Best Practice in Spoken Language Dialogue Systems Engineering* pages 1–16.

Arnold, D., L. Balkan, S. Meijer, R.L. Humphreys, and L. Sadler. 1994. *Machine Translation: An Introductory Guide*. Oxford: Blackwell.

Bos, J. 2002. Compilation of unification grammars with compositional semantics to speech recognition packages. In *Proceedings of the 19th International Conference on Computational Linguistics*. Taipei, Taiwan.

Bos, J., E. Klein, and T. Oka. 2003. Meaningful conversation with a mobile robot. In *Proceedings of the Research Note Sessions of the 10th Conference of the European Chapter of the Association for Computational Linguistics*. Budapest, Hungary.

Bouillon, P., M. Rayner, N. Chatzichrisafis, B.A. Hockey, M. Santaholma, M. Starlander, Y. Nakao, K. Kanzaki, and H. Isahara. 2005. A generic multi-lingual open source platform for limited-domain medical speech translation. In *In Proceedings of the 10th Conference of the European Association for Machine Translation (EAMT)*. Budapest, Hungary.

Bouillon, P., M. Rayner, B. Novellas, Y. Nakao, M. Santaholma, M. Starlander, and N. Chatzichrisafis. 2006. Une grammaire multilingue partagée pour la reconnaissance et la génération. In *Proceedings of TALN 2006*. Leuwen, Belgium.

Bresnan, J. and R. Kaplan. 1985. *The mental representation of grammatical relations*. Cambridge, MA: MIT Press.

Carter, D. 2000. Choosing between interpretations. In Rayner et al. (2000a).

Chappelier, J.-C., M. Rajman, R. Aragues, and A. Rozenknop. 1999. Lattice parsing for speech recognition. In *Proceedings of the 6th TALN*. Carges, Corsica.

Clarissa. 2006. http://www.ic.arc.nasa.gov/projects/clarissa/. As of 1 Jan 2006.

Doran, C., D. Egedi, B.A. Hockey, B. Srinivas, and M. Zaidel. 1994. XTAG system — a wide-coverage grammar for English. In *Proceedings of COLING-94*. Kyoto, Japan.

Dowding, J., M. Gawron, D. Appelt, L. Cherny, R. Moore, and D. Moran. 1993. Gemini: A natural language system for spoken language understanding. In *Proceedings of the Thirty-First Annual Meeting of the Association for Computational Linguistics*.

Dowding, J., B.A. Hockey, J.M. Gawron, and C. Culy. 2001. Practical issues in compiling typed unification grammars for speech recognition. In *Proceedings of the 39th Annual Meeting of the Association for Computational Linguistics*. Toulouse, France.

Dowling, William F. and Jean H. Gallier. 1984. Linear-time algorithms for testing the satisfiability of propositional Horn formulae. *The Journal of Logic Programming* 1(3):267–284.

Duda, R.O., P.E. Hart, and H.G. Stork. 2000. *Pattern Classification*. New York: Wiley.

Fikes, R.E. and N.J. Nilson. 1971. Strips: A new approach to the application of theorem proving to problem solving. *Artificial Intelligence* 3:251–288.

Gazdar, G., E. Klein, G. Pullum, and I. Sag. 1985. *Generalized Phrase Structure Grammar*. Oxford, England: Blackwell.

Jurafsky, D. and J. H. Martin. 2000. *Speech and Language Processing: An Introduction to Natural Language Processing, Computational Linguistics and Speech Recognition*. New Jersey: Prentice Hall Inc.

Kiefer, B. and H. Krieger. 2000. A context-free approximation of head-driven phrase structure grammar. In *Proceedings of the 6th International Workshop on Parsing Technologies*, pages 135–146.

Knight, S., G. Gorrell, M. Rayner, D. Milward, R. Koeling, and I. Lewin. 2001. Comparing grammar-based and robust approaches to speech understanding: a case study. In *Proceedings of Eurospeech 2001*, pages 1779–1782. Aalborg, Denmark.

Larsson, S. and D. Traum. 2000. Information state and dialogue management in the TRINDI dialogue move engine toolkit. *Natural Language Engineering, Special Issue on Best Practice in Spoken Language Dialogue Systems Engineering* pages 323–340.

Lemon, O., A. Bracy, A. Gruenstein, and S. Peters. 2001. Multimodal dialogues with intelligent agents in dynamic environments: the WITAS conversational interface. In *Proceedings of 2nd Meeting of the North American Association for Computational Linguistics*. Pittsburgh, PA.

Lemon, O. and A. Gruenstein. 2004. Multithreaded context for robust conversational interfaces: Context-sensitive speech recognition and interpretation of corrective fragments. *ACM Transactions on Computer-Human Interaction* 11(3).

Lewin, I. 2000. Acquisition of lexical entries. In Rayner et al. (2000a).

Martin, D., A. Cheyer, and D. Moran. 1998. Building distributed software systems with the open agent architecture. In *Proceedings of the Third International Conference on the Practical Application of Intelligent Agents and Multi-Agent Technology*. Blackpool, Lancashire, UK.

MedSLT. 2006. http://sourceforge.net/projects/medslt/. As of 1 Jan 2006.

Moore, R. 1998. Using natural language knowledge sources in speech recognition. In *Proceedings of the NATO Advanced Studies Institute*.

Moore, R., J. Dowding, H. Bratt, J. Gawron, Y. Gorfu, and A. Cheyer. 1997. CommandTalk: A spoken-language interface for battlefield simulations. In *Proceedings of the Fifth Conference on Applied Natural Language Processing*, pages 1–7.

Pereira, F.C.N. 1981. Extraposition grammars. *American Journal of Computational Linguistics* 7:243–256.

Pereira, F.C.N. and D.H.D. Warren. 1980. Definite clause grammars for language analysis – a survey of the formalism and a comparison with augmented transition networks. *Artificial Intelligence* 13:231–278.

Pollard, C. and I. Sag. 1994. *Head Driven Phrase Structure Grammar*. Chicago: University of Chicago Press.

Pulman, S.G.1992. Syntactic and semantic processing. In H. Alshawi, ed., *The Core Language Engine*, pages 129–148. Cambridge, Massachusetts: MIT Press.

Rayner, M. 1988. Applying explanation-based generalization to natural-language processing. In *Proceedings of the International Conference on Fifth Generation Computer Systems*, pages 1267–1274. Tokyo, Japan.

Rayner, M. 1993. *Abductive Equivalential Translation and its Application to Natural Language Database Interfacing*. Ph.D. thesis, The Royal Institute of Technology and Stockholm University.

Rayner, M., P. Bouillon, N. Chatzichrisafis, B.A. Hockey, M. Santaholma, M. Starlander, H. Isahara, K. Kankazi, and Y. Nakao. 2005a. A methodology for comparing grammar-based and robust approaches to speech understanding. In *Proceedings of the 9th International Conference on Spoken Language Processing (ICSLP)*. Lisboa, Portugal.

Rayner, M., P. Bouillon, B.A. Hockey, N. Chatzichrisafis, and M. Starlander. 2004. Comparing rule-based and statistical approaches to speech understanding in a limited domain speech translation system. In *Proceedings of the 10th International Conference on Theoretical and Methodological Issues in Machine Translation*. Baltimore, MD.

Rayner, M., P. Bouillon, M. Santaholma, and Y. Nakao. 2005b. Representational and architectural issues in a limited-domain medical speech translator. In *Proceedings of TALN/RECITAL*. Dourdan, France.

Rayner, M., D. Carter, P. Bouillon, V. Digalakis, and M. Wirén, eds. 2000a. *The Spoken Language Translator*. Cambridge University Press.

Rayner, M., N. Chatzichrisafis, P. Bouillon, Y. Nakao, H. Isahara, K. Kanzaki, and B.A. Hockey. 2005c. Japanese speech understanding using grammar specialization. In *HLT-NAACL 2005: Demo Session*. Vancouver, British Columbia, Canada: Association for Computational Linguistics.

Rayner, M., J. Dowding, and B.A. Hockey. 2001a. A baseline method for compiling typed unification grammars into context free language models. In *Proceedings of Eurospeech 2001*, pages 729–732. Aalborg, Denmark.

Rayner, M., G. Gorrell, B.A. Hockey, J. Dowding, and J. Boye. 2001b. Do CFG based language models need agreement constraints? In *Proceedings of 2nd NAACL*.

Rayner, M. and B.A. Hockey. 2004. Side effect free dialogue management in a voice enabled procedure browser. In *Proceedings of the 8th International Conference on Spoken Language Processing (ICSLP)*. Jeju Island, Korea.

Rayner, M., B.A. Hockey, and J. Dowding. 2002. Grammar specialisation meets language modelling. In *Proceedings of the 7th International Conference on Spoken Language Processing (ICSLP)*. Denver, CO.

Rayner, M., B.A. Hockey, and F. James. 2000b. A compact architecture for dialogue management based on scripts and meta-outputs. In *Proceedings of the 6th Applied Natural Language Processing Conference*. Seattle, WA.

Rayner, M., B.A. Hockey, F. James, E.O. Bratt, S. Goldwater, and J.M. Gawron. 2000c. Compiling language models from a linguistically motivated unification grammar. In *Proceedings of the Eighteenth International Conference on Computational Linguistics*. Saarbrucken, Germany.

Rayner, M., B.A. Hockey, J.M. Renders, N. Chatzichrisafis, and K. Farrell. 2005d. A voice enabled procedure browser for the International Space Station. In *Proceedings of the 43rd Annual Meeting of the Association for Computational Linguistics (interactive poster and demo track)*. Ann Arbor, MI.

Rayner, M., B.A. Hockey, J.-M. Renders, N. Chatzichrisafis, and K. Farrell. 2005e. Spoken language processing in the Clarissa procedure browser. Tech. Rep. ICSI Technical Report TR-05-005, ICSI, International Computer Science Institute (ICSI), 1947 Center St. Suite 600, Berkeley, CA 94704-1198.

Robinson, J.A. 1965. A machine-oriented logic based on the resolution principle. *Journal of the Association for Computing Machinery* 12(1).

Russell, S. and P. Norvig. 2003. *An Introduction to Artificial Intelligence (2nd edition)*. Cambridge, MA: Harvard University Press.

Starlander, M., P. Bouillon, N. Chatzichrisafis, M. Santaholma, M. Rayner, B.A. Hockey, H. Isahara, K. Kanzaki, and Y. Nakao. 2005. Practising controlled language through a help system integrated into the medical speech translation system (MedSLT). In *Proceedings of the MT Summit X*. Phuket, Thailand.

Stent, A., J. Dowding, J. Gawron, E. Bratt, and R. Moore. 1999. The CommandTalk spoken dialogue system. In *Proceedings of the Thirty-Seventh*

Annual Meeting of the Association for Computational Linguistics, pages 183–190.

Stolcke, A. 2002. SRILM - an extensible language modeling toolkit. In *Proceedings of the International Conference on Spoken Language Processing (ICSLP2002)*.

van Harmelen, T. and A. Bundy. 1988. Explanation-based generalization = partial evaluation (research note). *Artificial Intelligence* 36:401–412.

Wang, Y.-Y., A. Acero, and C. Chelba. 2003. Is word error rate a good indicator for spoken language understanding accuracy. In *Proceedings of Eurospeech 2003*, pages 609–612. Geneva, Switzerland.

XTAG Research Group. 2001. *XTAG Project*. http://www.cis.upenn.edu/~xtag/. As of 1 Jan 2006.

Yarowsky, D. 1994. Decision lists for lexical ambiguity resolution. In *Proceedings of the 32nd Annual Meeting of the Association for Computational Linguistics*, pages 88–95. Las Cruces, New Mexico.

Index